Go Web!
Dynamic Web Publishing
on the PC Platform

JOIN US ON THE INTERNET VIA WWW, GOPHER, FTP OR EMAIL:

WWW: http://www.thomson.com
GOPHER: gopher.thomson.com
FTP: ftp.thomson.com
EMAIL: findit@kiosk.thomson.com

WebExtra[sm]

WebExtra gives added value by providing an online version of the *Go Web!* resource guide, which will be updated as new information and resources become available.
Point your web browser at

http://www.thomson.com/itcp.html

A service of I(T)P

Go Web!
Dynamic Web Publishing on the PC Platform

David Harvey-George

INTERNATIONAL THOMSON COMPUTER PRESS

I⊕P An International Thomson Publishing Company

London • Bonn • Boston • Johannesburg • Madrid • Melbourne • Mexico City • New York • Paris
Singapore • Tokyo • Toronto • Albany, NY • Belmont, CA • Cincinnati, OH • Detroit, MI

Go Web!
Dynamic Web Publishing on the PC Platform

Copyright © 1996 International Thomson Computer Press

I ⓣ P A division of International Thomson Publishing Inc.
The ITP logo is a trademark under licence.

For more information, contact:

International Thomson Computer Press
Berkshire House
168-173 High Holborn
London WC1V 7AA
UK

International Thomson Computer Press
20 Park Plaza
Suite 1001
Boston, MA 02116
US

Imprints of International Thomson Publishing

International Thomson Publishing GmbH
Königswinterer Straße 418
53227 Bonn
Germany

International Thomson Publishing Asia
221 Henderson Road #05–10
Henderson Building
Singapore 0315

Thomas Nelson Australia
102 Dodds Street
South Melbourne, 3205
Victoria
Australia

International Thomson Publishing Japan
Hirakawacho Kyowa Building, 3F
2-2-1 Hirakawacho
Chiyoda-ku, 102 Tokyo
Japan

Nelson Canada
1120 Birchmount Road
Scarborough, Ontario
Canada M1K 5G4

International Thomson Editores
Campos Eliseos 385, Piso 7
Col. Polenco
11560 Mexico D. F. Mexico

International Thomson Publishing South Africa
PO Box 2459
Halfway House
1685 South Africa

International Thomson Publishing France
1, rue St. Georges
75 009 Paris / France

WebExtra is a Service Mark of Thomson Holdings Inc.

The programs in this book and its accompanying CD-ROM have been included for their instructional value. While every precaution has been taken with their preparation, the Publisher does not offer any warranties or representations, nor does it accept any liabilities with respect to the information contained herein.

Products and services that are referred to in this book and its accompanying CD-ROM may be either trademarks and/or registered trademarks of their respective owners. The Publisher/s and Author/s make no claim to these trademarks.

Please ensure that before using each program on the CD-ROM you read carefully and observe the conditions for its use.

British Library Cataloguing-in-Publication Data
A catalogue record for this book is available from the British Library

Library of Congress Cataloging-in-Publication Data
A catalog record for this book is available from the Library of Congress

First Printed 1996

ISBN 1-85032-251-1

Commissioning Editor Liz Israel Oppedijk
Cover Designed by Button Eventures
Typeset by Florencetype Ltd
Printed in the UK by Clays Ltd, St Ives plc

Contents

Acknowledgments

This book is the product of many peoples' efforts, despite the single name on the cover. I would like to thank the staff at International Thomson Computer Press, in particular Liz Israel Oppedijk and Jonathan Simpson. Kate Harvey-George, who read through the first drafts and offered much support and advice. Aileen Barry and Peter Flynn for proof reading and many helpful suggestions.

Di Winnett and Martin Hurren of Hewlett Packard, Bracknell were very helpful with the loan of a 3C scanner.

The many people of the Internet community at large, especially the authors and companies who contributed software to the CD-ROM.

Front cover:

Armfield (http://www.armfield.co.uk) courtesy Armfield Ltd.

Greyware (http://www.greyware.com) courtesy Jeffry Dwight.

1 Introduction

Unless you've been living on the dark side of the moon recently you can't have failed to notice that information publishing is undergoing a profound change. The way knowledge and ideas are disseminated has altered more in the last fifteen years than in the previous five centuries. Incredible advances in digital electronics have provided the means for this to happen. Clubs and small businesses use desktop publishing (DTP) and photocopiers to produce magazines without recourse to the print shop. High-quality color printing is also within the reach of these users. CD-ROM has replaced the floppy disk as the distribution medium of choice. Book publishers are already taking advantage of the audio-visual possibilities offered by CD-ROM. A CD-ROM press costs the same today as a laser printer did five years ago and a single CD can be stamped for a lower price than printing a book.

Print was introduced to the Western World in the 15th century with Gutenberg's Bible but it took a further 300 years before books were a familiar sight in every home. The digital age has brought cheap photocopiers, printers and the CD-ROM and in their wake an information explosion. About fifteen million journals were published from the 17th century to the early 1960s but in that decade alone the figure was doubled and it is doubling again every ten years.

The rise of the World Wide Web has been nothing short of meteoric. In a very short period it has grown from a research institute project to the defining application of the information age. Personal computers and laser printers gave

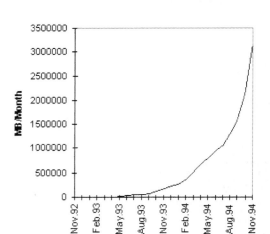

Figure 1.1 Growth of information delivered by the Web

individuals low-cost print production and CD-ROM gave them high-capacity random access storage. Now the Web closes the information loop by offering a mechanism for both production and global distribution. Anyone with a computer can become an information provider with a potential worldwide audience.

■ What is the Web?

Information isn't just knowledge hoarded on the world's databases. It implies communication. As the traditional media of newspapers, television and radio shifted their focus towards entertainment, computer networks have emerged as the primary carriers of information. The World Wide Web is an instrumental part of this change, leading some commentators to dub it 'the fourth medium'. The Web is a distributed information system based on the **Internet** computer network. Its primary strengths are the support for **hypertext**, **multimedia** and the **client–server** model.

- Hypertext is a way of organizing related knowledge by linking separate documents. These **hyperlinks** usually take the form of a high-lighted key word or phrase which when clicked loads the connected

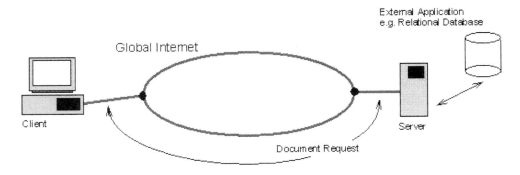

Figure 1.2   Client–server operation

document. Using the Internet, hypertext documents may span various computers in many countries forming a global information system.

- The Web extends the hypertext metaphor to include other resources. Any information for which suitable viewing software is available can be published on the Web. This includes pictures, sounds and video. The Web is better described as a **hypermedia** system.
- 'Client–server' is not just another piece of jargon but is key to distributing resources away from centralized and monolithic computing centers. The Web, like many other Internet applications, follows the client–server model. **Web servers** are responsible for processing

Media	Presentation	Organization	Portability	Cost
Print	High quality text and graphics. Good control over layout and presentation.	Random access at page level via contents and index.	No special issues.	High production costs. High distributions costs. Medium costs to end users.
CD-ROM	Combines text, graphics, audio and medium quality video clips.	Hypermedia. Possibility of direct random access within single CD-ROM	Limited. Multimedia capable laptop computer is required.	Medium production costs. Medium distribution costs. *Added Value* means high costs to end users.
The Web	Combines text and graphics. Limited control over presentation. Bandwidth is restricted.	Hypermedia. Possibility of direct random access to documents on remote computers.	Very limited portability, at present via laptop computer and low-bandwidth digital cell phone.	Medium production costs. Low distribution costs. No direct costs to end users.

Figure 1.3   Comparison of print, CD-ROM and the Web

requests for documents received from clients and for interacting with other applications.

The Web is interactive and also gives users a single interface to various Internet applications. In this way the Web and the Internet are symbiotic, one fueling growth in the other.

■ Out of Academia

The Web has been widely adopted in academic and, more recently, commercial circles. Many of these use computers running the powerful UNIX operating system. UNIX is popular in the research, education and business communities but in the home and on the desktop Windows is prevalent. Individuals and organizations who are already committed to Windows, '95 or NT, find it hard to justify running UNIX just for a Web server.

Fortunately the introduction of the NT operating system and the inclusion of Internet connectivity in the Windows 3.11 and '95 platforms has heralded a wave of Web software. This change is steadily moving the design and production of Web sites from a specialized technical role to a wider multi-skilled discipline involving information engineers, graphic and icon designers, technical authors, copywriters, typesetters and marketeers. Of course there is still a need for computer specialists when configuring the network and for programming tasks.

■ About this book

An old Greek guy once said something like, 'give me a firm place to stand and I will move the World.' In the shifting sands of information people are looking for that firm place, the ideas and innovations can be left to them. There is already an enormous quantity of on-line and printed documentation about designing and building Web sites. This books draws on that documentation and the author's own experiences to produce a concise and organized text for Windows users. Information is not obscured by references to other platforms. In the following chapters you will find what makes the Internet tick, learn how to prepare basic and advanced Web documents using familiar Windows software and discover how to integrate multimedia into the site. For more advanced users running a Web server on Microsoft's latest 32-bit operating systems, Windows '95 and NT are discussed. Web servers enable individuals and organizations to produce interactive documents and integrate these with

legacy systems. The recent advances in virtual reality and dynamic documents are presented in a separate chapter. Finally it will show how to build readership without breaking the rules of the Web. The aim has been to produce a book which is friendly, fun and easy to follow, one that can be read anywhere, not just sitting in front of a computer screen. The technical information has been interspersed with thoughts, insights and opinion to stimulate users on their own voyage of discovery.

▩ Conventions

Technical books are rarely read cover to cover. The information in *Go Web!* is presented in a logical progression, but to aid browsing margin icons have been used. ☜ Thumbs down illustrate problems that the site builder may encounter, ☀ bombs highlight security issues, ☝ an open hand indicates areas where caution should be exercised and finally ☝ thumbs up indicates a useful gem that makes the Web site an extra bit special. Where the information presented is incidental to the main flow but otherwise of interest it is contained in a separate panel.

▩ WebExtra and other value added features!

This book is accompanied by the following additional features:

- WebExtra, an on-line guide featuring updated information. To view, point your browser at `http://www.thomson.com/itcp.html`.
- A CD-ROM packed with much of the software you'll need to get your Web site up and running fast. A full description can be found in the Resources Guide at the rear of the book.
- Two reference guides. The HTML 3.0 card is a handy description of the HyperText Markup Language used to build Web documents. The Internet Assistant toolbar reference gives a quick guide to the toolbar icons used by this popular Web editor.

▩ The audience

The Web needs you! Although a tool of immense power it is still in infancy. This potential will be harnessed by a range of professionals drawn from the media and computer disciplines as well as people who suddenly find they have something to say and the tools to say it with. Some of the most interesting developments have been made by people who have recognized new areas and markets that can be exploited through the Web. The information should also be useful to experienced users, especially those who are migrating to the Microsoft platform. The only assumption is a familiarity with Microsoft Windows and an Internet connection.

2 Web basics

Before launching into the details of producing Web documents and running a server it is useful for the reader to have an overview of the Internet and how it integrates with the Web. This chapter gives a basic guide to the underlying technology and will help in understanding the rest of the book. It should also prove useful when reading other documentation which often assumes considerable familiarity with the subject.

To most people the World Wide Web and the Internet are synonymous. The explosion in Internet interest has been driven in large part by the commercial possibilities created by the Web. The Web is said to be the Internet's 'killer app'. That is, a single product which is so useful and popular it sells the whole. Many other applications and protocols use the Internet. Electronic mail (email), news discussion groups (Usenet News) and the file transfer protocol (FTP), which is used to retrieve files on remote computers.

The Web's popularity is further ensured by providing an interface to other Internet applications. Using a single program, called a **browser**, a user can navigate the Web, download files and applications, view many types of data, read News and send Email. This universal interface has led to developments in other areas. Moves are afoot to allow hyperlinks in news articles and email so that references to interesting material can be instantly followed. In this way the Web may subsume much of the present suite of Internet applications.

Although closely linked it should be remembered that the Internet and the Web are separate entities. Web documents can be created and usefully exist

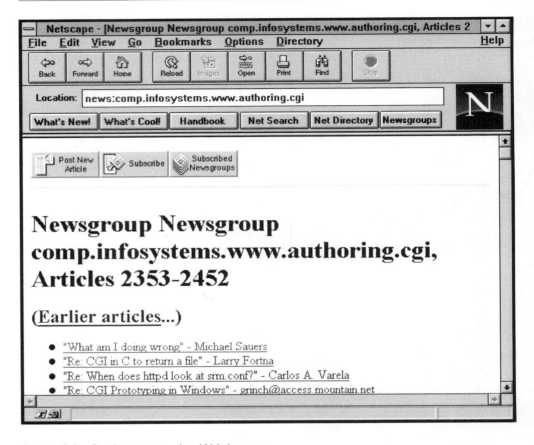

Figure 2.1 Reading news with a Web browser

outside of the Internet. They can be viewed directly with a Web browser, either from the local disk or from a shared file server. Even the HyperText Transfer Protocol (HTTP), the fundamental method of Web communications, is not restricted to the Internet and can be implemented on top of other types of network. For instance, Web browser software is available for CompuServe, a proprietary, non-Internet network. However most Web applications are based on the Internet Protocol (IP) suite and developers wishing to serve a wider audience or carry out more complex operations will have to run a Web server and be connected to an internet network.

▓ Protocols and the Internet

A protocol is a formal definition of how two parties communicate. If you were an Englishman meeting a compatriot at your favorite dining club you would extend your right hand and inquire about your friend's general state of health and then proceed to talk about the weather. As a response you would expect your friend to proffer his hand and confirm that he was in good health and reply that the weather 'is quite reasonable, considering the time of year.' Clicking heels, bowing and addressing ordinary people as 'Doctor' is not part of the protocol. In the same way when two computers communicate they must also follow a set protocol or risk being misunderstood, and in an analogy to our English gentlemen communications boffins have dubbed the initial exchange of information **handshaking**.

In the beginning there was the ARPANET, funded by the United States Defense Department. This linked a disparate array of networking technologies located at many sites. The Internet Protocol suite grew from a need to connect these diverse technologies into a single virtual network. The Internet Protocols allow connected computers, called hosts, to send packets of data to each other as though they were linked to the same local network. They were universally adopted by ARPANET hosts in the early 1980s and have proved popular because they are not oriented to any one particular operating system.

Many higher level protocols build on IP. Transmission Control Protocol (TCP) for the reliable transmission of data packets and the Simple Mail Transfer Protocol (SMTP) for email to name but two. The Internet can be viewed as a stack of protocols extending from the physical networks to the applications.

▓ The Internet

The sharp-eyed reader will notice that I've spelt 'internet' both with an upper and lower case. So just what is the Internet and what difference does the spelling make to the meaning?

The Internet has been called a network of networks because it links computers connected to a variety of local networks. These can be single machines connected by a modem and a phone line to an Internet Service

Provider, or a corporate enterprise network consisting of single or multiple Ethernets, Token Rings or other types of local area network (LAN). Indeed 'Internet' is a contraction of 'Inter-Networking'.

A more disingenuous definition of the Internet is, 'A fool at one end, a modem at the other,' misquoting Dr. Johnson's famous description of coarse fishing. Long hours spent burning the midnight oil (or the company's time) surfing the Web lend some credence to this skeptical view of affairs. In reality any activity carried to extremes can be harmful but when used intelligently the Internet and the Web offer enormous and unrivaled power as an information and communication resource.

The single defining factor of whether a computer forms part of the Internet is that each and every machine must communicate using the Internet Protocols. Computers connected to CompuServe or Microsoft's MSNet are not on the Internet proper but talk to the Internet through a gateway computer, a machine which converts the protocols used from one system to another. Users of these networks cannot run Internet applications directly but must rely on programs provided by their network operator. This software is called 'proprietary' because it cannot be used with any other system. A more nebulous term, **the Net**, can be thought to include other networks which offer some more limited form of Internet connectivity.

You don't have to be connected to the Internet to run the Internet Protocols on your computer(s). Local internets (note the lower case spelling) can run over an internal local area network or even on a single machine. The implication of this is that a fully functional Web site can provide an organization-wide information service with no connection to the wider Internet. A Web author can also fully test the site by running both server and browser software on the same machine.

■ Internet hostnames

'I am not a number, I am a free man', claimed Patrick McGoohan in the cult sixties TV series *The Prisoner*. How wrong he was, in the Information Age we are all numbers. Pin numbers, social security numbers and employee numbers all exist to make a computer's cyberlife easier. Numbers are behind all computer communications. Unlike *The Prisoner*, a.k.a. Number 6, we've all adapted, albeit with varying degrees of success.

The problem is that we humans are notoriously poor at remembering random sequences of numbers and judging by the frequency of misdialed phone numbers, even poorer at tapping them in. The short-term memory can hold about seven pieces of unconnected information and it's no coincidence that local phone numbers don't generally exceed this length. We eventually commit frequently used numbers to memory but phoning Great Auntie Vera who lives in Knutsford still has us reaching for the address book.

Numbers rule on the Internet too. When a packet is routed through the network the address isn't something you and I can readily understand but simply a number (one that is 32 bits long). Now you may already be familiar with and use Internet names of the form:

```
www.microsoft.com                  a Web site hostname
```

or

```
billyboy@microsoft.com             a personal email address
```

So there is obviously a bit of magic occurring. In fact it's quite straightforward. Somewhere there is a database that maps names, which humans find easy to remember and use, to those address numbers. In the days when the Internet consisted of only a few machines a single file called **hosts.txt** contained all the mappings. The Network Information Center (better known as the NIC) kept this file on their computer. The file consisted of name to address mappings much as the ETC\HOSTS file does on Microsoft systems, at least those with a Winsock interface:

```
192.42.172.1    pittsburg.edu

157.73.1.1      usaf.mil
```

Administrators would send the NIC the names and addresses of new machines and would periodically download hosts.txt to replace their own host file. This scheme is a bit like the local phone book that the telephone company updates and distributes annually. When a program needed to connect to a remote machine it looked up the address in the local copy of the host file.

Rapid growth of the Internet highlighted shortcomings with this scheme. Distributing a global name file is a bit like sending phone books for the whole world out to each telephone subscriber. In computer jargon 'it doesn't scale'. To resolve the problems a new scheme called the Domain Name System (DNS) was established.

■ DNS

DNS has delegated responsibility for parts of the hosts.txt file to specific areas of control on the Internet, called domains. If you are already connected to the Internet you will be part of a domain. For example, if you have a dial-up connection to an Internet Service Provider you will be part of their domain. My computer is called `threewiz` and is a member of the `demon.co.uk` domain run by Demon Internet Services in the United Kingdom:

```
threewiz.demon.co.uk
```

In turn Demon is part of the `uk` domain, one of the country-specific domains. Top-level domains also exist to represent bodies such as the US government (`.gov`) or commercial organizations (`.com`). Internet hostnames are resolved right to left. To access a machine on another network it is no longer necessary to look up the address in a copy of the global hosts.txt file but simply to ask Demon's **name server**. If it's another machine on Demon's network the address is returned immediately, otherwise the server makes an inquiry to some higher level server which will either resolve the address directly or point towards the server which controls the required domain. As a single domain can be large it is possible to split it into zones, each with its own name server responsible for a number of sub-domains. In the `demon.co.uk` example responsibility for the demon sub-domain has been delegated to Demon Internet Services and no longer forms part of the `uk` zone.

A domain can be a single local network or many networks spanning continents as is the case with the `.com` domain which covers hundreds of organizations all over the planet.

DNS is a sort of Internet directory inquiry service. When you call your local phone company inquiring about Great Auntie Vera's number they may have

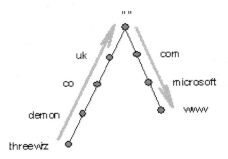

Figure 2.2   DNS lookup

the number in their records, if not they will have to contact the phone company responsible for that area or if it is in another country the International Directory Inquiry service, the root domain in DNS terms.

◼ Is DNS for me?

Unless you are running a phone exchange you won't want to provide a directory inquiry service and unless you are responsible for a domain you probably won't want to run a DNS server. You will be a user of DNS and with the Web nearly every document you access will involve a DNS inquiry. The Web places an enormous load on the DNS system. Failure to find a hostname can be due to the browser timing out waiting for a response or simply because the DNS server is off-line. If the problem lies between you and the host's domain you can try another server.

Windows and '95 are geared towards the client side and users will be consumers of DNS services. Microsoft's server-oriented operating system, NT, contains a partial implementation of DNS in the resource kit. Zone transfers, where a copy of all the hostname to address mappings is automatically transferred between servers, are not supported. There are commercial implementations of fully fledged DNS servers for NT.

◼ Multihoming

Multihoming enables many internet addresses to resolve to the same host. Thus the hostnames:

```
www.kimble.co.uk

www.threewiz.com
```

could really both be the same machine (with suitable addresses and routing entries in the **uk** and **com** DNS databases). The machine must support multiple addresses on the same network interface. This requirement is due to a limitation of the HTTP protocol. The site's Web server is responsible for returning the correct documents based on the address used. This service provides a professional image for customers not wishing to incur the problems involved in actually running a server.

An understanding of DNS is important for commercial Web sites which may be responsible for their own domain and have to set up services such as **multi-homing**.

■ Internet addresses

With Internet applications such as the Web it is possible to use an Internet address directly in place of the hostname, so:

```
threewiz.demon.co.uk
```

is the same as:

```
158.152.116.88
```

and we don't have to make a DNS lookup.

Internet addresses are 32-bit numbers but are written as four separate bytes (octets) in a **dotted notation**. Addresses are composed of a network and host part. The network part identifies the network to which the host is connected and the host part the particular machine on the network. Three network sizes are supported, these are called **Class A, B** and **C** networks and it should be remembered that these differ in topology from the underlying physical networks. With a Class C address the three leading octets identify the network

■ Dotted IP address notation

An Internet address not only identifies a host but each byte, or octet, conveys the type of network and also corresponds to components of the hostname. Unlike hostnames Internet addresses are read from left to right.

Network		Host		
10011110.10011000.	01110100.01011000			32-bit address
158.	152.	116.	88	Class B network
uk.co.demon.			threewiz	Hostname components

A leading **0** in the address indicates a Class A network, **1** a Class B network and **11** a Class C network.

and the final octet the host; it can support 256 individual machines and each machine will have an address of the form:

```
192.152.116.n
```

where the n is the machine number. Similarly Class B addresses identify the network by the leading two octets and Class A the first octet. Examples of each would be:

```
128.172.n.n  and  11.n.n.n
```

Even the smallest Internet network doesn't have to correspond to a real network. Using **subnetting** a single Class C network could be divided over different local networks.

If your local network is not connected to the global Internet you can pick any range of addresses but be warned. If you subsequently get connected you will have to change all these. It may be worth deciding in advance what Internet topology suits your network and registering your domain.

Machines which form a bridge between two internets, such as the company network and the global Internet, will have two Internet addresses. Every machine on the local internet requiring access will also need its own unique Internet address. Where an organization has been assigned a Class A, B or C network address these can be allocated directly from that block. Nowadays it's very difficult to get any more than a Class C network address.

Using the Web, it's possible to provide a range of Internet services to the whole company while only having a single Internet address and a point-to-point connection to the Internet service provider. This entails running a **proxy** server on the gateway machine. Addresses on the local network may be assigned without regard to the global Internet. The proxy provides services on behalf of other systems. If a Web browser requests a document the request is sent to the proxy rather than directly over the Internet. The proxy then contacts the remote host and downloads the document and forwards it onto the browser.

This type of operation is called **store and forward** and works equally well for other Internet services such as news and email. If the gateway machine is made ultra-secure by restricting who can use it and disabling unused Internet services this configuration can form part of a **firewall**. Hackers cannot directly access any machine on the local network because these machines are not actually part of the global Internet. They would have to crack the gateway and then break in from there. If the firewall is secure it may be okay to be fairly lax about internal security.

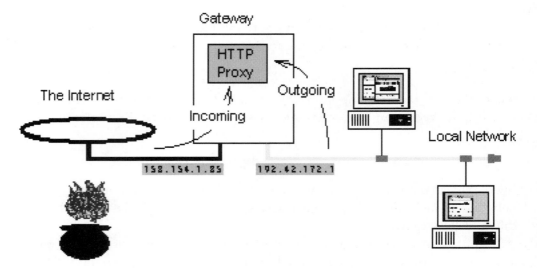

Figure 2.3 Proxy server

Running a proxy has a further benefit because it can store copies of previously requested documents locally. This store is called a **cache**. If this copy is up to date it is returned directly to the requester. This saves a potentially slow download over the Internet. Web browsers may also have a cache of documents but the advantage of a proxy's cache is that the local copies are available to everyone.

▪ The limits of growth

The 32-bit addresses used on the Internet have a range of 4 228 250 625, which is a shade over 4 billion hosts. This would appear adequate for the time being but life is never that simple. A single Class C network takes 256 addresses but depending on its size only a few addresses may get allocated. Class B and A topologies may exacerbate the problem where the organization has no immediate requirement for the range of addresses available. In reality the Internet address scheme is full of holes.

 Some Internet Service Providers have addressed this problem by using **dynamic addresses**. Rather than giving each dial-up user a permanent Internet address a dynamic address is allocated with each connection. Thus the host `chips.elan.net` may have the address `192.129.172.2` one day and `192.129.172.137` the next. Elan may have a Class C network with only 256 addresses available and as many dial-in lines but still be able to service

■ Internet packets and routing

An Internet packet is a bit like an envelope which features both a destination and return address and contains information. An envelope may be routed through many post offices and be carried by different modes of transport on its journey. The recipient can send a reply to the return address, but if this is incorrect it will get lost. The 'single IP address serves all' set-up described previously will suffer from a similar problem as only the gateway machine has a globally recognized address. It's a like bit deciding you don't like living at '13, Windy Drive' and choosing another address. It won't fit in with the post office's scheme and incoming letters will vanish.

Without a proxy server it may still be possible for a local machine to send outgoing packets, after all the destination address *is* valid. This is illustrated using the `ping` utility from a local host, the transmit data light on the gateway machine's modem will flash but the receive light will show that no packets are being returned. This sort of physical conformation is useful for diagnosing network problems.

thousands of users. A Web site could still be permanently connected to Elan over the phone line but unless Elan's DNS database can be updated with each connection Internet users won't be able to find the site. It's worth inquiring exactly what sort of connection you are being sold.

■ Reverse mapping

Given an Internet address it is possible to find the hostname of the machine by using a **reverse name server**. This is useful when analyzing Web server log files. If logging is enabled, the Web server will store an entry for every request made in a log file. This entry takes the form of a date and time, the machine accessed and the IP address of the foreign host. Programs that analyze these log files use reverse name servers to turn these dotted IP addresses into more meaningful hostnames. There are some interesting things to watch out for. If the foreign host was allocated a dynamic address this will not be resolved to a hostname. There will also be an unusually large number of requests from a few hosts. These hosts will either be proxy servers or gateways to networks outside of the Internet; in both cases the host is making requests on behalf of other users.

■ Internet, the Next Generation

A proposal exists for an extended Internet addressing scheme. Internet Next Generation (InNG), as the new scheme is boldly called, will have an almost infinite capacity (for mathematicians that's: ∞ – a bit) so that in future an everyday consumer item such as a toaster may very well have an Internet address. This is not quite so outrageous as it sounds. The drinks machines at MIT in Boston have long been Internet connected and inquiries can be made around the world as to how many cans of drink remain in the hopper. I was quite disappointed in 1991 when, having first checked the machine had a few cans of my favorite brew from the comfort of my desk in France, I found it was out of order when I arrived in Boston a day later! Companies such as SGS Thompson are already selling powerful RISC processors for use in mundane items like washing machines and refrigerators. Who knows, maybe the fridge of the future will run a Web server and you will be able to select tonight's TV (or is that Internet?) dinner with the click of a mouse! For the shape of things to come check out Paul's Fridge:

`http://hamjudo.com/cgi-bin/refridgerator.`

■ Other protocols

The Internet Protocols are fairly low level and it is normal for an application to access them through several higher level protocols. TCP is often directly associated with the Internet Protocol suite and statements such as 'The Internet is built using the TCP/IP protocols' are sometimes made. This is not entirely accurate. User Datagram Protocol (UDP) is another protocol used directly with the Internet Protocols and in fact provides little more than a programmer interface to IP, the abbreviation UDP/IP is used in this case. Web browsers and servers access these protocols through **sockets**, a standard library of network routines. Microsoft has its own implementation, the Winsock Dynamic Library or **Winsock DLL** for short.

■ Ports

Internet addresses provide a mechanism for routing packets to and from remote machines but they don't specify which particular application should receive the data. A further piece of information, called a **port**, names the application or service. If an Internet hostname is analogous to the address of a building then a port is like a floor number within that building.

Common servers typically use a **well-known port**, a quick glance at the local `etc\services` will list some of these. TCP Port 80 is assigned to Web servers, 21 for FTP and so on. You can make your Web server listen on any port which isn't already in use and note that a TCP Port of 80 is different from a UDP Port of 80! It is *very* bad practice to reuse well-known ports, even if you are not running that particular service. Some operating systems restrict access to ports below 1024, so 8080 is often chosen as an alternative for Web servers.

 If you have an active session with your Web server the internet utility `netstat` will show details of the connection:

```
C:\ netstat -a

Proto    Local Address       Foreign Address     State
TCP      kimble:80           threewiz:3102       TIME_WAIT
...
```

Here we see that the browser is running on threewiz and has its own port number of 3102. These two pieces of information are used to form the unique reply address.

▓ Web names

The location box in Figure 2.1 shows an example of the Web naming scheme called a Uniform Resource Locator or, more commonly, URL. URLs are used to access resources such as the news article shown in Figure 2.1 and can be typed directly into a Web browser or embedded within Web documents as hyperlinks. The URL is divided into two parts and the basic syntax is:

SCHEME:PATH

Scheme specifies the protocol to be used and **path** the location of the resource to be retrieved. The exact set of protocols available is browser dependent. The format of the path depends on the protocol used and an understanding of that protocol is useful when composing the path field.

For example news follows the newsgroup and article id format

```
news:comp.infosystems.www.authoring.cgi
```

will display a list of articles in the cgi newsgroup and

■ URLs, URIs and resources

The Internet is a community. Standards are not adopted by dictat but arise out of lengthy discussions. The kick-off is often a Request For Comments (RFC) document and this forms the basis for the standard. The document governing how resources on Internet hosts are located is called RFC1630. This proposes the Uniform Resource Identifier (URI) scheme. The Web's own Uniform Resource Locator (URL) is a specific form of URI. The word **resource** is used in preference to document because it is more general and encompasses all types of data.

```
news:3t4v37$s9o@comet.magicnet.net
```

shows the text of a particular article. The news scheme tells the browser to contact a news server using the Network News Transfer Protocol (NNTP) and retrieves the information specified by the path.

Other schemes use the convention of a hostname and port number to identify the host and server program. This is followed by some further information to enable the remote server to identify the requested resource. Supported protocols typically include but are not limited to: HTTP, FILE, FTP and MAILTO.

■ HyperText Transfer Protocol

HTTP is the protocol used by the Web to transfer resources from a server to a browser. The path component consists of a double forward slash followed by an internet hostname or address and an optional port number. A single forward slash separates this from the path of the requested document:

```
http://Hostname[:Port]/Document-Path
```

This is similar to the network path format used in Windows. The optional (signified by the square brackets) port number identifies a particular server on a machine (an internet service). The number 80 has been globally assigned to Web, that is HTTP servers, and is the default. If an alternative port is used make sure you are talking to a Web server.

The document path specifies the location of a Web document under the server directory tree. If omitted it normally defaults to a file such as `index.htm`

▨ Spoofing

It's possible to deceive Internet servers into thinking that you are their client by mimicking the protocol; this is commonly known as **spoofing**. The easiest way to do this is with the `telnet` utility. Telnet is normally used to connect to the `telnetd` service giving users a command line on the remote host but it can be used to connect to any other Internet service. You can tell if the port is for a Web server by connecting to the system using the telnet utility:

```
telnet www.microsoft.com 80
```

and spoofing the HTTP conversation by typing:

```
GET / HTTP/1.0
```

The server should return a header and possibly the default document at the root of the server's directory tree:

```
HTTP/1.0 200 OK
Server: HTTPS/0.96
Allow: GET HEAD POST
MIME-version: 1.0
Content-type: text/html
...
```

This header provides us with some interesting information including the type of server which is running, in this case the EMWAC HTTPS server for Windows NT. Using telnet in this way obviously requires some quite detailed knowledge of the protocols involved; users who are familiar with SMTP can send hoax emails. Watch out, that message from Bill Gates may not be all that it seems!

or `default.htm`; if there is no default document a complete listing of the directory may be returned by the server. On Microsoft systems path names are not case sensitive, thus:

```
http://www.kimble.co.uk:80/dOcS/dEfauLT.htM
```

is identical to:

```
http://www.kimble.co.uk/docs/default.htm
```

or:

```
http://www.kimble.co.uk/docs
```

Note that a forward slash '/' character is used for separating the directory hierarchy.

 If you move your documents to systems which are case sensitive the URLs and actual filenames must match. Several other characters have special meaning when given within the document-path component of a URL and these will be covered later.

 If the context of the document is known, for instance you are following a hyperlink to a local document, a **partial URL** can be given. This can be no more than a filename if the resource is in the same directory as the current document; in this case the above examples could refer directly to `default.htm`. When embedding URLs the partial form is preferred as it permits groups of documents to be moved.

■ File

Web browsers can view files on local or network disk drives directly using the file scheme. There is no request to a server, enabling a local web of documents to be constructed. The syntax is similar to HTTP:

```
file://[Hostname]/Document-Path
```

If a hostname is given it specifies the original location of the document. If the file is missing it may be because the current document has been moved. The browser will know this because the hostname will not match that of the current system. It may be possible for the browser to use a protocol such as FTP for retrieval. The special name of *localhost* can be used where the file should exist on all relevant systems. A good example is the Windows `AUTOEXEC.BAT` file:

```
file://localhost/C:/AUTOEXEC.BAT
```

On Microsoft systems the drive, in this example C, can be specified as shown.

■ File Transfer Protocol

F-T-P-ing is a popular and ancient net activity and is the preferred way of downloading software and other files. In days of yore users had to issue obscure incantations to terse and unfriendly programs to fulfill their software needs. FTP is a protocol for the safe transfer of files. Data is transmitted as a series of small packets with various checks, counts and retries to make sure nothing is lost in cyberspace.

Most Web browsers understand this protocol and can be used to fetch files, either directly from servers or from helpful hyperlinks within Web documents. FTP sites also require user names and passwords and so the syntax is a little different:

```
ftp://[Username[:Password]@]Hostname[:Port]/Document-
Path[;type=Code]
```

Most public FTP sites require a password of `anonymous` and your complete email address as the user name. This form of transfer is called **anonymous FTP** and the transfer may be recorded. If the username and password are omitted they default to the anonymous values with the email address being picked up from the browser configuration, for example the URL:

```
ftp://ftp.demon.co.uk/pub/winnt/gdit.zip
```

would download the file `gdit.zip` from Demon's anonymous FTP server.

If the final filename is omitted a complete directory listing is displayed. Files are either pure ASCII, that is text, or binary data. The content of a file can normally be deduced from the suffix: .TXT would be ASCII and .ZIP binary but there are no absolute standards which govern FTP sites. Binary data should not be transferred as ASCII because character mappings may be performed. The file type may be specified as A for ASCII and I for binary.

There is also a security breach Web builders should be aware of. The password, held as plain text, is clear for everyone to see, either on screen, in Web documents and even when the URL is sent over the Internet. To avoid passwords being compromised it is advisable to restrict Web usage to anonymous FTP. Sensitive material should be moved from the public FTP directories.

Support for FTP within Web documents has taken a lot of hassle out of downloading files and enables distributors to place links to software components within on-line documentation.

▓ Mail

The mailto scheme is useful for including contact information within Web documents or for sending email from a browser:

```
mailto:david@threewiz.demon.co.uk
```

The Web browser will display a mail form with the destination address already completed. Unfortunately there is no way of directly specifying the subject line. The browser (or email program) passes the message onto a mail server to be forwarded to its destination. Addresses follow the Internet mail format.

■ Summary

- The Internet is composed of computers which communicate with the Internet Protocol suite.
- The Web provides a common interface to many Internet applications.
- The Internet uses a 32-bit addressing scheme. Hostnames are converted to addresses by the domain name system.
- A single Web server can be known by many different names.
- Proxy servers improve both security and speed of access.
- The Uniform Resource Locator naming scheme specifies both application protocol and the target resource.
- Web documents are transferred from servers to clients using the HyperText Transfer Protocol.
- Web documents can be accessed locally.

3 | Creating pages

The lingua franca of the Web is the HyperText Markup Language (HTML). All Web documents are written in HTML. The language describes the structural elements of a document and combines this with the ability to make links to other resources. These hyperlinks can be text or graphics, usually they are selected with a mouse click, loading the linked resource. HTML is not a page description language like PostScript. You cannot specify that the body text is in two columns set in Garamond 11 point font. Instead you describe the structure of the document such as headings and lists and let the browser decide how best to render them. This makes Web documents portable over a wide range of hardware including: Braille and simple character-based terminals and high-end graphic workstations.

■ HTML

HTML is an application of the Standard Generalized Markup Language (SGML). SGML has the backing of the International Standards Organization and provides a formal definition of the HTML syntax. The generic nature and simplicity of the language means that a wide range of applications can generate HTML output and a huge selection of hardware can view that output. This is an obvious advantage over a proprietary format like Microsoft's Word or even standards such as Adobe's Portable Document Format (PDF) both of which require the purchase of special hardware and software even when the basic viewer is available for free.

■ Programming HTML

Creating Web pages can be seen in the same light as typesetting. The name of one popular HTML editor, HoTMetaL (the capitals spell HTML) harks back to the bygone era of compositors, molten lead and ink-stained fingers. People talk about HTML programming just as they speak of programming a video or microwave. This doesn't mean that HTML is a programming language with control constructs, Boolean logic and looping. Indeed, new tools like Microsoft's Internet Assistant (IA) for Word, allow Web authors to create HTML documents without even getting their fingers dirty.

An HTML document is written as text and contains descriptive markup tags. Thus a Web page can be created using a text editor and as it is not encoded before transmission the source of that page can be readily viewed by the end user. One of the best ways of learning new and interesting techniques is to view the source of the page in question. This also has the implication that any whizzy new ways you discover for arranging text will quickly become known to the Net community at large.

Even though HTML is designed to be simple and platform independent it is divided into 3 levels. Writing for level 0 ensures that everyone will be able to read the document. Level 1 adds images and special text effects such as highlighting. These may not be seen by text-only browsers like Lynx. Many Web users, especially those on dial-up or slow lines, also run their browsers in text-only mode. It's still possible to create a Level 1 document which Level 0 users can read and browse but care must be taken in the use of images. Some sites offer an alternative text-only page by placing a link near the head of the document. Level 2 introduces fill-out forms.

As with any living language the original syntax of HTML has evolved, fragmented into dialects and at some points recombined. The current standard is version 2.0. The now defunct HTML+ and its offspring HTML version 3.0 provide extensions including tables, mathematical symbols and better control over layout. Netscape, who have captured a good two thirds of the Web browser market, also have a set of extensions to version 2.0 which only their browsers understand. There is some compatibility with HTML 3.0 and Netscape have publicly committed themselves to implementing version 3.0 when the standard is ratified. In order to differentiate them from HTML, the Netscape extensions are more simply referred to as **Netscapisms**.

■ The Netscape controversy

There is a great deal of debate in the Web community as to whether the Netscape extensions are a good thing. Many users, seeing that the majority of the browser market belongs to Netscape, view the Netscapisms as a *de facto* standard. Much controversy and long threads of discussion revolve around such simple directives as the centering of text. Competition and evolution are undoubtedly beneficial but some of the new directives have smacked more of revolution to the HTML world. Netscape's dominant market position has forced the specification to adopt markup which is not altogether in keeping with the overall structure and objectives of the language.

With a majority of the market place the choice of using the Netscape extensions may not seem all that drastic if a job needs to be done. However the Net is a fickle place. Netscape built market share by offering novel features and through effectively making their browser free. Last year's browser of choice was Mosaic and next it could be Sun's HotJava. What looks good on today's top browser may appear disjointed and poorly organized to a growing band of users. To see just how fierce the winds of change can blow take a look at the forlorn lists of books with 'Mosaic' in the title. Not a good marketing decision.

Treading a middle path is probably the best compromise. Where HTML 2.0 proves too limited, use the Netscapisms. The extensions are benign and other browsers generally ignore them. They should not adversely affect the rendering of the document except where a particular effect is relied upon. Tables are an example, in this case mark the page as Netscape specific and if possible, offer alternative versions. If you are being really flash your server can detect which browser is being used and you can supply a Netscape or HTML 2.0 compliant page dynamically. Where Netscape also supports the HTML 3.0 syntax use that, a good example is when centering text. Finally check your documents with at least one other browser to make sure they are readable by the widest possible audience. A text browser is a really good choice for your second string.

■ HTML document structure

An HTML document is a combination of text and **markup tags**. A markup tag and an associated piece of text is called an **element**. The element is delineated by start tags: < > and end tags: </ >. For example:

```
<B>This Text is Bold</B>
```

will embolden the text between the tags. Some elements only have a start tag and other end tags, such as those for paragraphs, may be inferred by context and omitted. Where both start and end tags are used the element is called a **container**. Elements can be nested with a few exceptions, accordingly elements of a list can contain separate paragraphs. The tags contain a descriptive **name** which is case insensitive with no white space permitted before the leading '<' character. <HeaD>, <head> and <HEAD> are all legal tag names whereas < HEAD> is not.

An HTML document consists of three sections:

1. The **prolog** identifies the HTML specification the document conforms to.
2. The **head** gives an unordered set of information about the document.
3. The **body** contains the document itself.

The example below shows a typical document the structure tags are shown in bold for clarity:

```
<!DOCTYPE HTML PUBLIC "-//IETF//DTD HTML 2.0//EN">
<HTML>
<!-- HTML 2 Document Follows -->
<HEAD>
<!-- Head of Document -->
<TITLE>An HTML Document Example</TITLE>
</HEAD>
<BODY>
<!-- Body of Document -->
<H1>Simple HTML 2 document</H1>
<H2>Introduction</H2>
<P>This simple document illustrates the structure and
some tags used in HTML.
<H2>Document Structure</H2>
<P>An HTML document is composed of 3 sections:
<OL>
<LI>Prologue
<LI>Head
<LI>Body
</OL>
</BODY>
</HTML>
```

Figure 3.1 A typical HTML document

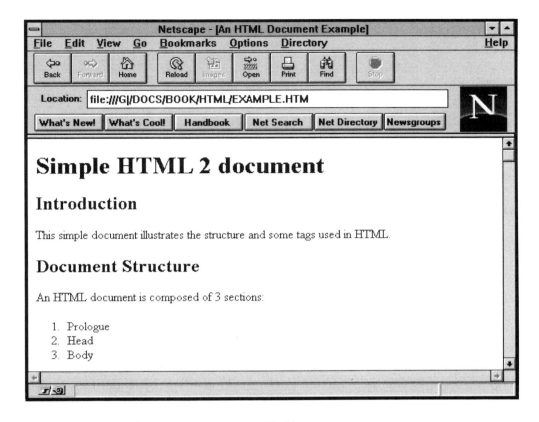

Figure 3.2 A typical document as interpreted by Netscape

In fact both the PROLOG, HEAD and BODY elements of a document can be omitted leaving the TITLE as the only mandatory part. A minimal HTML document is:

```
<TITLE>Small HTML Document</TITLE>
```

The TITLE isn't displayed within the document but is generally shown on the browser's title bar at the top of the window. Figure 3.2 shows how the example document from Figure 3.1 would be rendered by the Netscape browser.

If the DOCTYPE directive isn't present in the prolog then HTML 2.0 is assumed. In practice the head and body sections should always be included as it permits a browser to locate information like the TITLE without having to read the whole document. For brevity the examples shown in this book are partial and this style should not be emulated!

```
<HTML>
  <HEAD>
    <TITLE>...</TITLE>
  </HEAD>
  <BODY>
    <H1>...</H1>
      <H2>...</H2>
      <H2>...</H2>
    <H1>...</H1>
  </BODY>
</HTML>
```

Figure 3.3   Hierarchy of an HTML document

An HTML document forms a hierarchy of elements all of which should be specified in the correct order and place. The HTML element identifies the contents as HyperText Markup Language and contains the head and body of the document. Similarly the body may contain headings and these should begin with level 1 and continue in sequence. A document should not contain a level 1 heading and then skip to level 4 before continuing with level 1. The different tags are for marking the structure of the document not for rendering a particular style on a given browser.

The indentation is used to highlight the structure although leading spaces before a tag are ignored.

■ HTML 2.0

There are some documents that are still based around earlier versions of HTML but version 2.0 is the standard in use today. These earlier documents can be read with HTML 2.0 browsers and backwards compatibility is a basic aim of the HTML definition. The growing range and sophistication of editors allows simple documents to be created and converted with little direct knowledge of HTML. In particular the basic document structure and appropriate DOCTYPE directive will be inserted automatically by an editor. To get the best from these tools, a familiarity with the basics of HTML is useful. This section takes a look at the most important markup elements. A full description of HTML can be found in the specifications.

■ Writing HTML

HTML is not supposed to be difficult to write or read. Enough HTML to create simple documents can be learnt in five minutes! Existing text can be plugged in to the structure shown in Figure 3.1. The real skill is not in remembering and entering tag names but in having a good idea of how to structure a document and the effect each element has on that structure.

■ Comments

Apart from the DOCTYPE directive comments can also appear outside of the head/body structure. Any text within comment tags is ignored by the browser:

```
<!— This is a comment —>
```

The '—>' string is treated as the end of a comment and so cannot be nested.

■ The head

The head contains information about a document of which only the TITLE element is mandatory. Meta-information is so-called **information of a higher order**, that is, elements which may have an effect on a document but won't be displayed within the document text. As an analogy, paper quality and quantity of correction fluid provides meta-information for typed business letters, indicating the amount of value the writer places on the correspondence. Other meta-information includes: BASE, ISINDEX, LINK, META and NEXTID. The ISINDEX element may also be located outside of this section.

■ Title

Elements such as highlighting or paragraph information may not be nested within a title. These make no sense within the context as the TITLE element is used in the browser's **bookmark** list and its window caption.

■ Base

The BASE element can be used to specify the URL of a document.

```
BASE HREF="http://kimble.co.uk/book/intro.htm"
```

HREF is called an **attribute** and the text within the quotation marks refers to a URL. Quotes are only necessary where the text doesn't follow the proper syntax, that is it contains characters which should be encoded; an obvious example is the forward slash. Where partial URLs are used they are resolved relative to the current document. If the document has been moved or downloaded by a user it is said to be 'out of context' and this resolution will fail. If a base URL is specified it will be used when resolving all the partial URLs which follow it:

```
<A HREF="index.htm">Return to the Index</A>
```

In this example the hypertext anchor `index.htm` will be resolved as `http://kimble.co.uk/book/chap/index.htm`.

Usually the URL of the document will be specified using a BASE element located in the head, any trailing filename is stripped before the URL is appended.

If a downloadable version of the documents is available, perhaps as a ZIP file archive, the BASE element should be removed as resolution will be made to the on-line URLs and not the local documents.

■ Isindex

The `ISINDEX` tag marks the document as searchable. The browser will display a search field at the point of the `ISINDEX` tag:

```
<TITLE>International Widget - Product Support</TITLE>
<H1>Customer Support Database</H1>
<P>Check out our extensive product support database.
<ISINDEX>
```

Completing the field and hitting return will cause the URL to be resubmitted but with a search or **query string** appended. Alternatively the search string can be typed directly by the user without reading the `ISINDEX` document.

Searching for the keywords `i/o errors`, Figure 3.4, will generate the new request:

```
http://192.42.172.2/book/chap3/ISINDEX.HTM?i%2Fo+errors
```

This URL is processed by the server, either by invoking a script written by the Web site developer or by using a preconfigured search engine. This procedure is discussed in more detail in Chapters 8 and 9.

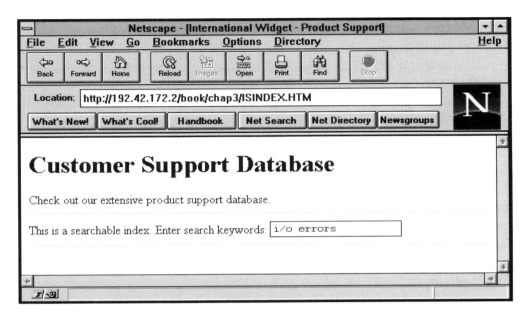

Figure 3.4 A document search

▨ Query strings

In the above URL the question mark '?' character separates the document path from a query string. Query strings are used to pass user data to backend server programs. Spaces in the string are replaced by '+' characters.

▨ Encoded characters

Certain characters are not permitted within a URL. The space character is one example and the forward slash character '/', which is used as a hierarchical path separator, another. These characters must be encoded. Character encodings are represented by a '%' followed by two hexadecimal (base 16) digits. These digits correspond to the character's value in the ISO-8859 or US ASCII character set. The preceding search example represents the slash as the encoding: %2F.

These encodings can present a security loophole. Where necessary checks on user input must cover both encoded and unencoded versions of characters. For instance the previous directory can be represented in a path by two dots '..' or the encoding: %2E%2E. This may enable a rogue user to break out of a given directory tree.

■ Meta

The META element encodes information which is not directly defined in the HTML specification. Meta information can be used by both clients and servers. One possibility is to embed information useful to a script. This information would have no meaning outside of the script's context. HTTP header fields can also be specified using named attributes:

```
<META NAME="Version" CONTENT="$Revision: 1.6 $">
<META HTTP-EQUIV="Expires" CONTENT="Mon, 19th
September 1995 18:07:00 GMT">
```

The server may choose to generate the HTTP header field:

```
Expires: Mon, 19th September 1995 18:07:00 GMT
```

if so configured. HTTP is covered in more detail in Chapter 7.

■ The body

The BODY element contains the text of the document. Markup directives may be embedded to structure and format the text.

■ Text formatting

HTML provides little control over the presentation of text, in particular type-faces and font sizes cannot be specified. The text formatting elements are primarily concerned with the semantic and visual appearance of characters within a paragraph. All of these markup elements are level 1 features.

The difference between **semantic** and **physical** markup is not immediately obvious. If we refer to a published document the convention is to render the reference in italic text: <I>Spinning the Web</I> but the semantic markup can also be used: <CITE>Spinning the Web</CITE>. This tells the browser that the contained text cites a publication. The difference is only obvious where the browser can't render italic text. In the first example all meaning will be lost but with the cited text the browser will find another way of making the reference apparent to the reader. For instance a braille terminal might choose to send a short electric shock through the reader's fingers! This simple example shows the essential difference between formatting and markup.

Table 3.1 Semantic markup elements and typical rendering

Citations	`<CITE>`Kramer v. Kramer`</CITE>`	*Kramer v. Kramer*
Code	`<CODE>`do. . . while`</CODE>`	`do . . . while`
Emphasis	`<EM>`will be done`</EM>`	*will be done*
Keyboard	`<KBD>`format a:`<KBD>`	`format a:`
Sample	`<SAMP>`Sample`</SAMP>`	`Sample`
Strong	`<STRONG>`Warning`</STRONG>`	**Warning**
Variable	`<VAR>`Variable`</VAR>`	*objectA*

Table 3.2 Physical markup elements and typical rendering

Bold	`<B>`Bold`</B>`	**Bold**
Italic	`<I>`Italic`</I>`	*Italic*
Teletype	`<TT>`Teletype`</TT>`	`Teletype`

▨ Character sets

The US ASCII or ISO-8859-1 character set is used. This has characters for most Western European alphabets. Where the keyboard doesn't explicitly provide a character, or the character may be interpreted as markup, a **character entity** must be given:

`&#214;`	`&Ouml;`	Ö	O umlaut
`&#60;`	`&lt;`	<	less than symbol

Character entities always use the ISO-8859-1 character set and can be entered either as the decimal index or a name. O umlaut is always represented by `&#214;` irrespective of the document's declared character set. Restricting HTML to 7-bit ASCII (codes between 1 and 127) makes documents highly portable between different systems.

■ Headings

Six different levels of headings can be represented in an HTML document:

```
<H1>Highest Level</H1>

<H6>Lowest Level</H6>
```

Figure 3.2 shows level 1 and 2 headings. Although the exact rendering is browser dependent the emphasis usually decreases with each level. Line spacing is used above and below a heading and paragraph breaks are implied before and after.

■ Text blocks

Paragraph markup must be used where a new paragraph is not implied by other elements:

```
<H1>Introduction</H1>
This is the first paragraph.</P>
<P>This is the second paragraph.
<BR>This is a line break. A second sentence 
won't be broken after the word <EM>sentence.</EM>
```

The end paragraph tag is optional. A paragraph is normally surrounded by vertical space. Line breaks, horizontal tab and multiple white space characters are ignored within the paragraph text. Line breaks can be forced using the <BR> tag. Horizontal tabs are converted to a single space. The no-breaking space: , character entity may be used to stop the browser starting a new line at a given word break.

Lines of text can be quoted using the BLOCKQUOTE element. This may cover many paragraphs such as an excerpt from a novel or poem:

```
Or as Descartes might have said
<BLOCKQUOTE>
<P>I'm pink, therefore I'm Spam.
</BLOCKQUOTE>
If he had a sense of humor!
```

Quoted text is typically displayed in an italic font. A BLOCKQUOTE element implies a paragraph break before and after the quoted text.

Tables and other data which require a fixed-width font can be enclosed with the preformatted text element: <PRE>. Preformatted text elements respect line break positions, multiple space and tab characters. Tab characters should space across to the next 8th column, e.g. 8, 16, 24 . . . character positions. Their use is not recommended and results can differ from browser to browser. The default line length is 80 characters but an optional WIDTH attribute specifies sizes of 40, 80 and 132 characters with other values being rounded to these amounts. Elements such as paragraphs, headings and address blocks are incompatible with preformatted text.

```
<PRE WIDTH="40">
<B>
Date          GOPHER       WWW</B>
Nov 1992      24,744       39
May 1993      103,870      17,298
Nov 1993      291,133      172,340
May 1994      555,708      799,163
Nov 1994      867,043      3,126,195

<B>Table 1:</B> bi-annual growth in information ser-
vices.
</PRE>
<HR><ADDRESS>
<A HREF="http://info.isoc.org/home.html">The Internet
Society</A><BR>
November 1994
</ADDRESS>
```

The above code fragment also shows how an address may be marked. The rendering of this code is given in Figure 3.5. A paragraph break is implied above and below the ADDRESS element.

Paragraphs, headings and similar blocks can be divided using horizontal rules represented by the <HR> tag. It's also possible to design and include custom rules using the IMAGE element. The disadvantage of this approach is that they won't be resized with changes to the browser window.

▓ Images

Text can be interspersed with graphics using the IMAGE element. Not all browsers can render images and some are restricted to just the CompuServe Graphics Interchange Format (GIF), although these often have the capability to send the image data to another program for display. As graphics tend to be

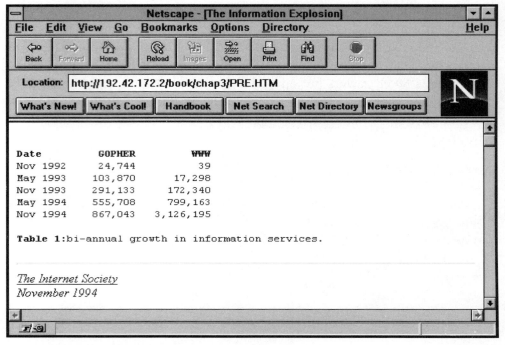

Figure 3.5 Preformatted text

large, bandwidth-conscious users may also run their browsers in **text-only** mode. In these cases the ALT attribute gives a text description of the image.

```
Mountain biking
<IMG SRC="bike.gif" ALT="MTB Icon" ALIGN="MIDDLE"> is a
pleasant way to see the countryside.
<P>
<IMG SRC="http://www.mtb.org/docs/bike2.gif" ALT="Bicycle
on hill" ALIGN=æBOTTOM"><B>Fig 1:</B> In the hills.
<P>
At home in the hills, mountain bikes are also a practical
way to negotiate potholed city streets.
```

An IMAGE element is treated in the same way as a text character. A line break before or after the element is rendered as a single space. Images do not imply a paragraph break and they can appear embedded in the text or at the start of a line.

The SRC attribute gives the URL of the image. This can be a local or remote file. The base URL will be appended to this attribute if the file is removed from

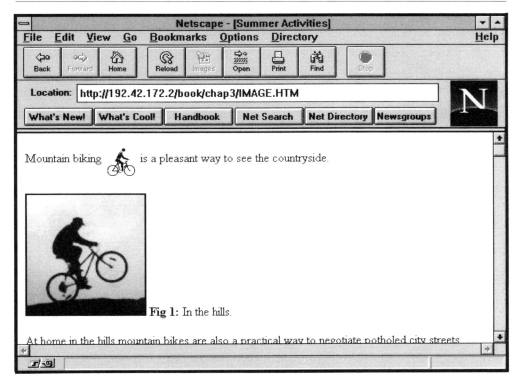

Figure 3.6   In-line images

its normal context. The surrounding text can be aligned with the TOP, MIDDLE
or BOTTOM of the image, which is useful for positioning captions. It should be
noted that subsequent lines begin below the image, not the text, so these alignment attributes cannot be used to make the text flow around the image.

■ Lists

HTML has five different list types. The syntax of simple (unordered), ordered,
directory and menu lists are essentially the same.

```
<UL>...</UL>          unordered list
<OL>...</OL>          ordered list
<DIR>...</DIR>        directory list
<MENU>...</MENU>      menu list
```

Each item within the list is marked with a list item `<LI>` tag and these are
surrounded by start and end list tags shown above. Lists can be nested and
elements such as paragraphs embedded in the item text.

```
<UL>
<LI>Item 1<P>This is a new paragraph.
<LI>Item 2<BR>This is a new line.
<LI>Last item.
</UL>
```

Simple lists of items can be contained in the unordered LIST element. Browsers separate individual items by white space and mark the start of each item with a bullet point:

- Item 1

  This is a new paragraph
- Item 2
  This is a new line
- Last item.

Figure 3.7   An unordered list

Ordered lists are essentially the same, replacing the bullets with sequential numbering. Ordered lists take the optional COMPACT attribute which, on some browsers, can reduce vertical spacing within the list:

```
<OL COMPACT>
```

Menu lists are a more compact form of unordered lists and normally use only a single line for each item, much like a Windows application menu. An item could be a link to another resource. Items in a directory list are up to 20 characters long and the browser may choose to arrange them in columns across the page.

Definition lists separate the item into a **definition term** and a **definition**. A glossary is a good example of a definition list.

```
<DL>
<DT>HTML<DD>HyperText Markup Language.
<DT>Anonymous File Transfer Protocol<DD>A standard way
of allowing public FTP access to a computer. A user-
name of <I>anonymous</I> and the user's <I>Email
address</I> as the password allow access to controlled
directory tree on the host.
</DL>
```

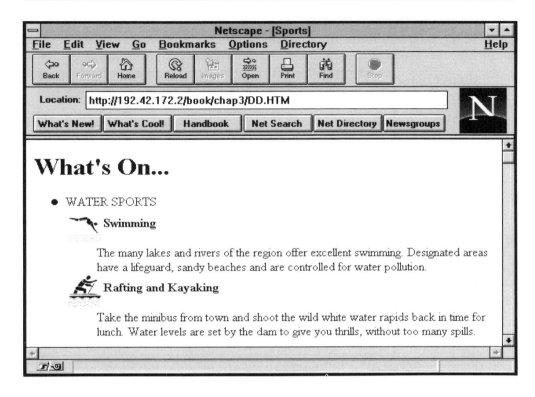

Figure 3.8   Images as definition terms

Definition lists offer a further twist in the list formats. The definition term can be an image file such as an icon or a custom bullet point. The layout is the same as for an unordered list.

▪ Hyperlinks

Structural markup is a powerful concept but the real utility of HTML is the ability to include hyperlinks in documents. A hyperlink is a marked section of text or image which points to another resource. An HTML hyperlink is a URL naming an internal, local or Internet resource. In the Windows environment, following the link by clicking it with the mouse causes the target to be downloaded. If it's an HTML document or an image file it may be directly displayed by the browser, otherwise the data is sent to an external application.

Hypercards or CD-ROM are familiar applications of hypertext. The URL addressing scheme extends the concept to any resource available on the

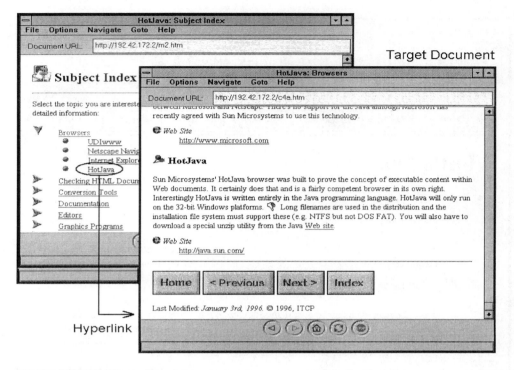

Figure 3.9 Hypertext documents

Internet. Links can and should be used pervasively in HTML documents. Any resource which can be sent over the Internet can be the target of a link. Resources mentioned in the text should be hyperlinked. Software, on-line documentation, organizations and people can all be the targets of hyperlinks.

The **anchor** element, <A>, marks either the destination or start of a hyperlink. The HREF attribute takes a URL as a parameter. The '#' character separates the URL path from a reference to a named anchor within a document:

```
<A HREF="http://www.stamford.edu/fusion.htm#
ColdFusion">
Fusion in a test tube</A> was announced...
```

If the link is within the same document only the **anchor name** must be given:

```
<A HREF="#ColdFusion"> Fusion in a test tube</A> was
announced...
```

The text or image before the closing </A> tag may be underlined or displayed in another color to show the link. In Figure 3.5 The Internet

Society is linked to its home page and on this browser the relationship is illustrated by underlining.

If a NAME attribute is used the anchor is the destination of a hyperlink. Other links can refer not only to a document but to a specific word or line within that document. As anchors can only be found by studying the source this sort of relationship is normally used in documents from a single author or a group of authors working closely together.

```
<A NAME="ColdFusion"> Fleischmann and Pons</A> claimed
that...
```

The TITLE attribute names resources which are not marked-up text such as images. The title string may be displayed by the browser when the cursor passes over the link or while the linked resource is being downloaded.

 The anchor element can also contain an image instead of, or in addition to, text. This is a useful feature for active definition lists and may also be used to display a **thumbnail** image. The thumbnail would be a smaller version of the image that it is linked to. The thumbnail gives an idea of what the image is without the user having to wait for large internal graphics to be downloaded. Clicking the thumbnail will display the larger image, either in-line or on an external viewer. Image links are highlighted by the browser underlining or surrounding the whole image with a border.

```
<A HREF="BIG.GIF" ALT="Climber"><IMG SRC="SMALL.GIF"
ALT="Thumbnail"></A>
```

Thumbnails can be generated from the original using the resample/resize feature found on many graphics packages.

Image maps extend this theme. The ISMAP attribute tells the browser that an image is divided into individual **hotspots**. Clicking on one of these sends the mouse coordinates to the server. Based on these coordinates the server can decide which resource to fetch. An obvious example is to make the image a map. Town names could then link to information about that town.

```
<A HREF="towns.map"><IMG SRC="japan.gif" ISMAP></A>
```

Image maps are described more fully in Chapter 9.

▧ Forms

HTML forms can be used for questionnaires, placing orders or as a front end to other applications including databases. The use of forms implies the

```
<H1>Widget Fault Report Form</H1>
Service Engineers Only

<FORM METHOD="POST"
ACTION="http://www.widget.com/fault.exe">
<P>
I.D. No: <INPUT NAME="number" SIZE="8">
Password: <INPUT NAME="passwd" TYPE="password" SIZE="10"
MAXLENGTH="10">
<P>
<TEXTAREA NAME="fault" ROWS="2" COLS="60">Enter a brief
description of the fault</TEXTAREA>
<P>
Checks Completed:
<INPUT TYPE="checkbox" NAME="level" VALUE="1">Functional
Test
<INPUT TYPE="checkbox" NAME="level" VALUE="2">Board Level
<INPUT TYPE="checkbox" NAME="level" VALUE="3">P.O.S.T.
<BR>
Severity:
<INPUT TYPE="radio" NAME="severity" VALUE="1" CHECKED>1
<INPUT TYPE="radio" NAME="severity" VALUE="2">2
<INPUT TYPE="radio" NAME="severity" VALUE="3">3
<P>
Click on product name or submit if unknown:<BR>
<INPUT NAME="image" TYPE="image" SRC="product.gif">
<P><INPUT TYPE="submit" NAME="submit">
<INPUT TYPE="reset" VALUE="Clear">
</FORM>
```

Figure 3.10   Example HTML form

existence of a Web server to process the data. This server can be part of the Web site, using a mixture of custom and standard applications to process the form. Alternatively the user input can be sent to a Web server anywhere on the Internet which may do no more than bundle and transmit the data to its destination using email.

Although not as powerful as custom screen painters like Microsoft's AppStudio or Powersoft's PowerBuilder, it is possible to use the forms mechanism as the client side of a client–server application. It has the added advantage that the application can be accessed from anywhere on the Internet from a very wide range of hardware using a standard and familiar interface. An example might be a system for making travel inquiries and booking tickets.

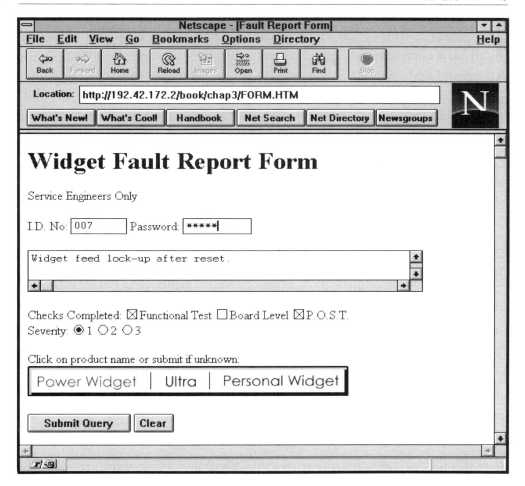

Figure 3.11 An HTML form

By using passwords or by checking Internet addresses access to certain areas of the system can be restricted to a subset of Internet users.

Form input fields can be embedded within other elements, including paragraphs, lists and images. This gives considerable scope for the overall layout. The input fields are contained within a FORM element, delimited by the opening <FORM> and closing </FORM> tags. A form has an ACTION attribute which takes the URL of the program which will process the form. If there is no ACTION attribute the URL of the current document is used. In this case the form may be generated by a script which will process the input and display a new, possibly altered form.

A single document may contain more than one form, but forms cannot be nested. The METHOD attribute takes the values GET or POST. POST sends the form data as a separate stream, GET simply appends the data onto the end of a URL as a query string. Figure 3.11 illustrates how the form defined in Figure 3.10 would be rendered.

■ Query strings

The form in Figure 3.11 can be submitted by clicking the *Submit Query* button or, alternatively, by selecting a product name from the image. Using the GET method and the values shown the query string appended to the URL is:

```
?number=007&passwd=bilbo&fault=Widget+feed+lockup+
after+reset.&level=1&level=3&severity=1&submit=
Submit+Query
```

The string consists of a set of **name/value pairs** separated by the ampersand '&' character. Each name corresponds to the string assigned to the NAME attribute and the values are appended after an equals '=' character.

■ Input fields

The default input field is for text. Input fields like TEXT and PASSWORD take optional size and maximum length attributes. The SIZE attribute specifies the width of the field on the screen and MAXLENGTH the total number of characters which can be entered. This value can be greater than the field size, in which case the text will be scrolled on screen. Even though the password field is blanked out by asterisks the password is sent as plain text from the client's browser across the network. In this case it's the word 'bilbo'. Obviously a hobbit fan.

Checkboxes (CHECKBOX) can be used to select a number of input items; compare these to radio (RADIO) buttons, where only one from the set can be selected. Attempting to push a second radio button will reset the first. Fields are grouped by name. The CHECKED attribute is used to preselect options and VALUE to set the initial value of input elements. In Figure 3.11 both the *level 1* and *level 3* checkboxes have been ticked and the default *severity 1* radio button pressed.

The CLEAR button will reset the form to its initial values and SUBMIT is used to send the form data to the resource named by the URL; in this instance a Windows **console application** running on the Widget's computer. Another way to submit this form is by clicking on the product image. This is like an image map; in this case the query string will be:

```
?number=007&passwd=bilbo&fault=Widget+feed+lockup+
after+reset.&level=1&level=3&severity=1&image.
x=287&image.y=21
```

The *submit* field is substituted for the coordinates of the mouse pointer on the image. It would be up to the script to decide exactly which region of the image was selected based on these (*x, y*) coordinates. The image file is specified by an SRC attribute which takes a URL as a parameter.

Multiline forms input

Multiline input is possible with the TEXTAREA container element. The initial text is contained between the TEXTAREA start and end tags. The height and width is set with the ROWS and COLS attributes respectively. The text box is scrollable. Care should be taken with the GET form method as long URLs may be truncated. Single space characters are replaced by the plus '+' sign within the query string.

Selection lists

A lists of items can be given using the SELECT element. This is normally displayed as a drop-down menu, the number of items displayed simultaneously being limited by the SIZE attribute. More than one selection is possible if the MULTIPLE attribute is used. Multiple and range selections are made using the standard Windows CONTROL and SHIFT-clicking operations.

```
<FORM>
<SELECT NAME="Bus Type" MULTIPLE>
<OPTION>ISA
<OPTION>EISA
<OPTION>VL-BUS
<OPTION>PCI
</SELECT>
...
</FORM>
```

Selecting ISA and PCI from this list gives the query string:

```
?Bus_Type=ISA&Bus_Type=PCI
```

■ Summary

- The HyperText Markup Language is concerned with content not presentation.
- The current standard is HTML version 2.0.
- The Netscape browser supports a popular dialect of HTML and offers greater control over presentation.
- HTML documents consist of text and markup tags.
- Markup includes headings, paragraphs, lists, forms and images.
- Hyperlinks can be embedded within HTML documents.

4 Further HTML

The Web is a rapidly evolving environment. The ink doesn't have time to dry on one standard before new ideas are proposed and implemented. Developments in the resource naming scheme, version 3.0 of HTML and the Netscape extensions are the most important to Web documents. As of today the Netscape extensions probably have the widest significance. Loath or love them the fact remains that the majority of Internet users have access to a Netscape browser and can create and view the new elements. The HTML 3.0 standard is still in discussion although a draft proposal exists. Browser support is limited but applications to create and view documents are slowly appearing. Extensions to the resource naming scheme will have great significance to the growth and organization of the Web as a whole.

This chapter discusses the proposed replacement for URLs, HTML version 3.0 and the Netscape extensions. It also compares the different paths taken by version 3.0 and Netscape.

▓ Extensions to document naming

As was discussed in Chapter 2, the Domain Name System was developed to cope with the growth in Internet hosts. Rather than using numerical addresses or relying on possibly out-of-date or inaccurate host files, DNS establishes a set of protocols for resolving a symbolic name from data held on a domain name server. Internet hosts are now largely represented by symbolic names rather than absolute addresses. Hostnames have the added advantage that a machine can move its physical location and Internet connection without changing its global name. The host: `microsoft.com` could be located in Seattle or moved to Cairo for cost or other unspecified benefits. Documents linked to this address will not notice the difference, unless the Internet connections to Egypt prove slower or less reliable!

The resource naming scheme used by the Web builds on the DNS protocols. If you establish a site with a name like `widget.com` you can easily move it from a third-party Web provider to an internal machine or on to another provider. The hostname, but not necessarily the physical address it resolves to, belongs to you. You won't be forced to update links from external documents when changing site.

DNS doesn't resolve the issue of moving documents to a site with another name, or of hosting the same document on different machines. Although browsers and proxy servers can cache frequently requested pages locally, multi-hosting Web documents can offer performance and reliability advantages. With some suitable addressing scheme a browser could find the nearest location for a resource; if the Web site is off-line for any reason the browser would then try the next closest site.

The uniform resource name (URN) discussion is an attempt to solve this problem. It defines a persistent name and resolution protocols for a resource. URNs will comply with the current URI standard and it is likely that an address will take the form:

```
urn:<path>
```

'Path' would be a symbolic name representing the resource; browsers and proxies would contact the appropriate server for the real location. The adoption of URNs will hopefully prevent the Web from becoming too tangled and broken.

■ HTML 3.0

The HTML version 3.0 specification has developed from Dave Raggett's original HTML+ document. Experience with HTML showed that many authors were abusing features of the language to obtain particular formatting effects. In addition support for certain markup was missing or deficient. Authors often had to resort to the tedious generation of in-line images when including mathematical symbols and HTML 2.0's preformatted text is a poor substitute for real tables.

The approach taken with version 3.0 differs from Netscape. It doesn't extend the control over presentation by providing new language elements. Instead the whole issue of document presentation is subsumed into separate **style sheets**. Existing elements are refined and new markup added to overcome current deficiencies. Version 3.0 attributes are more orthogonal than their predecessors, for instance alignment can now be used with a range of elements. Unlike Netscape, a version 3.0 document can be more readable to users without graphical browsers. In this way the original aims of content-oriented documents, readable on the widest range of platforms, are preserved.

HTML 3.0 is largely backwards compatible with version 2.0; however, to differentiate it, a new DOCTYPE directive is used:

```
<!DOCTYPE HTML PUBLIC "-//IETF//DTD HTML 3.0//EN">
```

And the file extension '.ht3' may be used on Windows operating systems. Web servers should generate the MIME content type: text/html; version=3.0, for version 3.0 documents if there are any compatibility concerns with version 2.0 browsers. Version 2.0 browsers will not render this content but will instead prompt for the whole file to be saved to disk. MIME is explained in Chapter 6.

▓ Style sheets

The Netscape extensions have proved popular because they give content providers greater control over page layout, something they are accustomed to with printed media. HTML version 3.0 recognizes this need but has placed the presentation information into separate style sheets. Style sheets are an idea borrowed from print and contain the formatting specification for a document. This information might include the default font and size, header fonts, line spacing and layout along with any particular formatting to be applied to individual elements. The raw document would be sent to the typesetter along with the style sheet.

The current proposal recommends using a lightweight version of the Document Style Semantics Specification Language (DSSSL), an International Standards Organization (ISO) standard for describing the presentation of SGML documents. Style sheet files take the extension '.dsssl' and can be referenced using the LINK element:

```
<LINK REL=StyleSheet HREF=mystyle.dsssl>
```

Using the LINK element a style can be easily applied to documents from many sources without the need for detailed internal changes. The style sheet specifies the intended rendering for individual elements where there are sufficient resources available on the browser. This maintains support for non-graphical displays, speech and Braille output.

House styles can also be defined in one sheet. Authors need no longer concern themselves with the presentation of documents. Performance benefits accrue where a single style sheet may be cached by a browser and then applied to all the documents which reference it. Provision is made for cascading sheets, enabling authors and end users to override elements in a style. Authors can also include individual overrides in a STYLE element contained in the document head:

```
<STYLE NOTATION=dsssl-lite>...</STYLE>
```

The NOTATION attribute specifies the style notation used. Style rules can alter the rendering of a whole class of elements, for instance all Level 1 headings can be set in 20-point text or only elements in a particular context, as an example all horizontal rules after list elements could use a particular image.

Elements take two new attributes which are associated with document styles. The ID identifier names an element and, borrowing an idea from the object-oriented world, CLASS creates a named subclass with a specific style. A subclass of paragraph may be a summary, this could be shown as centered and in an italic font. Extending this concept, the generic division <DIV> element can be used for new container classes.

```
<DIV CLASS=Summary>
<H2>Summary</H2>
<P>This is summary text
</DIV>
```

In this way the presentation of specific parts of a document can be closely controlled.

■ Navigation

Navigation hyperlinks, often represented by button images, are a standard feature of many Web documents. The browser's own 'back' and 'forward' buttons, which permit the user to navigate a stack of previously visited documents, can be supplemented with links internal to the site. An on-line book organized as a set of pages may include 'next' and 'previous' buttons as well as links to a table of contents, index and the author's home page. HTML 3.0 formalizes these standard buttons. Rather than providing custom

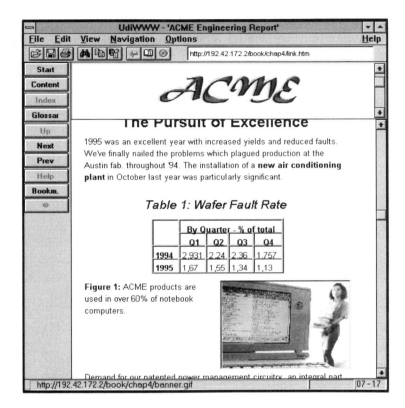

Figure 4.1 UdiWWW, A Windows HTML 3.0 browser

hyperlinks and button images within a document the LINK element is used to augment the browser's own navigation buttons:

```
<LINK REL=Next HREF=page2.htm>
```

The parameters to the REL attribute have been defined in HTML 3.0 as:

Home	home page or top of hierarchy
ToC	table of contents
Index	document index
Glossary	glossary of terms
Copyright	notice of copyright
Up	up one level in the hierarchy
Next	next document or page
Previous	previous document or page

Bookmark Provide entry points into an extended document
      (bookmarks may be labeled with the additional
      TITLE attribute)

Help   background help

The browser in Figure 4.1 shows the navigation buttons separately on the left-hand side. The highlighted buttons represent links contained within the current document.

■ Banner graphics

The BANNER element is used to hold information which should not be scrolled with the rest of the document. This can include graphics, contact information and hyperlinks. A typical use would be for a corporate logo. The banner information can be placed in a file to be cached and shared amongst a number of documents. This file is a standard HTML document and is referenced with the LINK element:

```
<LINK REL=Banner HREF=banner.htm>
```

Banner information may also be located directly within a document and is placed at the top of the document's body using the BANNER container element:

```
<BODY>
<BANNER>
. . .
</BANNER>
. . .
```

■ Alignment and flow of images and text

The ALIGN attribute can now be applied to a wide range of elements. For small images the LEFT and RIGHT parameters are used to make text flow down one side of an image. These are also supported by Netscape. It may be advantageous to use the FIGURE element for larger images. Another feature shared with Netscape is the ability to specify the HEIGHT and WIDTH of an image. This allows a small image to be scaled and to describe the basic page layout before the images have been downloaded.

The first image in Figure 4.2 has been enlarged by 100%; the image quality suffers proportionately but this technique can be used instead of a thumbnail to give a full size, low resolution representation of the final image. Compared

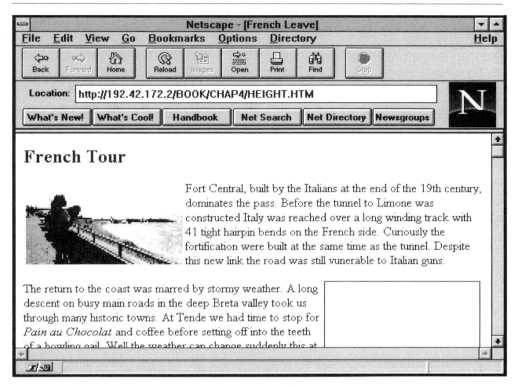

Figure 4.2 Scaling and page layout with **HEIGHT** and **WIDTH**

to the original full-resolution image it took less than half the time to download. The normal-resolution image could then be a link to this picture. Extending this idea, the non-standard LOWSRC attribute is understood by some browsers and is used to display a fast low-resolution image which is then automatically updated with the normal version.

Figure 4.2 shows that loading of the second image has not yet started, but the HEIGHT and WIDTH attributes have already established its location. The text will not be reformatted when the actual image is retrieved. The image dimensions can be determined using a graphics package.

HTML 3.0 images take the additional UNITS attribute which is either PIXELS or EN. En is a half-point unit and there are 72 points per inch. For example:

```
<IMG SRC="notebook.gif" UNITS=EN WIDTH=200 HEIGHT=140
ALIGN=RIGHT>
```

Here the image will be flushed to the right and text will flow in a single column to the left-hand side; this is illustrated in Figure 4.1.

Paragraph text may be centered, justified or left/right aligned. Rows of text can also be aligned vertically around the first occurrence of a decimal point. The decimal point character is changed using the DP attribute, a convenient feature for European languages. Automatic line wrapping is disabled using the NOWRAP attribute. The CLEAR attribute will start a new paragraph below a figure or table. This is useful where the side paragraph is a caption and brief description, the next paragraph not being directly associated with the figure. CLEAR takes the parameters LEFT, RIGHT and ALL but can also take a value in pixels or en. This gives the minimum width needed for the element. A style sheet could specify that no text will be placed to the side of a figure where the column is less than 1 inch (144 en) wide.

```
<B>Figure 1:</B> ACME products are used in over 60% of
notebook computers.
<P CLEAR=RIGHT>Demand for our patented power
management circuitry. . .
```

Images are centered by placing them within a paragraph container element:

```
<P ALIGN=CENTER>
<IMG SRC="logo.gif">
</P>
```

Heading text may also be positioned using the ALIGN attribute:

```
<H1 ALIGN=CENTER>Company Objectives</H1>
```

and the numbering style can be changed through a style sheet.

Figures and tables take the additional alignment parameters of BLEEDLEFT and BLEEDRIGHT. A **bleed** is an image that is placed outside of the usual text margin against the edge of the window.

■ Tables

Better support for tabular data was a principal aim for HTML 3.0. Table data and layout tags are placed within a TABLE container element. The cells can be drawn with borders and the whole table aligned relative to the page. A caption may be specified and aligned relative to the table. The body consists of header and data descriptions separated by table row <TR> elements.

Headers are specified by the table header <TH> element and data by the table data <TD> element. The size of a cell relative to its peers is controlled by the attributes ROWSPAN and COLSPAN. In Figure 4.3 the first header spans two

```
<TABLE BORDER>
<CAPTION ALIGN=CENTER>Table 1: Wafer Fault Rate</CAPTION>
<TR>
<TH ROWSPAN=2><TH COLSPAN=4>By Quarter - % of total
<TR>
<TH>Q1<TH>Q2<TH>Q3<TH>Q4
<TR>
<TH ALIGN=LEFT>1994
<TD ALIGN=DECIMAL DP=",">2,931<TD ALIGN=DECIMAL
DP=",">2,24<TD ALIGN=DECIMAL DP=",">2,36<TD ALIGN=DECIMAL
DP=",">1,757
<TR>
<TH ALIGN=LEFT>1995
<TD ALIGN=DECIMAL DP=",">1,67<TD ALIGN=DECIMAL
DP=",">1,55<TD ALIGN=DECIMAL DP=",">1,34 <TD
ALIGN=DECIMAL DP=",">1,13
</TABLE>
```

Figure 4.3 A table description

columns but contains no data, this leaves a blank left hand corner of one column by two rows. The second description provides an overall header spanning four columns. Figure 4.4 shows an example of a table within another table.

Header and data text take the same alignment directives as paragraph text. In addition the VALIGN attribute controls the vertical alignment of text within a cell. Header and data may include text and images and can embed other elements including line breaks, paragraphs or even other tables. Tables can be made to flow around other elements.

 Although it is possible to create tables by hand the exact formatting is tedious. Table markup is designed so that filters can easily be written for word processing and DTP packages and this would be the normal route for table production.

Column widths are automatically sized by the browser and depend on the contents and overall window size. The COLSPEC attribute specifies the width of a column in pixels or en. A browser would not have to size the whole table before rendering cells defined in this manner.

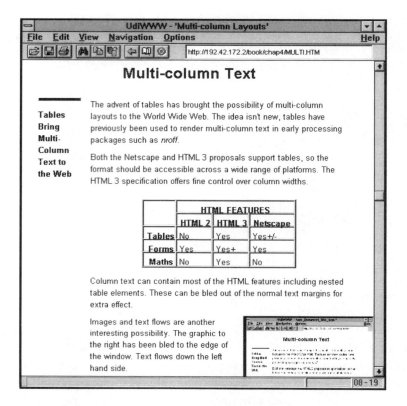

Figure 4.4 Using tables for multi-column text

■ Formulae

Considering its origins as a wide-area information server used in a physics environment it is surprising that direct support for mathematical symbols has only been introduced with version 3.0 of HTML. In the past this type of content had to be converted to image files and embedded in a document. The new markup is a bit esoteric, consisting of mathematical entities and HTML elements contained by the MATH element:

```
<MATH>
H(s)=&int;_0_^&infin;^e^-st^h(t)dt
</MATH>
```

The standard ISO 8879-1986 entity names are used for mathematical symbols. For brevity the subscript and superscript container elements can be replaced by the shortref characters '_' and '^'. The above formula is rendered as:

$$H(s) = \int_0^\infty e^{-st}h(t)\,dt$$

Figures

The ability to include graphics within a document has been greatly enhanced with the introduction of the FIGURE element. Figures not only enhance the graphical functionality of the original IMAGE element, they improve support for non-graphical browsers.

A figure can be built from separate images; this has caching advantages where many figures are composed of the same common set of images:

```
<FIG SRC="pc.gif">
<OVERLAY SRC="cdrom.gif" X=40 Y=20>
<OVERLAY SRC="floppy.gif" X=55 Y=50>
<OVERLAY SRC="harddisk.gif" X=40 Y=80>
<CAPTION>Fig 1: Home PC</CAPTION>
<P>
A typical example of a home personal computer.
</FIG>
<P>
<FIG SRC="workstn.gif">
<OVERLAY SRC="cdrom.gif" X=150 Y=10>
<OVERLAY SRC="harddisk.gif" X=20 Y=10>
<CAPTION>Fig 2: Office Workstation</CAPTION>
A high performance office workstation.
<CREDIT>Photo: ACME Technology</CREDIT>
<P>
</FIG>
```

The CAPTION and CREDIT text are displayed on both text and graphical browsers. The description text is intended for browsers which cannot render the image and is not limited to a simple string but can also contain HTML markup and hyperlinks. Thus the basic functionality of image maps is moved to the browser:

```
<FIG SRC="engine.gif">
<H1>4 Stroke Petrol Engine</H1>
<P>Component Parts:
<OL>
<LI><A HREF="cylinder.htm" SHAPE="rect
50,50,80,100">Cylinder</A>
<LI><A HREF="carb.htm" SHAPE="polygon
50,10,80,100,50,60">Carburetor</A>
<LI><A HREF="engine.htm" SHAPE="default">Engine</A>
</OL>
```

Users of non-graphical browsers benefit from these links as a full textual description will be displayed for each anchor element. The example above is given in the form of a numbered list. The SHAPE attribute marks the coordinates of a hotspot in the image. Clicking the mouse within the boundaries of this hotspot will load the corresponding resource. The list of available hotspot shapes is the same as for image maps and these are described more fully in Chapter 8. For completeness the IMAGEMAP attribute states that the mouse coordinates should not be processed locally but are to be returned to the server for processing. The NOFLOW attribute disables text flow around a figure and can be used in preference to CLEAR.

Figures offer the possibility of extending the capabilities of HTML to permit the embedding of information from other applications via object linking and embedding (OLE). This could take the form of an Excel spreadsheet graph and associated data. Sun's Java language may also use figures for referencing **applets**. These are programs which can be directly executed by Java-enabled browsers to provide dynamic content to Web documents. Sun's HotJava and Netscape Navigator 2.0 support applets.

■ Forms

The new SCRIPT attribute specifies the URL of a small program to be run locally by the browser. This program could perform some initial syntax checking on input fields and update their values before the data is submitted to the server. Hidden fields could be used to encode the field type information into the submitted form data. Local form scripts are probably most useful within a closed environment where the resources available to the client are known. A typical example would be to implement a front end to a database for an organization-wide information server:

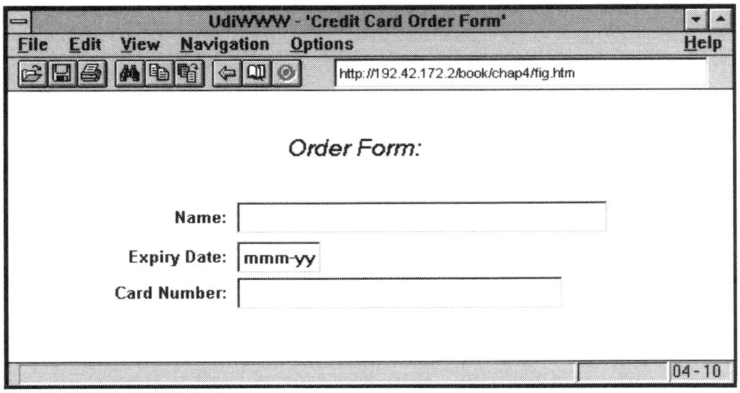

Figure 4.5　An HTML 3.0 form

```
<FORM ACTION="order.exe" SCRIPT="encrypt.exe">
<TABLE>
<CAPTION ALIGN=CENTER>Order Form:</CAPTION>
<TR>
<TH ALIGN=RIGHT>Name:<TD ALIGN=LEFT><INPUT NAME="Name"
SIZE="40">
<TR>
<TH ALIGN=RIGHT NOWRAP>Expiry Date:<TD
ALIGN=LEFT><INPUT NAME="Card" SIZE="8" VALUE="mmm-yy">
<TR>
<TH ALIGN=RIGHT NOWRAP>Card Number:<TD
ALIGN=LEFT><INPUT NAME="Card" SIZE="35">
</TABLE>
</FORM>
```

Tables may be embedded in a FORM element. This provides improved control over the layout of input fields. In the above example the sensitive credit card data is sent to a local program to be encrypted before being forwarded over the Net. This form is shown in Figure 4.5.

■ Searchable documents

The ISINDEX element has been extended to take the optional HREF and PROMPT attributes:

```
<ISINDEX HREF="search.exe" PROMPT="Enter Number:">
```

HREF is the URL of the script used for processing the query, in this case a Windows console application. The usual prompt text can be changed to some more appropriate value. This attribute is also supported by the Netscape extensions.

■ Text styles

The following styles are added:

`<S>. . .</S>`	~~Strikethrough~~
`<BIG>. . .</BIG>`	BIG
`<SMALL>. . .</SMALL>`	small
`<SUB>. . .</SUB>`	Sub$_{script}$
`<SUP>. . .</SUP>`	Sup^{erscript}

■ Lists

The standard list bullets can be overridden by custom images or icon characters. An image is referenced by the SRC attribute. Alternative bullet characters may be selected from the dingbat character set by giving the DINGBAT attribute. The numbering style of ordered list items is set by the style sheet and items are omitted using the SKIP attribute with a count parameter:

```
<UL>
<LI SRC="custom.gif">Item 1
</UL>
<OL>
<LI SKIP=3>Item 4!
</OL>
```

■ Backgrounds

The BODY element takes a new BACKGROUND attribute. This is used by browsers which don't support style sheets and is discussed further under the Netscape extensions.

■ The Netscape extensions

The Netscape browser is not HTML 3.0 compliant and the Netscape language extensions do not, by and large, form part of the HTML 3.0 specification. This specification is still far from being finalized and some important Netscapisms may eventually be included even though the general tone and direction has been set. Netscape and the HTML group should not be seen as warring factions. The developers at Netscape have contributed to the overall development of the HTML specification but, being commercially driven, their objectives are different with many of the latest features concerned more with presentation than content.

Use of the Netscapisms appeals to those with an artistic or graphic design orientation although they fall far short of desktop publishing standards. Many companies also demand a greater degree of control over page layout than is offered by HTML version 2.0. Netscape have implemented other interesting features for those wanting the most novel and 'cool' pages. With the Netscape browsers occupying around two thirds of the Internet marketplace it does appear to be the case of majority rule. Despite these powerful influences the Web author should always strive to reach the widest possible audience. It should be remembered that there is also a large non-Internet community on other networks including CompuServe, America On-line and Microsoft's own MSNet who don't run Netscape-compliant browsers. On the other hand the extensions do exist now and are available to a large number of users, unlike the HTML 3.0 style sheets. They can be learnt and used in a piecemeal fashion and are accessible by a lot of users.

Microsoft has licensed Netscape technology and the Windows '95 Internet Explorer browser supports some Netscapisms; other browsers may follow suit. Microsoft has some of its own extensions to HTML; the FACE attribute to the FONT element permits alternative typefaces to be specified. The Netscape deal may mean that these find their way into their own and other browsers.

Netscape have made a commitment to work with standards bodies and implement the HTML 3.0 specification when it is ratified. This doesn't imply that support for the Netscapisms will be dropped and they are already working on a document detailing their extensions to HTML 3.0!

■ Centering

Netscape supports the HTML 3.0 ALIGN=CENTER attribute but have added their own separate CENTER container element:

```
<CENTER>
<H2>Images</H2>
```

```
<IMG SRC="picture.gif">
A nice picture.
</CENTER>
```

All data between the tags will be centered.

■ Rules

Horizontal rules are often used in print media to break up sections or blocks of text. Netscape have added a number of attributes to the basic horizontal rule `<HR>` element.

SIZE	thickness of a ruled line
WIDTH	the width of the rule can be given in pixels or expressed as a percentage of the page size
ALIGN	the rule can be aligned to the LEFT, RIGHT or CENTER
NOSHADE	draw the rule as a solid bar

■ Lists

Netscape browsers automatically change the bullet type when unordered lists are nested. The TYPE attribute will override this progression with a particular bullet style: DISC, CIRCLE or SQUARE. This is similar to the HTML 3.0 list DINGBAT.

With ordered lists TYPE changes the numbers into letters or Roman numerals; the first item is set by the START attribute. TYPE may be used with the item elements to change individual lines. The current value of an ordered list item can be set by the VALUE attribute, this is similar in function to the HTML 3.0 SKIP.

```
<OL TYPE=a START=2>
<LI>List 2, Uses Small Letters and starts at 2
<LI TYPE=I>List 2, Item 2, Uses Roman Numerals
<LI VALUE=5>List 2, Item 3, Roman but Skips to position 5
<UL>
<LI>List 3, Item 1
<LI TYPE=CIRCLE>List 3, Item2, Bullet is a Circle
<LI TYPE=SQUARE>List 3, Item 3, Bullet is a Square
</UL>
</OL>
```

■ Images

Netscape supports text flows and alignment parameters in the same way as HTML 3.0. The original TOP, MIDDLE and BOTTOM alignments have been further augmented by:

TEXTTOP	aligns the image with the tallest piece of text on a line, not the tallest item!
ABSMIDDLE	aligns the middle of the current line, not its baseline, with the middle of the image.
BASELINE	aligns the baseline of the current line with the bottom of the image (this is the same as BOTTOM)
ABSBOTTOM	aligns the bottom of the image with the bottom of the line

These correct some deficiencies in the original implementation of the IMAGE element. Text can be moved down below the image using the break <BR> element's CLEAR attribute. This is the same as in HTML 3.0.

```
<BR CLEAR=LEFT>
Next line . . .
```

■ Font size

The text size is altered using the FONT element. Currently seven sizes are supported, the default is three. The BASEFONT element will set the default:

```
<BASEFONT SIZE=2>She sells
<FONT SIZE=5>Sea shells
<FONT SIZE=-3>On the sea shore.
```

The sizes are relative, not absolute values.

■ Copyright and trademark

There are a couple of new character entity names:

&reg;	registered trademark	®
&copy;	copyright	©

These are equivalent to the standard © and ® respectively.

■ Line breaking

The no break <NOBR> element will stop the browser automatically inserting line breaks, the word break <WBR> tag is a hint to the browser that it can insert a word break at this point with no break text:

```
<NOBR>
This text should be kept on a single line,<WBR> except
where there is a comma.
</NOBR>
```

The behavior is subtly different from the HTML 3.0 break <BR> tag and no wrap attribute. The break tag always forces a line break. The same effect as the Netscape elements is achieved in HTML using a sequence of no break space ( ) characters except where a line break might be appropriate.

■ Tables

Netscape have implemented the bulk of HTML 3.0 table syntax but have extended it to provide greater control over presentation. These modifications have been submitted to the HTML 3.0 working group for consideration.

Netscape tables can specify a border width; zero gives very compact tables. The space between cells and the space between cell contents and border can be set with the CELLSPACING and CELLPADDING table attributes. The width of a table is set using the WIDTH attribute. The parameter can either be expressed as an absolute value in pixels or as a percentage of the overall page width.

The differences between the Netscape and HTML 3.0 implementation of tables can make it difficult to produce a single table which will be rendered correctly on both types of browser. In particular the use of markup within cells should be avoided if the table is to be viewed with Netscape browsers.

■ Backgrounds

The BACKGROUND attribute to the BODY element is used to apply a background color or graphic to a document. This can establish site identity or differentiate between different documents on the same site. Microsoft use a light gray logo graphic for their background and the *Financial Times* light orange to mimic their newsprint color.

```
<BODY BACKGROUND="logo.gif">
<BODY BACKGROUND="#FF0000"
```

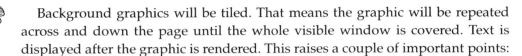

Background graphics will be tiled. That means the graphic will be repeated across and down the page until the whole visible window is covered. Text is displayed after the graphic is rendered. This raises a couple of important points:

1. Graphics files take some time to download so background images should generally be small as the browser will not display anything until the background is rendered.
2. Resizing the browser's window with a tiled background may cause effects which the page designer didn't intend. Tiling also magnifies minor blemishes and mismatches at the edges of a background image.

Backgrounds may also detract from the general legibility of the document and won't be visible to non-graphical clients. Their use should be restricted, some would say banned altogether. A cue can be taken from printed media where the actual information is usually rendered black on white. Logos (in a subtle contrast of grays), uniform patterns and blends are all good possibilities for backgrounds. Where maximum page length is predictable a blend, where one color or shade changes to another over a series of steps, can be made from a long, thin image. Although the image is small it will be tiled horizontally across the page to build a smooth background.

Netscape have extended the HTML 3.0 BACKGROUND attribute to allow a uniform color to be specified in terms of its 'red', 'green' and 'blue' components. These are given as a hexadecimal (base 16) value: #RRGGBB; #008000 would be a medium green. Many graphics packages will give these values for a given color although the numbers may have to be converted from decimal (base 10). Alternatively there is a script in Chapter 9 which will display the color given any set of values.

If images included in the document have transparent backgrounds they will use the color or image which is defined in the BODY element as their own background. Transparent images are discussed further in Chapter 6.

As is their wont Netscape have added further attributes to the BODY element to define TEXT, LINK and VLINK colors:

```
<BODY BACKGROUND="BACK.GIF" TEXT="#000000" LINK=
"#ff0000" VLINK="#00ff00">
```

TEXT controls the overall text color, LINK the hyperlink text color and VLINK the color of links which have already been visited by the user.

■ Summary

- Universal resource names move location details from Web addresses to a server database. This can be maintained separately from the document.
- HTML 3.0 extends control over presentation but continues to support non-graphical browsers. This is achieved using separate style sheets.
- HTML 3.0 has new elements for rendering tables and mathematical formulae.
- Netscape provides better control over presentation by extending version 2.0 of the HTML specification.
- The Netscape extensions are largely incompatible with HTML 3.0 and should not use either the version 2.0 or 3.0 DOCTYPE directive.

5 HTML tools

Arguments about the best tools for creating Web pages rage like pandemics across the Internet. Some HTML maestros claim that nothing beats the utility and speed of a simple text editor. A UNIX pilot's favorites are Emacs or the abstruse `vi`. The name of this editor is apparently short for 'visual' because you can actually see the text you are writing. No doubt *real* aficionados would prefer to enter their HTML with toggle switches and nothing but an LED display for feedback.

Even Windows users, who generally have a lower pain threshold, spend many hours transcribing markup tags into Notepad. Though the HyperText Markup Language is designed to be human writeable it is all too easy to make mistakes and often hard to visualize the result. HTML disciples might refute the second objection claiming that creating Web pages is the process of describing the structure of a document, not of formatting. This claim is not without foundation as the actual look of a document will vary from browser to browser. This last point is an important one, for it implies that there is no such thing as a true WYSIWYG HTML editor, at least not in the traditional DTP sense. Style sheets go some way to addressing this problem by enabling editors to mimic a browser's rendering of a document. Unfortunately editors which can use style sheets are firmly in the professional category.

The specialized HTML editors take a couple of approaches to the problem of creating documents. They either show the HTML tags directly within the document, sending the page to the user's choice of browser for previewing, or

■ Religion, flame-wars and vitriol

Amongst Internet users debate about the merits of various tools, be they browsers, servers or editors, rapidly degenerate into flame wars in which not only the opinions, but the sanity of people holding those opinions, are called into question. The choice of which HTML editor is largely a matter of personal preference and budget. All of the editors discussed in this book can produce fully compliant HTML but the unwary must be aware that only some of them guarantee this.

It should be noted that one general-purpose editor, Emacs, transcends all such debate and has entered into the realms of religion. Versions are available for all major operating systems, even DOS. Peter Flynn remarks that running in 'psgml-mode, it provides full HTML validation with hide and reveal of tags.' Emacs is beyond the scope of this book but the interested reader can take comfort in the knowledge that if they have any trouble configuring psgml they can always use the artificial intelligence capabilities of Emacs' in-built LISP engine to solve the meaning of life, the universe and HTML programming!

they give a sample rendering and hide the tags. Again it must be reiterated that this rendering will only be accurate for the one browser/editor combination. Users should not be lulled into creating documents which are readable with only the one browser.

Editors that use a browser for previewing the document are easier for programmers to write. As a consequence they are often first to implement the latest language features. This is not always a good thing as they may present users with a curious mix of tags taken from the various HTML versions. Unless the editor can parse the HTML document type definitions it may be difficult for users to ensure that the document complies with any particular standard or that markup is being used in the correct place and order. However, in skilled hands they are excellent tools for the production of Web pages.

Editors which hide tags and provide a sample rendering are easy for anyone who has at least a passing acquaintance with Windows word processing packages. Software companies have rushed to bolt filters onto their desktop publishing and word processing applications. Microsoft's Word and Novell's WordPerfect both offer HTML output and are ideal for anyone familiar with these or similar products. The Web community has also written a gamut of filters for these and related applications and third-party support exists for Excel, Quark XPress, Frame and PageMaker.

All of these products can convert existing document formats with varying degrees of success, largely dependent on how much structure was found in the original. For instance, if headings were represented as large, bold text rather than a heading style, they will not be converted to HTML headings by the filter. If there is no particular requirement to add hypertext links existing documentation can be converted and updated by unskilled operators. In this case standard HTML links and structure may be encoded in a template or macro, or added later by a script.

Another class of utility takes an existing document format and converts it to HTML. These utilities usually run from the command line and can process a single file or a batch of files. Filters are available for FrameMaker MIF format, rich text format (RTF), ASCII text, Quark tagged files, PostScript and Lotus Notes. These filter programs may be linked to a Web server script to perform conversions on the fly. This has the advantage that documents can be held in a single format with the latest versions always available on-line.

Using any one of these tools should ensure that the end product is valid (if not compliant) HTML whereas even the most skilled coder would have made mistakes using a simple editor. The disadvantage is that support for certain language features may be missing, although they can normally be encoded by hand. Filters also lack the intelligence of a skilled operator and may make a poor job of converting the original document to HTML format. Where editors or filters cannot guarantee a document's compliance with HTML an external verification program can be employed.

The rest of this chapter will look at two different approaches to editing HTML followed by more detail on conversion and proofing tools.

▓ Internet Assistant for Word

Microsoft released Internet Assistant for Word 6.0 early in 1995 as a free add-on package. Internet Assistant enables Word to save documents as HTML files and in addition allows Word to function as a Web browser. The browser is a little slow for extended use as all HTML documents must be converted to the internal Word format. Internet Assistant can easily switch from edit to browse mode which is a useful feature for testing.

Release 1.0 only supports the 16-bit version of Word but will run on all the Windows platforms. The only restriction is that file names follow the DOS 8.3 upper case format. Version 2.0 of the HTML specification is supported. Release

2.0 of Internet Assistant was made in the autumn of 1995 and is only for Microsoft's 32-bit operating systems. As such it won't run on Windows 3.1 or with 16-bit versions of Word. Being a full 32-bit application it can process data in bigger chunks and offers a much-needed performance boost.

The latest version of the software can be found at Microsoft's Web site `http://www.microsoft.com` and is a little over 1 megabyte in size. The complete package is supplied as a single self-extracting archive file, effectively a command line executable (`.EXE`). Running this program unpacks the components including a `README` file, which should be checked before installation. This process is straightforward, being driven by a standard Windows setup program.

The most obvious differences when Word is run for the first time after installation are altered menus and toolbars. These reflect the new functionality required for creating HTML documents. Apart from these changes Word functions as usual. Markup is not displayed. Instead, text is entered and formatted using the toolbar icons and menu options. Taking a WYSIWYG philosophy,

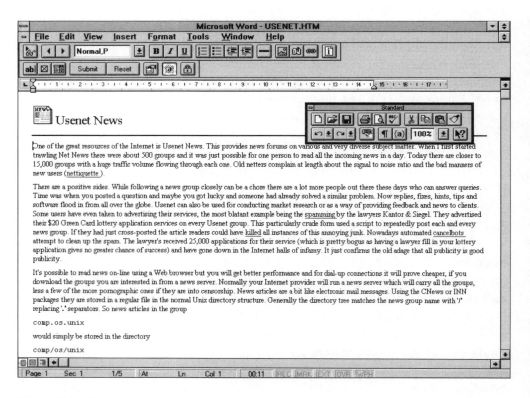

Figure 5.1   Internet Assistant for Word

Standard Toolbar

Formatting Toolbar

Forms Toolbar

Figure 5.2   Internet Assistant toolbars

Word attempts to display elements as they would appear to a user and when using the Word browser the document formatting is identical.

The individual toolbars can be hidden or revealed using the Toolbars option from the View menu. The toolbars can be moved or dragged to a floating position on the display. Toolbar icons provide convenient shortcuts to many commonly used menu options.

▨ Converting documents

Word can be used to convert a number of existing document formats to HTML. Standard import filters include WordPerfect, Write, rich text format and plain text files. The accuracy of the conversion is governed by:

- how much structural information can be obtained from the original;
- the degree of support offered by HTML 2.0 for the formatting used.

Conversion will typically preserve paragraph layout with bold, italic and underlined text being converted. Information such as font type is lost as are styles such as headings that are implied by the presentation and not the structure. A great deal of structure and presentation can be converted where the original document is constructed properly.

Word 6.0 heading styles, numbered and bulleted lists, text styles, bookmarks, summary information, forms and tables can all be converted. Heading, list and text styles are coded directly in their HTML equivalents. Bookmarks become hypertext anchors. Document summary information is used for the TITLE and META elements. If no title is given in the summary the first line of the document is also used for the title. As tables are not directly supported by HTML 2.0 they are first converted to preformatted text with any caption encoded as a separate line.

■ Internet Assistant report card

Some document conversion packages make a better job of conversion compared to Internet Assistant. Word could convert its own bitmap images to GIF format and reference them as **IMAGE** elements. It should also be possible to convert indexes and tables of contents directly to hypertext. Even considering these limitations Internet Assistant remains a useful tool for document conversions.

Certain styles cannot be readily converted to HTML:

- drawings, including table borders and shading
- footnotes, headers and footers
- frames
- page and section breaks
- index and tables of contents
- embedded pictures

■ The template document

Internet Assistant automatically generates an empty HTML template document. Meta-information identifies both the Author of the document and Editor used; however, a title is not added by default.

```
<!doctype html public "-//IETF//DTD HTML//EN">
<HTML>
<HEAD>
<META NAME="GENERATOR" CONTENT="Internet Assistant for
Word1.0Z">
<META NAME="AUTHOR" CONTENT="David Harvey-George">
</HEAD>
<BODY>
</BODY>
</HTML>
```

■ Meta-information

The document TITLE element and other meta-information can be added using the Title toolbar button. This displays the Head dialog box; the Advanced

Properties allow the BASE URL, ISINDEX and NEXTID elements to be set. Meta-element text is entered using the HTML Markup dialog box which is accessed using the Meta button. These elements are contained within the head of the HTML document.

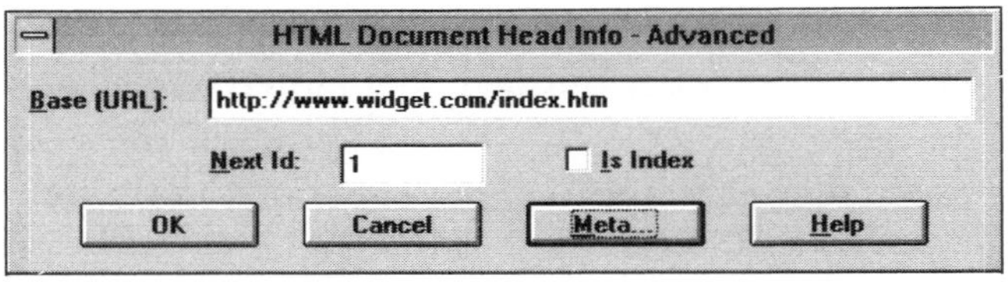

```
┌────┬────────────────────────────────────────────────────────┐
│ ─┃ │        HTML Document Head Info - Advanced              │
├────┴────────────────────────────────────────────────────────┤
│ Base (URL):  │ http://www.widget.com/index.htm │             │
│                                                              │
│        Next Id:  │ 1 │          □ Is Index                   │
│    ┌────────┐  ┌────────┐  ┌────────┐   ┌────────┐           │
│    │   OK   │  │ Cancel │  │ Meta.. │   │  Help  │           │
│    └────────┘  └────────┘  └────────┘   └────────┘           │
└──────────────────────────────────────────────────────────────┘
```

Figure 5.3   Adding meta-information

▓ Special characters

Character entities can be entered from the Symbol dialog box found under the Insert menu. Some of the symbols shown don't correspond to entities in the HTML specification and they may not be visible on every browser. For example the trademark symbol is encoded as the unused value ™. This gives the correct character under Netscape but was ignored by an HTML 2.0 compliant browser.

▓ Images

An HTML document can be a mixture of text and graphics. Graphics are inserted using the Image button and are displayed in-line. The file type list covers the CompuServe GIF and the JPEG file formats, two formats commonly in use on the Web. These files have the extensions .GIF and .JPG respectively. The standard extensions can be overridden to insert images of any format recognized by the Word filters. The image file is selected using a file browser, inserting an IMAGE element with a partial URL to the document:

```
<IMG SRC="../images/graphic.jpg">
```

The SRC is located relative to the current document, which must be saved first.

■ Building a Web with Word

A bottom-up approach should be taken when building documents. Resources such as images, sound and movies are created first so that links can then be made to them. Next, documents at the lowest level, or ones with the fewest external links are built. Usually a couple of iterations over each level must be made. Where a number of documents link back to a single **home page** it may be easier to first create a dummy file to represent this document. Other documents can then be added before the home page is completed.

Before links are made to images and other documents it's best to establish the directory hierarchy for the various files. This will avoid a lot of internal changes at a later date. You may decide to store each type of resource under separate sub-directories:

```
c:\http\ images
        scripts
        files
        sounds
        movies
```

This layout would not necessarily reflect the organization of the HTML documents to each other. A hierarchy of documents could all exist in the same directory with the structure imposed by the hyperlinks. For large sites good organization of the many files involved is critical.

Microsoft has introduced a new protocol for image files located on different drives:

```
<IMG SRC="LOCAL:e:/images/logo.gif">
```

A warning message is displayed before making such a link. This bit of ad-hocery is peculiar to Microsoft. The correct form of URL is:

```
<IMG SRC="file://localhost/e:/images/logo.gif">
```

 Of course this will only work for browsers that have direct access to the document. Files present on the local disk drive(s) may not be the same or even present on another system's disk drives. Where documents are made available over the Internet using a Web server they should all be located on the same drive and referenced using relative filenames.

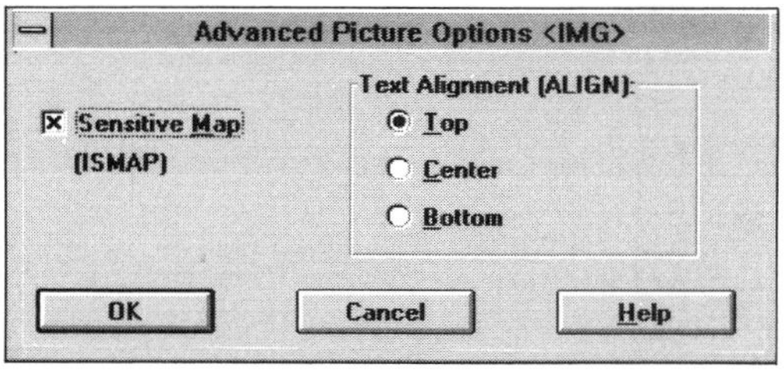

Figure 5.4 Advanced picture options

The text alignment and image map attributes are set through the Advanced Picture Options dialog box.

■ Making links

The Named Anchor (bookmark) button is used to create a hyperlink target within a document: The text or image which is to form the anchor is first selected and then a name is entered from the Bookmark menu. If a previously defined name is used the Anchor is moved from its current location to the new location. It makes no sense to have two Anchors with the same name within a single document.

Named Anchors are made visible within the edited document using the HTML Hidden button; this surrounds the anchor point with large square brackets. Double clicking this area brings up the Bookmark menu and the Name can be edited or removed.

Anchors enable hyperlinks to locate a particular section within a document. A table of contents, endnote or index could use these links. The start of a link

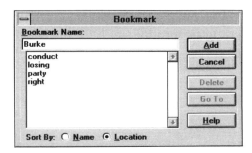

Figure 5.5 Adding hypertext anchors

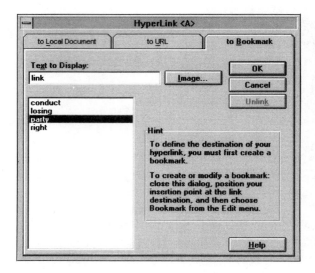

Figure 5.6 Creating a hyperlink to a named anchor

will be a section of text or an image. This is first highlighted using the mouse or cursor and the Link button pressed. This displays the Hyperlink dialog box, giving the user a choice of three kinds of link. As a link is always a type of URL, the links could all be made through the URL tab. The other tabs simply provide an easier interface for building certain kinds of URL.

- For a named anchor (bookmark) a list of current anchors within the document is displayed and one of these can be selected. The link text and image can also be given within this dialog box. A link can be both an image and text. Internet Assistant always places the image before the text whatever the original order in the document. This, as they say, is a feature not a fault.
- Named anchors in other documents must be given in the URL tab. The URL can be partial or full, depending on location, with the anchor text typed after the '#' character:

```
doc2.htm#product
http://www.widget.com/doc2.htm#product
```

Other URL formats can also be given here:

```
mailto:bill@acme.com
ftp://ftp.verlaine.edu/pub/windows/jiffy.zip
```

■ URLs and Word

Even though the 16-bit version of Word 6 is restricted to the DOS FAT filename format the URLs are not. The only restriction is that placed by the software accessing the file. If the URL refers to an NT server using the NT file system there is no restriction to the size of filename or extension although special characters will have to use the equivalent HTML entity. If the filename refers to a local file on a FAT file system the 8.3 standard will prevail.

A list of URLs which have already been used is shown; there can be many links to the same resource within one document.

- A web of documents located on disk drives that are directly accessible to the browser can be built using the Local Document option. This presents the standard Windows file browser dialog box. Relative links are made to files on the current drive using the partial URL syntax:

```
<A HREF="index.htm">Index</A>
<A HREF="../spec/rollout.htm">Autumn</A>
```

The 16-bit version of Word enforces the FAT short name format for files selected using the Local option. As with Images, Internet Assistant uses its own LOCAL protocol for files on different drives:

```
<A HREF="LOCAL:d:/http/java.htm">Link Text</A>
```

and once again this is unique to Microsoft. Documents built with this protocol will not work with other browsers. The standard format is:

```
<A HREF="file://localhost/c:/http/java.htm">
```

This must be typed directly, using the URL dialog tab. Normally all local documents are contained on the same drive under one directory tree, so this isn't a major problem. A complete Web site that will be accessed from a network drive can be constructed using local links. In this case there is no requirement to run a server.

Links are shown by underlining and text is also displayed in a different color. They can be changed or deleted using the Link button by first selecting the highlighted area and then altering the attributes through the Hyperlink dialog box.

■ Text blocks

A user enters text just as with a normal document. Lines are automatically filled and broken by Word. The final arrangement of lines is browser dependent and may not match that displayed while editing. A new paragraph: <P>, is started by the ENTER key and a line break: <BR>, by a combination of SHIFT and ENTER. Other styles are inserted by selecting the text or line and using the Styles list. Toolbar buttons are provided for Bold, Italic and Underlined text.

 Depending on the configuration Word may impose some of its own rules on the text. For example it is customary to leave two spaces after a sentence. Word can be configured to automatically remove double spaces. This may not be desirable.

■ Lists

Creating lists with Internet Assistant is a breeze. Lists should be entered before the formatting is applied. With the list items highlighted use the appropriate toolbar button or select a style from the drop-down menu. Unlike a normal Word document, ordered and unordered list items cannot be toggled with the toolbar buttons, to return to normal text mode select Normal from the Styles drop-down menu. This is why it is easier to apply formatting after all the text has been entered and this is a good general rule for many operations.

When creating a directory list, tab characters are used to separate items. This is a hint to the browser to display these items in a row. Tabs are also used as a separator when entering definition terms and definitions:

■ Nested lists

Lists of the same type can be nested by highlighting the desired sub-list items and pressing the Increase Indent button. The numbering is only changed when the document is closed and reopened, and even then it is in an unusual format, namely *number.number*, you won't see this style outside of Word. Lists of different types can be nested by highlighting the desired items and applying the appropriate list style. However Word prevents definition and directory lists from being nested or from containing other lists.

```
Definition Term A<TAB ->Definition A
Definition Term B<TAB ->Definition B
```

The list body should be highlighted and the Definition or Definition Compact style selected from the drop-down menu. The definition term can be an image, text or combination of the two. Lists may also contain hyperlinks but Word prevents paragraphs or line breaks from being entered directly, a line break always begins a new list item although the markup can be hand coded using the Markup dialog box found under the Insert menu. This markup is preserved when the document is reloaded.

▪ Building forms

Word already has the ability to define forms within a document. This capability has been modified to support HTML forms. Word inherits direct toolbar support for Text, Check Box and Drop-Down input fields from its own native forms. The definition of other HTML form fields is slightly more convoluted.

A new form is created by selecting the Form Field option from the Insert menu; this must be done outside of any previously defined form. The HTML specification does not allow forms to be nested. A dialog box prompts for the type of form field to be created, either Text, Check Box or Drop-Down list, the same as represented directly by the toolbar icons. Selecting Cancel will create an empty form. The boundaries of the form are clearly shown by double lines and the text 'top[/bottom] of form'. The Form toolbar icons will only insert items into a form, they will not create a new FORM element. The Options button allows attributes of the field and other types of input to be defined.

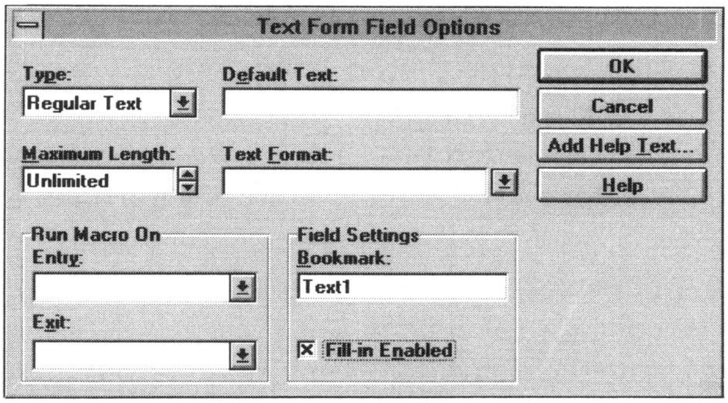

Figure 5.7 Text field attributes

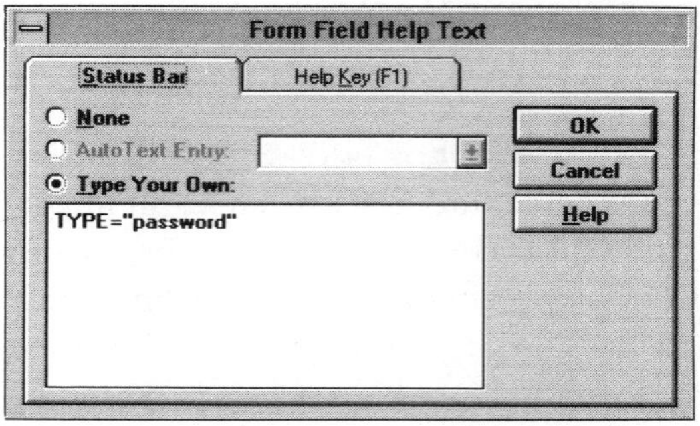

Figure 5.8 Help Text dialog box

The text field button generates a Text input field, the default type for a form:

```
<INPUT NAME="Text1" VALUE="" >
```

Unique names are assigned automatically by Internet Assistant and follow the pattern *Name#*, where # is replaced by a number, starting at 1 and counting in sequence. Naming is unique to the whole document, not just the current form. *Text1* will only occur once, even if multiple forms are defined. To make editing easier form fields can be highlighted using the Shading button.

The attributes are changed by selecting the field and using the Input Attributes button or by double clicking the desired field with the mouse. For Text input, only the Maximum Length and Default Text have meaning, the other fields can specify the type of text and enable input checking within the Word environment but have no relevance in the context of HTML 2.0. The default text is displayed within the input field.

Other attributes are defined using the Add Help Text button. Password and Hidden fields are selected using this option, relying on the fact that the text input type is not explicitly defined in the generated HTML. The button brings up the Help Text dialog box and the new type can be entered directly in the Status Bar tab. A Password field is specified in Figure 5.8.

TEXTAREA elements are also defined through this dialog box. Normal text input is converted to a text area by entering the number of rows and columns in the Status Bar field:

```
ROWS="5" COLS="40"
```

The Default Text is contained within the element tags. It's possible to change the names which are automatically assigned by Internet Assistant from the Help Text dialog box.

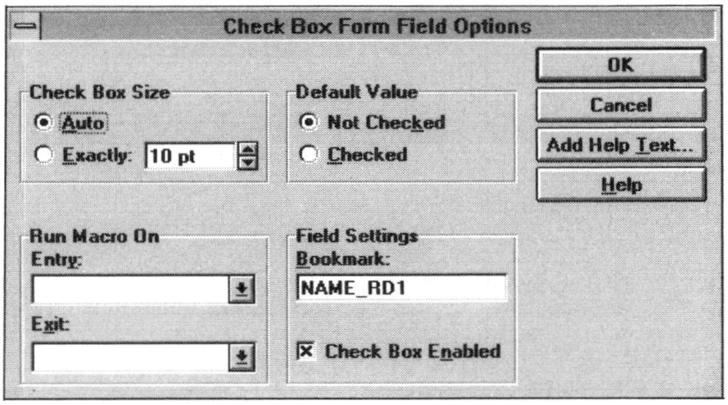

Figure 5.9 Check Box dialog box

The Check Box button generates the code for a checkbox input type:

```
<INPUT TYPE="CHECKBOX" NAME="Check1" >
```

This field can be converted to a Radio Button from the Check Box dialog box by changing the Bookmark to NAME_RD#, where the # uniquely identifies the button group. Radio buttons are grouped under this name. The button default value is also set from the Check Box dialog box.

SELECT elements are created using the Drop-Down button:

```
<SELECT NAME="Dropdown1" ></SELECT>
```

OPTION elements are added with the Drop-Down dialog box with other attributes being defined with the Help Text dialog box as before.

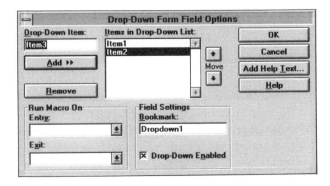

Figure 5.10 Drop-Down dialog box

■ Internet Assistant, version 2.0

The latest version of Internet Assistant for the 32-bit version of Word has direct support for some Netscapisms:

- The **CENTER** element is supported.
- Background pictures and colors can be included.
- The **TEXT**, **LINK** and **VLINK** colors can be set.

It is also possible to view the entire HTML source.

The Submit toolbar option defines the Form's ACTION, METHOD and ENCTYPE attributes in addition to creating a Submit button. With Internet Assistant there can be only one Submit button for a form. The functionality of Submit has been extended to allow an image SRC to be specified and this may be used in place of the text. This feature is not supported by all browsers and there is no easy way to define the standard Image input type with Internet Assistant. The Reset icon adds a standard Form reset button.

■ Support for Netscape and HTML 3.0

Internet Assistant doesn't yet support the Netscape or HTML 3.0 extensions. Unsupported markup can be entered from the HTML Markup dialog box under the Insert menu. This dialog box allows unrecognized elements to be hand coded, unrecognized attributes can also be entered but will be stripped by Internet Assistant when the document is reloaded. This means that: <CENTER></CENTER> can be added to documents directly but <P ALIGN=CENTER> will be stripped. All unrecognized markup is highlighted by the words: <<Unknown HTML tag>>. Clicking this brings up the Markup dialog box with the unknown tag.

■ Templates and macros

The standard HTML template can be customized for a particular project or a set of documents and can include a standard document layout. Images may be included but unlike a Word document they cannot be imported into an HTML template, instead a relative or LOCAL link is made to the image. For general working this effectively means that the relative positions of the

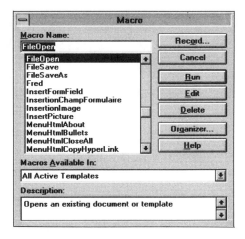

Figure 5.11 Macro dialog

document and template directory must be the same with respect to the image directory. An alternative is to store the template document as a straight HTML file under the project directory.

Word supports a powerful macro language called Word Basic. Related to Visual Basic it provides a standard scripting mechanism across the whole Microsoft Office product range. Word Basic macros are stored in templates. Word experts can redefine and augment the functionality of Internet Assistant and write Wizards to aid with the creation of standard documents. For example the usual File Save As menu option could be modified to recognize the file extensions `.htm` and `.ht3`. The HTML template would first be opened and then the Macros dialog box from the Tools menu selected. This displays a list of all the macros defined in the current HTML template. File Save As can be edited, the new code declares a File Save As record and initializes the name and format fields. The filename is selected from the file browse dialog box and saved using the HTML (9) format.

```
Sub MAIN
   Dim FSArec As FileSaveAs
   GetCurValues FSArec
   FSArec.Name = "*.htm,*.ht3"
   FSArec.Format = 9
   Dialog FSArecFileSaveAs
   FileSaveAs FSArec
EndSub
```

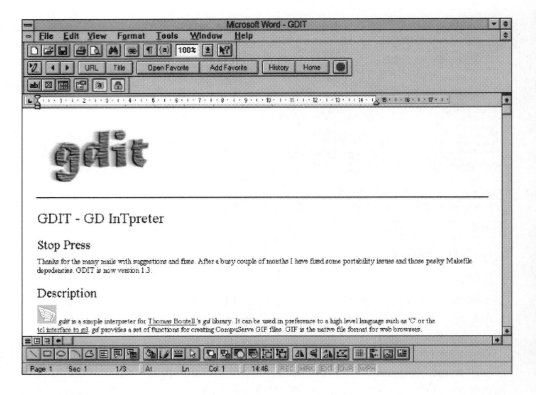

Figure 5.12   Internet Assistant in browser mode

This fairly contrived example does show the power of the Word scripting language. Further explanation is beyond the scope of this book but there are many good references.

■ Surfing the Web with Word

Internet Assistant turns Word into a fully fledged Web browser which understands version 2.0 of the HTML specification. The full URL syntax is supported, even where long filenames are used by a site. Word can surf both NT and UNIX sites and supports intermediate proxy servers. The full range of Word image formats are supported in-line, however the transparent and interlaced GIF modes are not used.

Word files can also be viewed directly and may contain links to other Word and HTML documents. All the Word formatting is preserved. Thus a Web of

Word documents can be published to anyone with Internet Assistant or the separate Word viewer. Unfortunately native Word documents are quite bulky, even an empty .DOC file occupies over 6,000 bytes! This mechanism is probably best suited to local use or for a few specific files.

The main disadvantage with Word as a Web browser is that it is incredibly sluggish. The input filter must convert all HTML files to the internal Word format before being displayed. Unless a blindingly fast computer is used, hyperlinking is more like a stroll through molasses than a leap into cyberspace. The latest 32-bit version does address this issue. It also provides better proxy support through a new dialog box.

▨ Other packages

▨ Web Author for Word

Quarterdeck spotted the same need as Microsoft for easy-to-use Web tools. Capitalizing on the advanced scripting features of Word 6.0 they have produced a very similar product to Internet Assistant. The principle advantages are:

- a specialized dictionary oriented to the Web;
- a syntax checker for proofing existing documents;
- improved forms and list creation tools.

Unlike Microsoft, who make profits from the sale of Word itself, Quarterdeck can't offer Web Author as a free loss leader but the additional features and support may make it interesting. Details of Web Author can be found on Quarterdeck's Web site: `http://www.qdeck.com/beta/WebAuthor-highlights.html`.

▨ WordPerfect

Novell have a couple of Web publishing solutions for WordPerfect. Internet Publisher is very similar to Word's Internet Assistant. It provides an HTML template for WordPerfect, converting it to a competent HTML editor. WordPerfect SGML edition offers full support for the SGML standard. Support for the SGML Document Type Definition turns WordPerfect into a fully compliant HTML editor. DTDs are available for HTML versions 2.0 and 3.0; there is also a Mozilla DTD for Netscape. Full SGML support offers a powerful and flexible solution.

■ Beyond HTML 2.0

Netscape support is already widespread amongst HTML editors and some are even implementing the latest HTML 3.0 specification. Versions of these products can be obtained on a shareware 'try before you buy' basis. Sometimes more advanced features are restricted or disabled ('crippleware') others have a time limit or reminder screen ('nagware'). Hot Dog, HoTMetaL and WebEdit are all good examples of this genre of editor and have similar functionality. HoTMetaL is the oldest and most mature of these products and has such advanced features as import filters for foreign file formats (try saying that after a few beers!).

■ Hot Dog

The recently introduced Hot Dog editor has a particularly attractive interface and supports both the Netscapisms and HTML 3.0. Like Internet Assistant, frequently used markup is accessed using toolbar buttons. However, no attempt is made to hide the underlying HTML tags and these are clearly displayed within the document. A good working knowledge of HTML is necessary to use this editor, especially the various HTML attributes' names. Hot Dog offer a Professional version with near WYSIWYG capability.

Hot Dog will create a basic document template for free. Text is added to the BODY element and markup is inserted from the toolbars and menu items. Hot Dog has pretensions to being an HTML 3.0 compliant editor and produces the appropriate DOCTYPE directive. Users should be aware that this specification is still not finalized and in any case should not be used if Netscapisms are present in the document.

For an experienced user marking up text for HTML documents can be easier with this sort of editor compared to a word processing package. The native (and sometimes extraneous) word processor functionality isn't mixed with HTML-oriented features, consequently the dialog boxes are cleaner and easier to understand. The main problem is the mixing of elements from the Netscapisms and HTML 3.0. Either a good knowledge of the specifications or a syntax checker is required to determine if the document conforms to any particular HTML version. The various SGML-derived editors get around this problem by effectively providing different personalities through the Document Type Definitions and the 16-bit version of Internet Assistant restricts authors to version 2.0 tags.

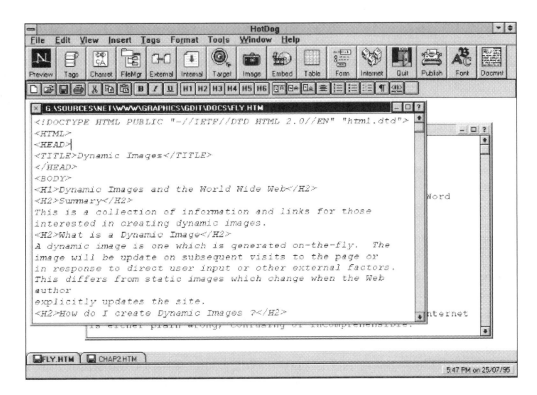

Figure 5.13 Hot Dog standard edition

```
<!DOCTYPE HTML PUBLIC "-//IETF//DTD HTML 3.0//EN"
"html.dtd">
<HTML>
<HEAD>
<TITLE> type_Document_Title_here </TITLE>
</HEAD>
<BODY>

</BODY>
</HTML>
```

Figure 5.14 Hot Dog's template document

With Hot Dog, text is marked up by highlighting the appropriate section and selecting an element from the Tags menu. Useful dialog boxes for inserting Images and creating Forms, Tables, Lists and Hyperlinks can be found under the Insert Menu.

Images

The Insert Image dialog box lets the user choose between an HMTL 2.0 or Netscape IMAGE element and an HTML 3.0 FIGURE element although not all of the current set of figure attributes are supported directly. There is support for all of the Netscape text alignment attributes and a browse window can be opened to select both the image and its LOWSRC proxy.

Forms

The Insert Form dialog box defines elements of an HTML form. If there is no current FORM element in the document the user is prompted to create and define the attributes of a new form. These include the optional HTML 3.0 script URL. The properties shown in the dialog box vary for each item type.

Tables

The Create Table dialog box is very useful, taking a lot of the strain out of formatting TABLE elements. The overall dimensions of the table are set with

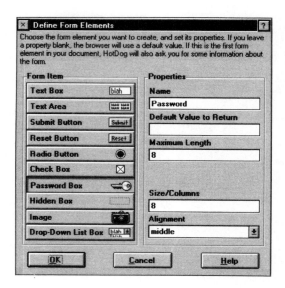

Figure 5.15 Define Form Elements dialog

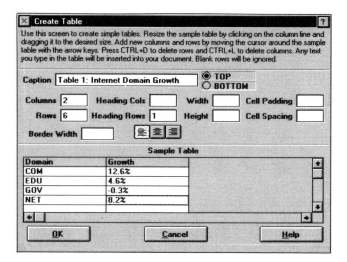

Figure 5.16 Create Table dialog

the Rows and Columns fields, these are then divided between heading and data. Figure 5.16 shows a table with one header row. The domains could have been marked up as a header column by entering a '1' in the corresponding field. Headings cells are grayed out.

HTML 3.0 column specification attributes (COLSPEC) are inserted with the Width and Height fields and Netscape cell formatting with the Padding and Spacing fields.

Lists

The Create List dialog box is similar to the Forms dialog box. The properties displayed for each list type change depending on which of the List radio buttons is selected. The first list item is marked but subsequent items must be inserted manually from the Tags menu.

Hyperlinks

As with Internet Assistant three separate dialog boxes are provided for document linking and these are:

1. a local document, FILE
2. a local anchor, #*Name*
3. a Web document, HTTP

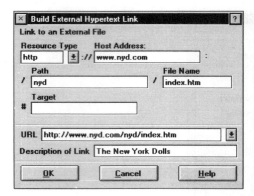

Figure 5.17 Building an external hyperlink

An additional dialog box allows the URL of an internet resource to be specified; this is the more general form of 3, above. This can either be a simple URL or another Internet service. The second dialog box features a drop-down menu of supported schemes, the properties of the path component depend on the chosen scheme and the dialog fields are changed to reflect the selection.

■ HoTMetaL

SoftQuad have used their undoubted expertise with SGML to produce a range of products targeted at HTML. The principal advantage with SoftQuad's editors is that they are fully HTML compliant. Not only will they assist in writing HTML tags they will ensure that elements are in the correct place and order.

Author/Editor is SoftQuad's top-of-the-range SGML editor. It can be used for many publishing applications, not just HTML. For instance, text books can be created from the same source as HTML documents using the DocBook DTD. It's fully WYSIWYG, a term which must be used with caution as far as the Web is concerned. Unfortunately this kind of power comes at a price, it's hard to escape the rule: YGWYPF (You Gets What You Pays For). Author/ Editor is beyond the scope of this book but should be considered by anyone who is serious about information publishing.

HoTMetaL is aimed at users who are just interested in creating HTML documents. Like its older brother, Author/Editor, it enforces correct HTML document structure. For example, it won't let you insert a form within the document head. Unlike Hot Dog the list of elements available is context

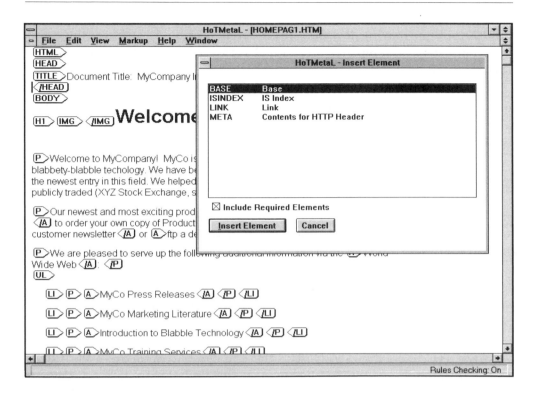

Figure 5.18 HoTMetaL follows the DTD rules

dependent. Figure 5.18 shows the elements which can be inserted within the document head.

This type of interface can seem alien to users more familiar with the DTP 'anything goes' strategy and it does require some knowledge of the various HTML tags. However, adherence to an HTML DTD should ensure that the information is available to the widest audience. The point about correct structure may not be obvious, especially when the user can view a malformed document without problem on one particular browser. Correct use of the HTML elements does matter, and some browsers will not be able to display incorrectly structured documents. It will also make life easier when moving documents from one HTML version to another, a worthwhile consideration for a large site. HoTMetaL can't read DTD files directly, instead it uses its own binary file format. New DTDs must therefore be obtained directly from SoftQuad.

Of particular interest to novice Web publishers are the range of templates available. These are predefined document outlines; the text can be edited by the user without having to insert any markup. Figure 5.18 shows the home page template. The templates are normal HTML files and therefore could be used with other editors.

An evaluation version of HoTMetaL is available but the full-blown professional version 2.0 does cost money. It also features dialog boxes for editing tables and forms as well as improved hide and reveal of tags for direct previewing.

▪ Checking the Document

Used carefully HTML editors can assist with the production of syntactically correct Web pages. They are not always so good at spotting certain kinds of structural error or unrecognized markup in existing documents. They won't highlight attributes which should be included such as the alternative text for IMAGE elements and some editors won't differentiate between elements from various HTML versions. Lastly they won't check for incorrectly specified or missing hyperlink targets.

Some browsers and editors will highlight tags that they don't recognize. The UDIwww HTML 3.0 browser displays these in red, Quarterdeck's Web Author will walk through an existing document displaying HTML 2.0 syntax errors and Internet Assistant strips attributes it doesn't recognize. This level of validation is reliant on the individual interpretation and support of the standard.

A more rigorous approach is offered by editors that can use the HTML Document Type Definitions directly. These definitions exist for standard HTML versions 2.0 and 3.0, Netscape's Mozilla and Sun's HotJava. Obvious candidates are Novell's WordPerfect SGML edition or SoftQuad's Author/Editor. Using a DTD the editor will produce markup strictly compliant with the standard.

There are on-line validation services based around SGML parsers. HAL software systems has an HTML syntax checker which uses the above DTDs and can check for even stricter compliance. Users are presented with a Web form and have to choose a conformance level and enter the full URL of the document to be checked. The document must be accessible to HAL and this requires the user to run a local Web server.

Individual HTML elements can be checked by typing these in a separate section of the form. In this way a whole document can be validated locally using cut and paste. The output from HAL is not altogether easy to understand, although sufficient on-line documentation is available.

■ Perl

Programmers often use Perl (Practical Extraction and Report Language) for developing Web tools as it is free, powerful and offers wide cross-platform support. Versions of Perl are available for all the Windows operating systems as well as flavors of UNIX and VMS. Perl is an interpreted language geared to pattern matching and text manipulation.

On-line checkers are favorite tools of net pedants who can easily validate other people's pages. News announcements of 'cool' or 'clever' sites are swiftly followed by a listing of bad markup. This form of abuse is normally reserved for particularly crass posts which break **netiquette**, the rules of net conduct and good manners.

Checking documents on-line is not always convenient. The HAL software is available for download, although no Windows versions are currently available. Other utilities exist and although these don't offer the power of SGML-based tools they are useful for validating the basic structure and elements.

Weblint is a popular syntax checker written in Perl. It's name is inspired by lint, the C programming language validator and it is equally verbose. Weblint is conveniently supplied as a ZIP archive, and assuming Perl is already installed is easy to configure and run:

```
C:\perl weblint test.htm
```

The program name is given as the second command line argument to Perl. Subsequent arguments are passed to Weblint. If Perl complains about missing libraries, the environment will need to be configured or the location can be given with the -I flag. NTPerl requires an installation program to be run by the system administrator to update the user registry with this information.

The following simple document:

```
<TITLE>Test Document</TITLE>
<CENTER>
<H1>Heading
<P>
New Paragraph
<H3>Heading 3</H3>
<IMG SRC=http:///fred.gif>
```

produced a multitude of errors and warnings:

```
test.htm(1): outer tags should be <HTML> .. </HTML>.
test.htm(1): <TITLE> can only appear in the HEAD element.
test.htm(2): <CENTER> is netscape specific (use "-x netscape"
to allow this).
test.htm(6): bad style - heading <H3> follows <H1> on
line 3.
test.htm(7): IMG does not have ALT text defined.
test.htm(0): no closing </H1> seen for <H1> on line 3.
test.htm(-): expected tag(s) not seen: HEAD BODY
```

Many of these would have been missed by a casual inspection. Weblint can detect the following types of errors in a document:

- basic document structure
- unknown elements
- illegal nesting and overlapping
- heading order
- mismatched tags
- missing end tags
- local hyperlink targets
- click 'here' hyperlinks

Support is provided for HTML versions 2.0, 3.0 and Netscape.

Weblint won't spot errors in non-local hyperlinks. These may be mistyped or can simply go missing. This often happens where links are made to student projects which have been deleted by faculty at the end of term. Missing and broken links give the site an unprofessional image.

Programs which traverse links are called robots or spiders. The CMU Lycos search engine (http://www.lycos.com) is a good example. Given a URL, Lycos will periodically visit and index a site. Users can perform a keyword search on the URLs held by Lycos and the database currently boasts millions of links. Some administrators object to these spiders crawling all over their sites consuming resources and a standard exists for barring specific robots http://web.nexor.co.uk/mak/doc/robots/norobots.html.

A robot can also be used locally to validate links in a document. Many examples of this type of utility exist and again they are often written in Perl. An alternative for Windows users is the shareware program, Webwatch, of which both 16- and 32-bit versions are available. Webwatch is a utility which can be launched directly from the program manager. It displays a dialog box in which a file containing the hyperlinks to be monitored is specified. This can be a normal HTML file. Webwatch will visit each hyperlink in turn building an output file showing the resources which cannot be reached and files which have been modified since a given date:

- Widget Home Page
  Error: Server Error: 500. Internal Server Error.
- Acme Technical Support
  Error: Client error: 403. Forbidden.
- Kimble
  Error: Retrieval timed out

The time-out and date can be configured; if the current date is used, only the broken links will be shown. The output file is an HTML document which can be viewed locally with a browser. Webwatch can also be set to run periodically, producing a bookmark list as items are updated on favorite sites.

Webwatch won't traverse links like a true robot. These can start from a given URL and search outwards, potentially building a picture of the whole Web. Parallel operation improves traversal speeds as this includes a lot of dead time waiting for connections. Robots can be used to check a whole Web site in one go by limiting the scope of the search. Peruser is a link validator for the NT platform. It runs from the command line and will scan an HTML document until it encounters a URL; it then tests if the document or image can be accessed. If it is another HTML document it opens this and repeats the process. A list of all the invalid URLs is then printed to the console.

▥ Conversion filters

▥ Lotus Notes

There is some overlap of functionality between the Web and Lotus Notes. Both are used to build local or wide-area information systems. Although the Lotus star may have waned of late, Notes is still seen as a strategic product by many corporations. Naturally Lotus has been keen to give Notes Internet connectivity and there are also products to make documents and databases available to the Web.

InterNotes is a Notes server application which talks to an NT Web server using the standard CGI script interface described in Chapter 9. It can automatically convert Notes documents and views allowing Web users to navigate the existing Notes structure. Many Notes artifacts are converted or preserved including bitmaps, tables, links and attachments. Aimed at the commercial marketplace InterNotes isn't cheap.

An alternative is TILE, which does have support for both Windows 3.1 and OS/2. TILE source code is included and the converter consists of two parts. A cross-platform program extracts data from Lotus Notes into HTML and a post-processor tidies up this output.

■ Rich Text Format

Rich Text Format (RTF) is a document exchange language developed by Microsoft. The specification is freely available and there is widespread support. It is often used as a common format to transfer documents between different applications and combines information about document structure and formatting.

RTF2HTM is a DOS command line utility written by Chris Hector to convert Rich Text Format to HTML. It does a remarkably good job of it too. With a properly structured document it can convert heading styles, writing a table of contents HTML page to a separate file. Bold, italic, underlined and courier (teletype) are all correctly tagged, including any combinations of these styles. Tables are converted to preformatted text and lists are also converted to their text equivalents rather than HTML. Headers and footers are lost but footnotes are stored in a separate file and hyperlinked from the document. Embedded images are output as separate Windows metafiles (.WMF) but as suitable viewers are not common on the Web they are linked in the document as GIF files. These files can be converted with a separate graphics package.

Support is included for the latest Word 6.0 RTF files, and the conversion of table of contents and footnotes may make it more suitable for processing technical documents than Internet Assistant. It can also take a wide range of existing RTF output and many other packages including WordPerfect and FrameMaker will generate these files.

■ Other converters

Converters exist for a range of document formats including Frame MIF, WordPerfect, Excel and PostScript. References to these can be found on any of the Web listing sites, Yahoo (http.//www.yahoo.com) or the W3 consortium (http://www.w3.org) being good starting points for any search.

PStoHTML was developed by Italy's National Research Council at Florence. It can convert PostScript files generated by the Windows 3.x drivers to HTML. Text styles are converted as are embedded bitmaps. A PostScript converter is useful where an HTML version is required and the original document is lost.

▓ Summary

- HTML can be coded directly using an editor such as Notepad.
- Specialized HTML editors provide a production framework and offer a basic level of syntax checking. Their interfaces are also cleaner than output filters for other packages.
- Output filters for existing DTP packages and word processors are less powerful but are easier to use. They can also import and convert a range of external formats.
- Command line utilities are available to process a range of file formats, they can generate documents on the fly or be used for batch conversion.

6 Multimedia

Web documents would be pretty boring if they were restricted to text only. This chapter discusses how the Web supports multimedia using an open delivery mechanism over which any data format, including those yet to be conceived, can be sent.

Like CD-ROM, Web documents can mix text, graphics, audio and video. The only requirement is that the client has suitable viewing software. In fact the Web markup language, HTML, is just another form of data. In this case the browser is the viewer.

Some purists dislike all this frippery, especially when they are forced to download bloated image files. When talking about the Web the old adage of a picture being worth a thousand words might be better phrased 'an image costs ten thousand bytes'. Salvation for the real puritans can be found by running their browsers in text only mode. While it is true that many graphics add little of direct value to the information content they do act like road signs, guiding the eye to points of interest. Video and audio are also important for aiding the understanding of certain concepts and existing legacy documents can be delivered within the Web context without prior conversion to HTML.

Graphical content is also important from a commercial viewpoint. Companies are used to having a high degree of control over style and layout. Although there is an appreciation that the Web is more of an information as opposed to an advertising medium people who have grown up with glossy brochures and a diet of MTV like to be greeted by graphically interesting pages.

■ MIME

The Web is true to its roots on the object-oriented NeXT computer system. Rather than reinventing the wheel the NeXT operating system encourages reuse of existing software components. Likewise the Web provides its multimedia capabilities by borrowing the Multipurpose Internet Mail Extensions, better known as **MIME**.

Internet email is a text-only system. If binary data, for example an image file, is sent it will arrive corrupted. The binary characters will have been reduced to ASCII text. To transmit binary data it must first be mapped onto the ASCII character set. The recipient then does the reverse trick and must also know the file type. As email usage has grown this process has become very annoying. MIME solves this problem and is an extension of the existing Internet mail format. This format consists of a header separated from the data by a blank line (carriage return/line feed [CRLF]):

```
From: Bill Bloggs <billb@acme.com>
To: A N Other
Date: Tuesday, 16-May-95 15:56:29 GMT
Body of message.
```

MIME adds the following fields to the header:

```
MIME-Version: 1.0
Content-Type: type/subtype
```

The version header informs clients what version of the MIME standard the message complies with. The current MIME version is 1.0. The content type identifies what is in the body of the message. The types include text, image, audio, application and video. There is a range of subtypes for each type, for example those for image include jpeg and gif.

■ HyperText Transfer Protocol

MIME provides all the facilities necessary for implementing a multimedia retrieval system. HTTP, the Web communication protocol, uses an extended form of MIME for sending messages between clients and servers. Clients make requests to servers in the form of a *method*, a Uniform Resource Identifier (URI) and a protocol version:

```
Method Request-URI HTTP-Version
MIME Like Header
CRLF
Body
```

This is followed by a MIME message which can include client information and request modifiers. The Server responds with a *status* line, a *protocol version* and an *error code* followed by a MIME message and, optionally, the requested content in the message body:

```
Status Line
MIME Like Header
CRLF
Body
```

HTTP is more flexible than mail about the `Content-Type` field because the client and server have the opportunity to negotiate as to what is acceptable. In particular the practice of preceding unregistered subtypes with the string 'x-' is neither required nor encouraged by HTTP although this syntax is still widely used. New non-experimental subtypes should be registered.

Figure 6.1 shows a typical client–server conversation. The user asks the browser to fetch the URL <http://www.acme.com/default.htm>. The browser opens a connection to the server and sends a simple `GET` request (remember how we did the same with our telnet spoof back in Chapter 2?). When requesting a resource physically located on the server there is no need to send the server name as part of the request. If the server locates the resource it responds with a status line (code: `200` means okay), a MIME header which says what type of resource is being returned, in this case HTML text, and the message body. The user's browser displays the line `Some Text`. Setting the `Expires` date to be the same as the `Date` field tells the browser not to keep a local copy of the document. The browser will have to re-request the server if the user wishes to view the document again. The same effect can be achieved with the field `Pragma: no-cache`.

HTTP is what's known as an **application level** protocol. Although Web programs use the Internet's TCP/IP communication protocol HTTP could be built on top of other network protocols.

That's a very brief look at how the Web supports a variety of media types. We'll come back to this topic when we look at dynamic documents in Chapters

The client requests the file: default .htm from the server: www.acme.com and the server returns the requested resource.

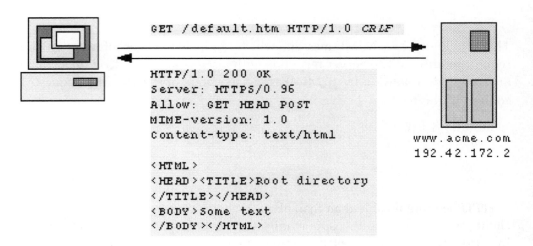

Figure 6.1 HTTP conversation

Application	HTTP
Session	WinSock Library
Transport	Transmission Control Protocol (TCP)
Network	Internet Protocol
	(IP)
Link	Local Ethernet, Internet Backbones, Phone Lines

Figure 6.2 WWW network layers

8 and 9 but for now we know enough to look at the other formats and make choices about what should be included on a particular Web site.

▓ In-line graphics

Two image types are supported directly by most Web browsers. These are CompuServe's Graphics Interchange Format and the Joint Photographic Expert Group format usually just called **GIF** and **JPEG**. GIF was devised by CompuServe's software engineers in the latter part of the 1980s as a hardware independent protocol for the on-line transmission of raster graphics. The JPEG standard, as the name implies, is concerned with the problem of compressing high-quality photographic images. It looks set to become the Web standard for this application though it is not quite so well supported as GIF.

GIF is popular because although CompuServe retain the copyright they have published a detailed description of the format. Software based on GIF must simply acknowledge CompuServe. GIF is straightforward to implement and there are only a couple of variations, GIF87 and GIF89. This makes it popular with developers and most graphics software supports one of the two standards. GIF allows 256 colors out of a palette of over 16 million (2^{24}) to be used. This seems quite limited by current standards but in practice there is little difference between a 256-color (8-bit) image and true color (24-bit) image when viewed on a monitor. Compression is defined as part of the standard and uses a patented **Lempel–Zif** compression algorithm (LZW). LZW replaces patterns of bytes with a variable length index and stores the pattern in a table. When similar patterns are encountered they are replaced by the index and this achieves the compression. It's not the most powerful algorithm and a problem with the patent holder has now threatened the whole format.

JPEG supports true color images. A color is composed of red, green and blue components. Computer monitors display color using a group of three such **pixels** (pixel is a contraction of picture element). From a normal viewing distance these blend to form a single colored point. JPEG can set one of 256 levels for each color, from off to full on. It's a bit like the dimmer control used in house lighting. The total number of combinations, and thus the total number of colors, is 256 x 256 x 256 which is a shade over 16 million (no pun intended). This has been dubbed **true color** or **photorealistic** and is deemed the minimum number of colors required to adequately render photographs. To represent all of the 16 million colors available to a JPEG image simultaneously the image would have to be 4000 x 4000 pixels in size. Compare that to a GIF where an 8 x 8 image can represent the whole range of colors. The 256 different levels

Figure 6.3   The limits of perception

of each color can be squeezed into a single byte, so three bytes are required for each pixel. True color is thus alternatively referred to as 24-bit color (1 byte contains 8 bits).

The JPEG standard uses a clever compression algorithm which is much better than the LZW system used in GIFs. One compression technique it employs is to exploit limitations in human perception. The retina at the back of the eyeball is made up of two types of cell which are sensitive to contrast and color. Contrast is more important when visualizing an image. Looking at a scene human eyesight is drawn to the regions which display the greatest contrast. Loss of small areas of color are therefore less important than equivalent areas of contrast. Figure 6.3 demonstrates how easily eyes can lie, the small squares appear to be different shades of gray but are in fact identical.

The JPEG standard doesn't specify how the resulting image should be saved to file. There is no guarantee that the compressed image from one program will be readable by another. To solve this particular problem the industry has developed a further standard called **JFIF** (JPEG File Interchange Format). Files complying with this standard should have the extension .JIF instead of .JPG but it looks as if .JPG will continue to be used for some time. Most JFIF-compliant software supports both extensions.

An obvious question is why use one of these formats when bit-mapped images would be a lot easier for developers to implement? Both GIF and JPEG formats specify a hardware-independent method for transferring images and also feature data compression. Although compression slows down rendering it is very important where data is sent across a slow communications link. A 100 x 100 image supporting 256 colors will require 1 byte per color, giving a file size of 10,000 bytes (plus a few hundred extra bytes for the color table and other descriptive information). The GIF LZW algorithm can achieve compression ratios of 4:1, shrinking the file's size to 2,500 bytes. This will take about a second to download over a V34 modem link compared to four seconds for the equivalent bit-mapped file. Quite some difference. JPEG can achieve even better compression ratios, typically 4:1 over LZW, shrinking the file a down to a tiny 600 bytes.

This image was saved with a quality factor of 75. The file size is 8,680 bytes compared to the original size of 109,122 bytes. This gives a 12.5:1 compression ratio. It would take about four seconds to download on a V.34 modem (28,800 bps). The image quality is very close to the original.

The quality factor has now been reduced to 25. There is a slight loss of definition. The image size is 3,924 bytes giving a compression of 28:1. The image could be downloaded in two seconds on a V.34 connection.

With a quality factor of 1 the image is displaying the typical JPEG slabbyness. The image is still recognisable (and was even better in color!) and could be used where a small, low-quality image is required. The size is now 978 bytes giving a 110:1 compression compared to the original. It would take less than a second to transfer.

Figure 6.4 Comparison of a JPEG image at various quality factors

A good rule of thumb is that an in-line image (one that a user automatically downloads when not in text-only mode) should take no more than 5 seconds to transfer. This is especially true for home page **banner** graphics. This limits image size to about 20,000 bytes on a V34 modem line. Web designers should always strive to make images as small (in terms of transmission time) as possible. Users are paying to download these graphics and will not appreciate bloated images. A small effort on behalf of the Web designer has a large Net benefit (pun intended).

So if JPEG is so good why bother with GIF images at all? Well as has already been mentioned the JPEG scheme exploits limitations in perception to remove

Figure 6.5 JPEG distortion

certain details which would be expensive to store. It is a 'lossy' compression scheme. The amount of loss can be specified as a quality factor (QF). The highest quality of 100 is practically indistinguishable from the original and would typically achieve a compression ratio approaching 10:1. The lowest quality settings result in blocky looking images. Most graphics programs settle on 75 for average quality. Graphics programs use different terms for specifying quality, PaintShop Pro (described in the following chapter) has a compression factor ranging from 0 to 100 and another popular shareware program LView Pro allows users to crank the quality down as far as 20. This gives a file maybe 50 times smaller than the original by trading off some loss in definition.

 A bit of loss doesn't sound like too high a price for those sorts of compression ratios. However, remember that JPEG loses small details. Single pixel lines, corners and text at small point sizes will be blurred. These features don't tend to occur in real-world scenes where even sharp edges blend with the background colors but they do occur in images like line art and icons. GIF is often better at compressing large areas of uniform color and images with only a few different colors. GIF may also be considered for black and white pictures. JPEG is excellent for photographs and for any image requiring more than 256 colors but higher QFs will be required when overlaying text. Figure 6.5 shows a fringing effect around text on an image compressed with a QF of 75. QFs of 85 and above would eliminate a lot of this 'noise' and would still give a smaller image than the equivalent GIF file.

The reader may be wondering just how many people will be using machines which support 24-bit graphics. True-color cards are still quite expensive as they employ fast graphics chip sets and need a lot of RAM memory, 2 megabytes for a reasonable 800 x 600 screen resolution. Wouldn't it be better just to stick with GIFs when rendering pictures? A scanned photograph is unlikely to be composed of less than 256 individual colors. Even wide expanses of what appears to be the same color, say blue sky or a cornfield, is actually made up of a near-limitless number of shades. Even the most powerful graphics system will have to map colors onto its available palette; 24-bit color provides a photo-realistic rendering of an image and this is the color depth supported by JPEG. If the number of colors is reduced to 256 by saving that image as a GIF file colors will be converted to the closest match in the new palette. This process is called **quantization** and results in some loss of quality.

If the recipient has an 8-bit graphics system a number of the available 256 colors of the palette will have already been used by Windows or by other images and applications. Indeed some browsers limit the number of colors which can be displayed in an image to a fraction of the total palette, 64 would be a typical figure. This avoids the problem of the first image grabbing the whole palette and leaving a lousy choice of colors for subsequent images. If a further level of quantization has to be performed there may be a very poor mapping between the original 24-bit colors and the final 6-bit colors. As an example, a light green in the original JPEG may get mapped to a darker shade when the image is saved as using GIF. The recipient's viewer might map this to a still darker green but might also support a shade that is closer to the original color. For real-world images it is better to transmit them as JPEG and let the recipient's computer perform the whole quantization process. The higher quality nature of JPEG means that compliant viewers often make a better job of quantization on 8-bit graphics systems than other software. It also permits users with better graphics capability to view higher quality images.

 GIF does have a further use. The more recent GIF89a variant supports **interlaced** and **transparent** images. Interlaced images are built up over four passes. An initial low-resolution version is displayed and as the rest of the image data is downloaded the full image is overlaid. This is a useful technique for giving a very fast representation of a Web page. Transparent GIFs are useful for displaying text or other non-square images allowing the background color of the browser window to show through the image's own background. Figure 6.6 illustrates the effect of a transparent background with the two custom headline graphics. The JPEG format supports a similar technique to transparent GIFs called progressive JPEG but it is not yet widely supported by Web browsers.

Thus the GIF format has proved more tenacious than the baddy in a Stephen King book. The final nail in the coffin may come from the patent issue. The Lempel–Zif compression algorithm is a patented process owned by the computer giant Unisys. Recently Unisys has reached an agreement with CompuServe over royalties for LZW. Commercial packages must now pay Unisys for using the compression and decompression algorithms. This will impinge on Web browsers as well as many popular graphics programs.

Figure 6.6   Transparent backgrounds

If the Web is an open-ended multimedia system then why not use another format altogether? For the vast majority of image applications designers will want to stick to the internal formats and this means GIF and JPEG. Other formats require users to obtain and configure an external viewer. Documents which rely on special graphics content will be unusable until this is done. This requirement is acceptable for limited areas where the user has a high motivation to find and configure a display program. Examples would be audio and video clips which are often incidental to the document.

Life after GIF

A solution to the problem of finding a good, general-purpose graphics format for Web browsers may be the proposed **PNG** standard. PNG stands for portable network graphics and in the style of the Free Software Foundation (FSF) is a recursive acronym: **PNG** is **Not GIF** although the designers have joked that this infringes the FSF's recursive acronym patent! PNG proposes a full-color image format while retaining and improving upon features such as interlaced display and transparent colors. It will use, but not be restricted to, the legally unencumbered compression algorithm LZ77, the same one that is used in PKZIP. This improves on the LZW compression ratios. The reference code is freely usable in commercial applications and support is already appearing in browsers and graphics packages. PNG is a lossless compression scheme. It is expected that JPEG images will still give smaller file sizes, especially where quality is less critical.

External file formats

Many people and organizations will have existing documents which they wish to put on-line. There are tools to convert various different file formats to HTML. Microsoft Word can import foreign word processor documents such as WordPerfect files and, using Internet Assistant, save them as HTML. There are external conversion programs available for Rich Text Format and FrameMaker. The success of the conversion process depends on how closely the original document can be rendered in the HTML language. Mathematical formulae, special characters, font information, pictures, diagrams and tables may all be lost during conversion resulting in an unusable document. Converting large numbers of **legacy documents** is time consuming and tedious.

The Web allows the designer to deliver any file format, even those not explicitly recognized by MIME. If there's a requirement to display some Excel spreadsheets as part of the company corporate accounts pages they can simply be transmitted as a native Excel document although the success of this strategy depends largely on who the audience is.

Web designers building an internal information system should have a good idea what software their users have available. For reasons of logistics and economy organizations often standardize on a small set of packages.

■ To buy or not to buy?

A good example of where users may be prepared to buy special viewing software is for a company selling geological maps. Currently these are supplied on paper and CD-ROM. The CD-ROM version is just a set of data points in a proprietary format, the map being constructed by a special piece of software. The company may decide that the Internet is an effective sales and delivery mechanism. As the maps have a high value users will have to purchase data sets on a pay-on-view basis. As part of this initial arrangement the special viewing software can be made available either on-line or delivered separately with any paper documentation. In contrast if the organization served the sales documentation as a Lotus WordPro file rather than converting it to HTML it would find Internet-driven sales very disappointing. The target audience is immediately restricted to those who have already purchased WordPro and have configured their browser to view such documents.

A company may have chosen to go the Microsoft route and equip every PC on the network with MS Office. The designer can then deliver PowerPoint presentations and Excel files directly and convert all Word documentation to HTML. This is enabled by defining MIME content types for PowerPoint .PPT and Excel .XLS files on the Web server and configuring each browser to launch the appropriate external application when viewing these files. The currently defined set of MIME content types is given in Appendix B.

 This strategy will be less successful when serving an external audience. Users may be running Apple Macintosh, NeXTSTEP or X-Windows systems. Even when there is cross-platform support for the external applications chosen by the designer it is unlikely that more than a small fraction of the audience will run them on their systems. Unless users have a high motivation for viewing the information, documents that involve a major purchasing decision should be avoided.

The problems of converting certain information to HTML may place too many restrictions on some applications. For instance, how to deliver that latest report full of tables, diagrams and formulae without laboriously converting large chunks to in-line images? HTML 3.0, the latest specification, provides a fuller range of formatting but is restricted by the availability of applications supporting the standard. Another alternative is to convert the document to a PostScript file.

▓ PostScript

PostScript is a page description language. It is used to render pages which have been produced by computer applications on to raster devices such as printers and computer displays. This is performed in a device-independent manner.

The language itself describes graphic *objects* rather than *bitmaps*. A string of text will have characteristics such as font, size and position associated with it. Every device capable of rendering a PostScript file has to run a PostScript language interpreter called a **rasteriser**. It is the responsibility of this program to translate the page description into an image. PostScript solved the problem of drawing fonts at different scales by describing each character as a series of lines and curves rather than as a bitmap. The rasteriser draws the font at the appropriate scale and then decides how best to fit this onto the output device's raster (or bitmap). Microsoft's TrueType fonts address a similar problem. The rasteriser must have character information for every font style in the document. This font information can either be stored in a separate computer file or in the case of printers, in a memory chip. If there is no description for a particular font a default style will be used. It is possible to download the font information with the file, but this makes the file bigger and normally the rasteriser's own fonts produce better characters.

PostScript printer drivers are readily available for the Windows operating systems. To create a PostScript version of a file install the appropriate driver from the print manager. For Windows there is a single driver file called PSCRIP.EXE available from Microsoft's FTP site (ftp.microsoft.com). The Windows NT installation disk contains various print drivers, the Hewlett Packard HP1200 C/PS gives good results. If a PostScript printer isn't connected locally then printing to file can be selected as the default. Configure this from the application by:

1. selecting Print from the File menu;
2. changing the Printer to the newly created PostScript device;
3. from the Print Set-up dialog box decide whether the driver should download font information; select Options for the Options dialog box and then Options again for the Advanced Options dialog box.

 Bitmaps should not be compressed. Some viewers can't cope with these. TrueType fonts may be downloaded if fonts outside of the usual Helvetica, Times Roman and Courier range are used. If a viewer doesn't have font information for the document it will substitute a default font. The Free Software

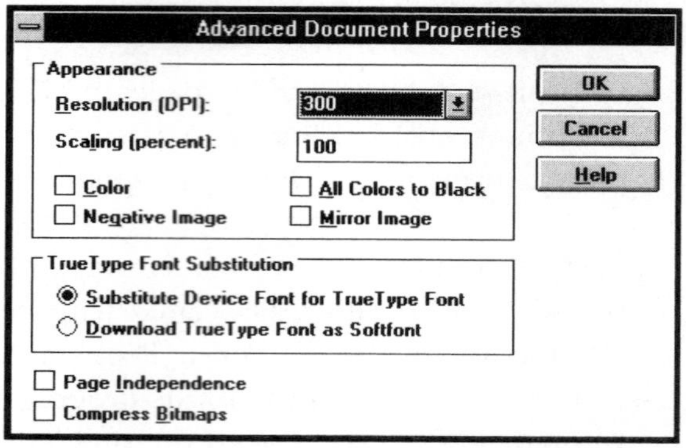

Figure 6.7 PostScript document conversion

Foundation's GhostScript viewer program GhostView uses the appropriately named Ugly font.

As PostScript is a widespread format many Web servers will recognize the `.PS` (PostScript) and `.EPS` (Encapsulated PostScript) file extensions and will supply the appropriate MIME content type of `application/postscript` to the browser. This would not be understood directly but many browsers allow an external application to be configured that will be sent the returned data. In Netscape a helper application is defined from the Options/Preferences menu or when the file is first accessed. As the PostScript MIME type is already known to Netscape this is simply a case of giving the path to an installed viewer such as GhostView.

Netscape launches GhostView (`GSVIEW.EXE`) to display the document. If the server doesn't know about PostScript both the MIME content type for the specific file extension on the server (e.g. `.EPS`, `.PS`, `.AI`) and the corresponding helper application on the browser will have to be configured. This applies to any new format, not just PostScript. The server will return a default MIME

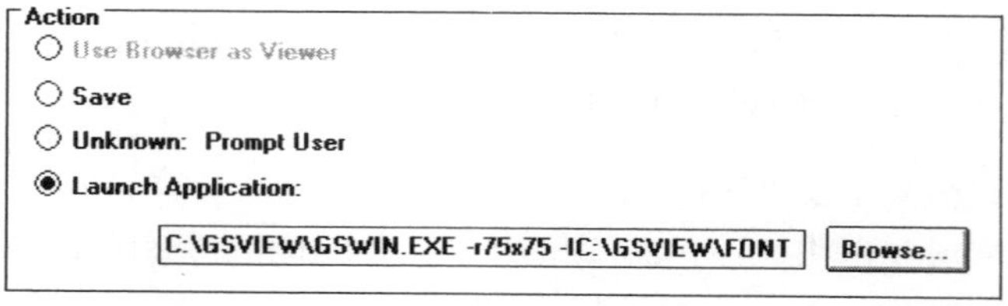

Figure 6.8 Configuring GhostView under Netscape

content type for unrecognized file extensions and the browser will perform the action for this default, not for the corresponding file extension. For example, the EMWAC's HTTPS server returns the default content type of application/octet-string and the browser performs the action for this type irrespective of any alternative action configured for the file extension.

It is easy to produce PostScript documents and providing the appropriate font information is available these will be exact representations of the original document. PostScript viewing software is readily available for a range of platforms and some Windows systems such as NeXTSTEP and NeWS have in-built support. As was mentioned previously the Free Software Foundation's GhostView is a popular choice for the Windows platforms. Many existing documents are already stored in PostScript format but note that Mac PostScript files will have to be converted to MS-DOS PostScript format.

PostScript remains an external format. There is no support for hypertext and it is not integrated into Web browsing software. There are no interesting links to follow either within the document or to external files. Thus much of the power of the Web is lost. A development from PostScript is Adobe's Acrobat. The Acrobat Portable Document Format (PDF) supports hypertext and an industry consortium including Netscape will integrate it into their browser technology. Adobe also makes PDF viewers available for free which should aid its wider adoption. The limiting factor is the availability of applications which can produce PDF files. All this power comes at a price, both Acrobat PDF and PostScript files can be considerably bigger than their HTML equivalents.

■ Sound and movies

With the increasing popularity of CD-ROM more people are buying multimedia-capable personal computers. These are usually high-specification machines and include graphics accelerator and sound cards. The computer case may even contain a microphone and stereo speaker system. As the technology to play sound and movie data is more recent than for images *de facto* standards are still emerging. Web authors have to pick from a bewildering array of formats.

Most multimedia systems running Windows already have the software available to play the Microsoft standard Wave Audio Files (.WAV) and Video for Windows (.AVI). These are extensively used on CD-ROMs and the playback software is usually supplied with the package but using these formats exclusively on a Web site will restrict the audience to the Windows community.

A more mature standard is QuickTime. Originally developed by Apple, viewers are available for both Mac and Windows platforms. Mac QuickTime files take the extension .QT and those for Windows .MOV. The difference is that the Windows viewers require what is termed a single fork data stream for video and audio. The Apple QuickTime file should be flattened. Shareware is available to reduce the video and audio to a single fork. There is a lot of support for the production of QuickTime movies and consequently this is less complicated than with other formats.

Mosaic and Netscape have bundled audio playback utilities with their browsers, but a supported sound card is still required. Mosaic's player understands the Sun and NeXT .AU format, which is an 8-bit mu-Law encoded data stream suitable for speech. Netscape also supports this format and also plays Mac and Silicon Graphic's .AIFF files. This features 16-bit samples suitable for music. Both formats are common for sound-only files on the Internet.

An emerging standard is that from the Moving Pictures Expert Group or **MPEG**; like JPEG the file format is named after the committee. MPEG covers audio, video and a combination of the two; the file extension types reflect these differences. .MPG is used for video, .MPA or .MP2 for audio and .MPS for the combination of audio and video. The MPEG I standard is concerned with how a video signal can be compressed onto a 1.5 Mbps data stream. Video compression uses standard techniques for shrinking each frame. Additionally there is often little change between subsequent frames in a movie. For instance the background may remain static over a number of images. MPEG leverages off this fact by only transmitting the differences between frames. It achieves better compression ratios than the other standards and viewing software is available for many platforms. Often these are evaluation versions of commercial software with some features disabled or a limit placed on file size.

Computer audio works by digitizing an analog signal. The original signal is a continuously varying voltage. An analog-to-digital converter takes a series of snapshots of the signal. The signal quality depends on the frequency of samples. To prevent aliasing the sampling rate must be twice the highest frequency found in the signal. Digitization also introduces harmonic distortion, or 'hiss', because the smooth input wave form has been changed into a series of steps. Humans are sensitive to frequencies up to 20 kHz so for high-quality digital reproduction the signal will be filtered above this frequency and sampled at 40 kHz. In fact compact discs use a sampling rate of 44.1 kHz, that's two 16-bit samples every 22 microseconds! Many sound cards allow for audio sampling and using a Digital Signal Processor (DSP) they can take direct digital input from a compact disc or digital audio tape (DAT) player.

■ Musical Instrument Digital Interface

Another way of encoding music is with the Musical Instrument Digital Interface (MIDI) format. Just as PostScript represents graphic data as a set of objects rather than a bit map MIDI stores music as a sequence of instruments and notes. MIDI data files are much more compact than their sampled data equivalents. A piano note may take several seconds of sampled data but is a single instruction to play a certain note using MIDI. MIDI files can be played on sound cards or routed over a MIDI local area network to a set of connected instruments. A couple of codes could instruct synthesizer 2 to play a honky-tonk piano A7 and the drum machine to strike a hi-hat beat. The original MIDI LAN ran at about 31 kHz over a simple serial connection. It's quite possible to send MIDI in real time over the Internet and some musicians are already having on-line jam sessions. MIDI is restricted to the sounds which can be reproduced on electronic musical instruments but could be an interesting inclusion on music-oriented sites.

Digital video is produced by capturing a series of frames from a video signal with a special piece of hardware called a **frame grabber**. A video signal occupies several Megahertz of bandwidth so it's quite some feat to compress this onto a 1.5 Mbps digital channel.

Both these techniques produce huge quantities of data. Lower sampling rates, fewer frames per second, black and white and smaller picture size can all reduce the amount of storage needed. As a very rough rule of thumb a couple of JPEG images are the same as eight seconds of audio sampled at 44.1 kHz or 1 second of MPEG audio/video at 30 frames per second.

■ Other formats

Although it is inadvisable to deliver proprietary file formats over the Web some free viewers can be found for certain documents. Microsoft provide external Windows viewers for PowerPoint and Word files. These can be downloaded and configured in the same way as for GhostView, described earlier. The Word viewer may be used to make a Web of Word documents available over the wider Internet, much like Adobe's PDF files. The main problems are the proprietary nature of Word documents and their inherent size.

It is a good idea to include a link to viewing software whenever an external file is presented in a document. This can either be within the current page or on a separate resource page.

■ Summary

- Rather than reinvent the wheel the Web builds on existing technology to provide multimedia support. The method used is both extensible and open. Any file format can be delivered.
- HTTP is a lightweight protocol and is not limited to a specific network but is normally associated with the Internet's TCP/IP.
- JPEG or GIF are used as the default image formats. JPEG compression is 'lossy'. JPEG is used for photographic scenes and GIF for icons, line art and images with few colors. Consider GIF for black and white images.
- Always strive to make images as small as possible without sacrificing too much quality.
- Use PostScript or Acrobat where documents contain many diagrams and special characters. PostScript currently has wider support than Acrobat, but Acrobat should offer better integration with the Web.
- Use MPEG for video and possibly audio file formats. Sun's AU audio is also supported by the popular Mosaic and Netscape browsers.
- As a courtesy provide hyperlinks to viewers for any external file formats used.

7 Graphics

There's no doubt that a very functional and informative Web site can be built entirely around text pages, but the inclusion of suitable graphics can make it more attractive and easier to navigate. Photographs add support and credibility to the text; after all, the camera doesn't lie.

The graphical content depends largely on the nature of the site. The pages of a research center may differ enormously from those of a commercial site. A research site may restrict itself to a banner logo, which establishes the site identity, and to some navigation icons, the other pages being on-line versions of its published papers. The compelling reason for users to visit the site is the need for information. Anything which detracts from or hinders this purpose may be viewed as unnecessary baggage. Commercial sites are driven more by the requirement to entertain rather than inform; the adjective **edutainment** is often used to describe this genre of material. The home pages of a record store will look more like *MTV* than *Scientific American*. A whole spectrum lies between the purely academic and the obviously commercial.

The overwhelming majority of new sites will feature some graphical content. This is encouraged by good in-line image support from the latest browsers and new features, such as background images. A big problem facing Web authors is the creation of these graphics. For traditional media the production of graphics would have been given to a trained artist or designer. Artwork would have been delivered on paper or film. More recently graphic designers have adopted computer technology and artwork is nowadays supplied on floppy or

Syquest disks. Large format transparencies are also an important medium and some design studios are even installing fast Integrated Services Digital Networks (ISDN) connections.

Where available these are all useful sources for the site builder but existing images are rarely in the correct format for the Web. Graphic designers have almost universally adopted the Macintosh as the computer system of choice and their ISDN lines are usually for point-to-point connection with print shops, not the Internet. To use existing artwork, whether on film or on-line, it must be converted and this can require capital expenditure in the form of hardware and software.

Web builders may feel that existing sources are too staid and don't convey a suitably hi-tech image. In this case they would be well advised to work with a graphic designer to adapt existing images or to produce entirely new versions. If the designer has no Web experience a demonstration and tour of some of the best sites is advisable. Unless cost is the only consideration, it is better to use a graphic designer with no Web experience than a 'techie' with no design experience!

Graphic design is an important skill and it is likely that the Web will create its own specialists as has already happened with icon design. As the Web matures an increasing number of graphic artists will specialize in this area. The Web itself places a different set of artistic constraints to those of printing. The previous chapter highlighted some of the shortcomings of the image formats used. It is important that designers understand and work within these bounds. Delivering artwork in the correct format, either by email or floppy, is always preferable to some post conversion or scanning process.

The reader may well be wondering where all these Web graphic specialists will be found. The answer is: on the Web of course. Use a search engine and look at their home pages to see what they offer. A Web designer should have a good on-line portfolio to demonstrate. Apply the shareware maxim and try before you buy.

■ Graphic design

Traditionally graphic design would cover the layout of the page and ultimately the document as a whole. Elements such as font style, the placement of graphics and location of white space are important. HTML affords limited, and browser-dependent, control over these areas. Graphic design within the HTML framework is largely concerned with the production of graphical (that is image) elements on a page.

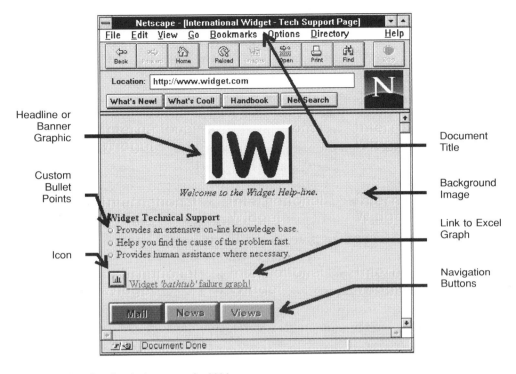

Figure 7.1   Graphical elements of a Web page

Figure 7.1 shows the main graphical elements of a Web page. A page may also feature other in-line graphics including diagrams, charts, scanned photos or cartoons.

■ Headline graphics

If the site is for an existing organization some graphics can be taken from promotional material or company reports. Logos and images are often closely associated with the company they represent, for example think about the golden arches of McDonalds or the ellipse and lettering of Ford. It may be worthwhile modifying the logo to create a different Web presence but remember that any change to corporate image will have to be approved at the highest level.

The international exposure any Web site receives has to be considered. The company may trade under different names and employ a different design for each country. Exxon is unknown in Europe where it uses the familiar 'Esso' brand name and logo. This global reach makes it important to clearly identify the origin of the site, especially where there is a possibility of conflict. As an example Hoover is owned by Maytag in the United States but by the Italian firm Candy in Europe and the Middle East.

If new graphics are required it is worth remembering that while full-color images are simple to produce for the Web they can be costly to print. A color image will require a four-color print process for any hard-copy literature and as the site establishes itself the logo will be associated with any related activity. Color inkjet and laser technology may be used to reduce these expenses but they too are costly for large print runs. Any competent graphic designer or printer should be able to advise on the cost to reproduce a design and this should be factored in to the overall site budget.

The legal status of any graphic should be confirmed before it is used. It is often erroneously assumed that an organization will own or have permission to use anything in its existing promotional literature. Photographic agencies often charge a rate per thousand copies. This will be hard to monitor on a Web site and the agency may not be happy about unregulated electronic distribution. The Web knows no national boundaries and laws on intellectual property rights do vary. A case in point is the text of Hitler's manifesto *Mein Kampf*, which can be published in the United Kingdom without reference to the copyright holder, the Bavarian state. In the United Kingdom copyright extends to only 50 years after the author's death but it would fall foul of the law in Germany which currently stands at 75 years.

With the ever-increasing commercial interest in the Internet expect to see some interesting test cases. The globalization of the world economy is also forcing harmonization in the area of copyright law either through trade blocks such as the European Community or international organizations like the GATT.

HTML 3.0 includes a new banner element. A banner graphic will retain its position on the visible page even when it is scrolled. These 'floating' areas can be used for the corporate logo and information. A modified and smaller form of the banner logo may be produced for any subordinate pages to reinforce the site identity.

■ Icons

Icons are small images, usually 48 x 48 pixels or less, which are used to represent a subject or concept. As the dimensions of an icon decrease it becomes increasingly difficult to sensibly depict a topic. Microsoft use a size of 19 x 17

(24 x 22 including border) for their toolbar icons but even this may be too large for use in an HTML definition list.

 There are many excellent sources for standard icons on the Web. These can be downloaded via FTP but as with anything on the Internet don't just assume that they are in the public domain. Any icons or graphics displayed by a browser can be captured. The Netscape browser makes this easy by clicking the right mouse button over the desired image. A floating menu will pop up allowing the image to be saved to a file. CD-ROM collections provide another convenient source and will often have a useful companion book and index. The image formats can be converted to GIF using a package such as Paint Shop Pro, described later in this chapter. This can also be used to modify icons by changing colors or adding borders.

 Unless the site is restricted to internationally recognized symbols, like traffic signs, the meaning of icons may be unclear to other users. It is a good idea to back them up with a text description. Icons which look like buttons should also have some associated action; the icon button in Figure 7.1 will pop up an Excel generated graph.

Navigation buttons

Navigation buttons are used to move around the Web site. They provide a more organized structure than hyperlinks contained within the text and extend the navigation capabilities of browsers which are restricted to scrolling backwards or forwards through a chain of visited pages.

Typical uses for navigation buttons include:

- returning to the home page;
- movement through a sequence of structurally linked pages (e.g. a report);
- links to new and interesting features;
- display of email response forms;
- submitting data for local processing.

Charts and pictures

Scanned pictures can be used to aid text descriptions. Illustrations will show objects with more structure than a picture. The International Widget support page may include a photograph of a Widget but might use a line art drawing to illustrate the component parts. The illustration could be taken directly from a CAD package, either by screen grabbing or by saving the image in a format which can be converted to a GIF file. Line art can also be scanned but the more exacting nature of the image gives less satisfactory results compared to photographs.

Clip Art is another useful source but should be used judiciously to avoid building pages with tired and hackneyed images. Clip Art can be combined or manipulated with a graphics package to personalize it for the site.

Charts are used to convey trends and make comparisons. In Figure 7.1 the chart icon would link to a graph showing failure rate of widgets plotted against time, the famous 'bathtub' curve. Graphical data can be culled from sources such as spreadsheets or can be generated directly from other data sets using scripting.

■ Page furniture

Backgrounds

Backgrounds are a feature of the latest Netscape browsers and are also supported by the HTML 3.0 standard. Where used they shouldn't intrude on the text. Great care must be exercised in color schemes, especially if the font color is changed from the default of black. Black on light gray or white is not a random choice by computer manufacturers but has shown itself to be the most readable combination. Don't trade readability for flashy pages. Backgrounds can be used to reinforce the identity of a site or a collection of pages.

Rulers

The HTML horizontal rule can be replaced by a custom image. As with background images different rulers reinforce a site or page identity. Pages and documents may even be color coded in this way. There are some very flashy rulers used on the Web ranging from rainbow lines to barbwire. Many sites carry rulers which can be freely downloaded. Care should be taken over width as browsers will resize their internal rules to cope with page width but won't do the same job with custom rules.

Custom bullets

The custom bullet points shown in Figure 7.1 are only 8 x 8 pixels. An obvious question is why use custom bullets when HTML already provides them with unordered lists? One reason is where two different lists are to be represented on the same page. The strain on the communications link is not huge as a bullet GIF is only a few bytes in size and can be cached locally for use on other pages.

▧ Rolling your own images

There will be few Web sites which can survive on existing graphics alone. Site builders are then left with the choice of finding a designer or producing their own images. As has already been stressed, the production of good graphics really needs an accomplished designer. Naturally some Web spinners may also be accomplished artists but for every good jack-of-all-trades there are another ten where the builders are graphically out of their depths.

Most of us have an inherent feel for what constitutes good design, if we didn't there wouldn't be work for design consultancies. Although realizing a concept may be beyond our drawing abilities there are a whole range of images which can be created using the standard capabilities of a graphics package. It's a semantic difference, like painting the Cistine Chapel and laying the bricks.

Users who are already producing graphics probably have a favorite piece of software. Packages such as CorelDraw or Illustrator can all be harnessed to create stunning Web images. Both are powerful illustration tools but have a steep learning curve to be able to use them effectively. Designers use Adobe Illustrator to create wonderful drawings from little more than blends and bezier curves.

These sorts of packages are not ideally suited to common Web tasks. It's a bit like using a power drill to fix screws into wood; in the hands of a skilled operator it is fine for the big jobs. Paint and photo-retouching software offer a better platform. They feature a range of built-in filters and effects and are great for laying out text, knocking up icons and bashing out buttons. Adobe's Photoshop is undoubtedly the best but the price of the Pro version puts it a little out of reach for most people. The LE version is bundled with many scanners and can be a good jumping-on point.

A widely used alternative is Paint Shop Pro (PSP), a shareware package available from many FTP sites. At a twentieth of the price of Photoshop and allowing users a 30-day evaluation period it is an ideal starting point. The major limitations are:

- the lack of a blend tool;
- no channel separation, so the red, green and blue (or CMYK) components of an image can't be worked on separately.

The latest release (3.01) supports transparent GIF files and the emerging PNG format; it also accepts the Photoshop plugins. These are the standard for Windows and are little external applets used to perform some process on an image. They are much more powerful than user-defined filters. Unfortunately shareware versions are much rarer for Windows than, say, for the Macintosh platform. This problem is shared by both Photoshop and Paint Shop.

The range of effects available can be bewildering to a neophyte. The usual temptation is to load a scanned picture, perform some range of filtering (embossing is my personal *bête noire*), turn out something close to the dog's breakfast and think, 'hmmm, magnificent but is it art?'. The answer is of course, no! The mistake has been to work on too broad a virtual canvas and that usually leaves the novice disappointed with the utility of the tool. While these packages are great for retouching and converting real-world images their real power is obtained by the successive application of filters to simple original artwork. Often the key is to work in black and white and only apply color at the final stage.

The next section takes a closer look at Paint Shop Pro and the most important features from a Web graphics viewpoint. These basic techniques can also be applied to more powerful packages although many users prefer the simple utility of PSP (and the price!).

■ Paint Shop Pro

Figure 7.2 shows PSP in action. There is the standard Windows style menu and toolbar. The toolbar icons are hot keys for frequent tasks. In addition there are floating toolbars, those for Select and Paint are shown. These can be hidden or moved anywhere on the screen. The on-line help is very extensive and should be used. Context-sensitive help is available for each class of operation.

While the help is very good at explaining what the functions are it is not a tutorial and gives little guidance as to how best to employ the functionality. PSP can be broken down into three areas:

1. acquisition
2. creation
3. manipulation

■ Acquisition

PSP understands a wide range of image formats including Windows Bitmap and Clipboard, Mac and Microsoft Paint, UNIX Portable Pixel Maps, Word

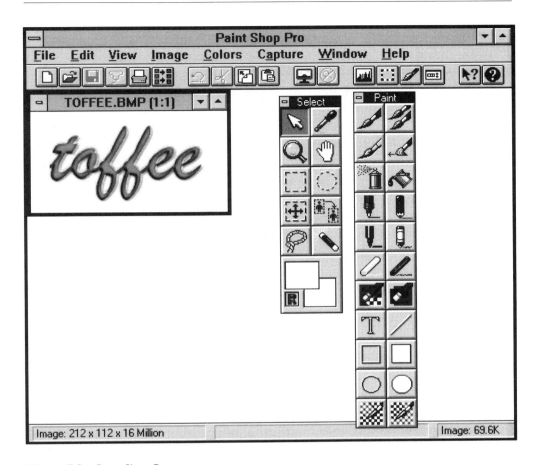

Figure 7.2 Paint Shop Pro

Perfect, Photoshop, TIFF, Corel Draw, Hewlett Packard Graphics Language, PNG and of course GIF and JPEG. This list is by no means exhaustive and doesn't include formats supported by external import filters. PSP can convert all of these file formats to Web in-line graphics, either GIF or JPEG.

 Any graphic which can be placed on the clipboard can also be converted to Web formats. For instance, from within Excel select a graph, type CONTROL-C to copy it to the clipboard and, in PSP, CONTROL-V to paste it. The image can be saved as a GIF file for inclusion within a Web document as shown in Figure 7.3. If the image can't be captured in this way it may be possible to save it in one of the supported formats. An alternative solution is to use the Capture menu option to grab a window or area. A hot key must be configured to use this.

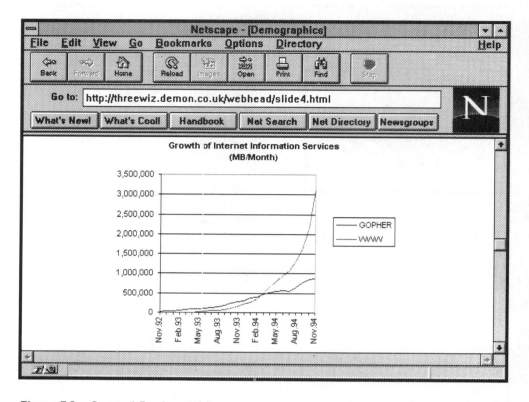

Figure 7.3   Captured Excel spreadsheet

The 16-bit version of PSP (or any similar utility) on '95 or NT will only be able to capture images from other tasks running in the 16-bit sub-system.

TWAIN-compliant devices are supported. TWAIN is a standard way for software to talk to image devices such as scanners. An alternative cheap and simple way to digitize photographs is to have a Photo CD (PCD) pressed. Photo CD is a standard developed by Kodak which permits 100 high-quality images to be stored on a multisession CD-ROM (a multisession drive is needed to read these disks). During the development process film is scanned at 2,000 dpi. A 35mm image produces an 18-megabyte file and a further four files are made each one half the resolution of the last. The final 24 megabytes of data are then compressed to 6 megabytes. As the CD-ROM is multisession and recordable a further hundred images can be stored at later dates. The system is widely available and inexpensive if carried out at the same time as development. Paint Shop supports the PCD format.

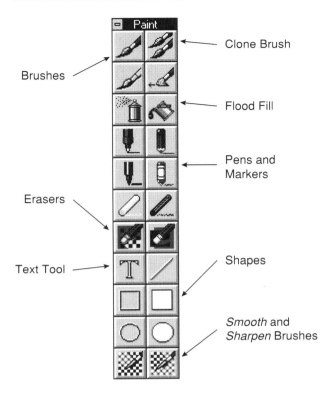

Brushes

Clone Brush

Flood Fill

Pens and
Markers

Erasers

Text Tool

Shapes

Smooth and
Sharpen Brushes

Figure 7.4   The Paint toolbar

▨ Creation

Although not in the same league as Corel Draw or Illustrator, Paint Shop Pro has still acquired a following amongst icon designers. It is ideal for simple painting operations where complex tints and blends are not required. Drawing with PSP is like building a collage. Shapes are overlaid on a canvas to construct the overall picture. As with any computer activity the design should be sketched off-line before committing mouse to monitor.

A new image is created from the File menu and can have any dimensions. The number of colors is specified at the same time and ranges from two color to true color. The filter operations can only be applied to true color or 256-gray-level images, however, the number of colors can be changed later from the Colors menu. Icons should only use the 16 Windows colors, this saves memory and avoids dithering on low-specification systems. Navigation buttons and text can be drawn in monochrome and colored later. The background color for a new image is set from the Select toolbar.

■ Dithering

In a similar fashion to the red, green and blue (R, G, B) pixel triads on a color monitor, dithering places areas of different color in close proximity in the hope that the eye won't notice and they'll blend to form a new color. It's not usually very successful and ruins small images.

The Flood Fill tool is particularly useful for coloring line art. Choosing the foreground color from the Select toolbar and clicking the cursor on any area surrounded by a solid line will flood fill to the boundary. Pens, Brushes and Erasers are useful for altering and retouching images. Selecting the Text tool and clicking on an image brings up the Text dialog box. The font, style, size and orientation can be set and the text positioned on the image. The *anti-alias* checkbox produces smoother text by blending steps on curves ('jaggies'). The shadow effect will draw shadow text in the background color and may be used, but always sparingly. Underlining should generally be avoided, for emphasis use italics or boldface instead. TrueType fonts are better than their bitmap equivalents.

Graphics should not be so large that users have to scroll their browser horizontally or vertically to view them. Screen dimensions are typically 640 x

■ Custom headlines

Headlines in special type can be very effective but don't overdo it. A general rule is no more than 2 fonts on a page: the HTML text (which is generally rendered in Times Roman) is one of these so pick another for headline and subheading text. The font can be used to convey the tone of the document. Unless a special background is used the background color should be set to Windows light gray (R 192, G 192, B 192) and then saved as transparent. Anti-aliased fonts show a strange fringeing effect on transparent backgrounds, this is especially noticeable where a background color or image is used. Light text on a dark background is unreadable in small font sizes and when using these remember that the size is specified in pixels not points so can be illegible at different screen resolutions. Use HTML for large blocks of text, don't render them as images.

480 pixels and Netscape defaults to somewhat less than this width. A good rule of thumb is that graphics should be no more than 400 pixels square and even this is too big for headlines. There is no easy method for deciding the font size, a 72-pixel-high font will fit into a 72-pixel-high box but for proportional fonts the width is governed by the type and the characters used.

GIF files can be saved as either normal, interlaced or transparent from the Save As dialog box under the File menu. Interlacing is useful for larger images giving a faster representation of the picture. The Preferences can also be set from this menu. The compression factor used for JPEG images can be changed in the Saving tab found in the General Preference dialog box. The lower the number the higher the quality. The working copy of any image should always be saved in a lossless format, not as JPEG. JPEG losses are cumulative, each time a file is loaded and changed the amount of loss increases. The dots per inch (dpi) setting has no effect on displayed image size. Plugin filters can be configured from the General tab and anti-aliasing, which works on selected portions of the image, can also be enabled here.

▦ Manipulation

Paint Shop Pro provides a number of useful image manipulation routines as standard and third party plugins can also be used. The manipulation routines are found under the Image menu and the color routines, logically, under the Color menu.

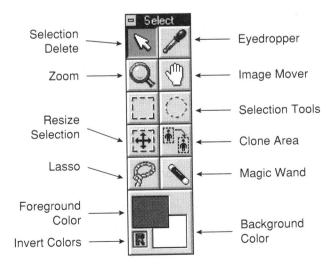

Figure 7.5 Select toolbar

The Select toolbar is an important resource for image manipulation. All of the filter processes can be bounded by a selected area. In addition to the Square and Round selection tools there are freehand Lasso and Magic Wand. The Wand will select an object, such as a blue square or an individual letter. This will cramp the style of the many filtering routines which need to work beyond the confines of the original object: blurring is an obvious example.

Selected areas can be cloned (copied) or moved and the selection is canceled by the *Arrow* (Selection Delete). Resize enables the bounds of the selection to be changed or the whole selection moved. Freehand and Magic Wand selections cannot be resized. The Eyedropper identifies the red, green and blue components of the pixel under the cursor and the color index value for 256-color images. This is useful for editing a specific color in the palette. The information is displayed in the middle of the Status (bottom) line shown in Figure 7.2.

■ Colors

All of the filtering operations must be performed on true color or true gray images. Filters need to work on real pixel values, not an index into a color table. The color menu lets you change the number of colors in a palette. Reducing the number of colors in a GIF palette from 256 to 16 can save memory, especially where a lot of small images are used. Palettes of 256 colors or less can be edited, this is useful for changing a large area of color, say a uniform background. When the number of colors in an image is increased there is no actual change to the colors displayed. However certain choices have to be made when reducing the number. The palette choice is between one which gives the best match and one containing the 16 standard Windows colors. For a 256-color palette the latter will also contain 250 optimized colors. The matching algorithm used is one of Nearest Color, Error Diffusion (pixel dithering) or Ordered Dither (pattern dithering). Dithered colors may be fine when printed but look poor on a monitor. Nearest-color matching should be used.

This doesn't guarantee that the selected colors won't be dithered on some other display. In the previous chapter we discussed how 8-bit graphics cards will only display 256 different colors, if the image palette doesn't match the current palette the image will be dithered. Some browsers allow an even more limited palette for each image in an attempt to stop one picture hogging all 256 colors. Reducing GIF files to the standard 16 Windows colors avoids this problem but may be too limiting for many purposes. Where 256 colors are

■ JPEG color depth

All this talk of reducing the number of colors used is irrelevant to JPEG images. JPEG is a true-color image format. People talk about 256-color JPEGs because they believe that by reducing the number of unique colors to 256 with a package like Paint Shop Pro they have also reduced the number of colors displayed. In fact the number of unique colors displayed depends on the rendering software. Still not convinced? Take a JPEG, count the colors used and reduce the total to 256. Save the image and reload in Paint Shop and count the number, it won't be the original value and won't be 256. Open in another package and you will almost certainly see a different value.

required the Standard (Windows + 250) palette should be selected. If multiple GIF images are to be displayed on the same page the designer should consider using the same palette for all images. This can be achieved by either working with the standard palette or by saving a Custom Palette and then applying this palette to all the images used. The Standard Palette can be applied to an image by changing it to true color and then reducing to 256 colors.

The usual set of color adjustment tools are provided. Gamma correction is handy for enhancing scanned photos, especially those from less expensive scanners. Solarize and Posterize are useful in combination with other filters but can produce a proverbial cat's supper when used indiscriminately. The Negative adjustment combined with Embossing gives an etched, rather than a raised effect.

 It is usually easier to work on monochrome images rather than try and maintain the desired color through a range of filtering processes. Although it should be noted for the record that embossing a grayscale image causes a general protection fault with PSP version 3.0 and certain combinations of graphics

Color	R	G	B	H	S	(L)
Red	255	0	0	0	240	120
Green	0	255	0	80	240	120
Blue	0	0	255	160	240	120

Figure 7.6 Hue, saturation and luminance equivalents

Crazy Deals!

Figure 7.7   Rotated text

drivers, which, if the image hasn't been saved (checkpointed) is often followed by that other military-sounding problem, major disaster! Colorization is the easiest way of adding a color. Colors are specified in terms of their hue and saturation. Up until now colors have been described in terms of their red, green and blue components. A color can also be described by its **hue** (tint), **saturation** (how pure it is) and a third component, **luminance** (how bright it is).

Unfortunately the ways in which Paint Shop Pro specifies these components differ between the color adjust menu (percentages), the color dialog box (value from 0–240) and the Colorize menu (value from 0–255). The Colorize menu doesn't allow the luminance to be set, it uses the current pixel value instead.

The Rotate dialog box found under the Image menu allows the orientation of an image to be changed. The Flip and Mirror functions can both be applied to selections on true color images but Rotate always operates on the whole image. Borders can be added automatically in the current foreground color. These increase the overall size of the image by twice the width of the border line.

The Mask features are particularly interesting when preparing graphics. They can be used to apply strange shadows and shadings or to create

Figure 7.8   Deformations

translucent text. Like a selection, a mask restricts the area over which Filter and Color operations work but it can also specify the strength of an operation for each pixel. A Mask applies a transformation to an image where a black pixel is full off and white full on.

Deformations bend and twist images in weird and wonderful directions. Operations such as the Circle shown in Figure 7.8 work harder at the periphery than the center so an image may have to be cropped for maximum effect. If Eight Ball had been a single line at the middle of the square it would hardly have been changed by the deformation.

▦ User-defined filters

All of the standard filtering processes are implemented by applying a mask to a given area and recalculating the target pixel based on the surrounding values. For the mathematicians, this is like a Laplacian transform operation. PSP extends this concept by offering user-defined filters. These are found under the Image menu.

PSP uses a 5 x 5 filter matrix and employs the following algorithm:

1. Working from top left to bottom right, the matrix is centered over each pixel in turn.

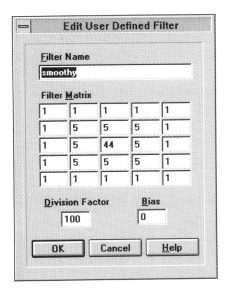

Figure 7.9 User-defined filters

■ Filter configuration

Filters can be configured by observing the following points:

- Smoothing-type operations use a positive center value and positive values in the surrounding matrix.
- Sharpening filters have a negative center value.
- The strength of a particular filter is governed by the difference between the center value and the surrounding matrix.
- The division factor keeps the result within the 0 to 255 bounds.
- The division factor would normally equal the sum of all the matrix elements.
- Bias can be used to boost the result in either direction. Positive values tend towards white and negative to black.

2. The value in the matrix is then multiplied by the value of the pixel. A grayscale image will have pixel values between 0 and 255; for a full-color image each of the red, green and blue components can range from 0 to 255. The filter may be applied to any or all of the color channels.
3. The individual products are then summed and the resulting pixel value is placed in the corresponding position of a new image.

By using separate input and output images Paint Shop Pro ensures that the results from previous pixel calculations are not added to the filter causing exponential feedback. User-defined filters are quite difficult to set up and the common set of operations, smoothing, edge enhancing and blurring, are already built in to Paint Shop Pro.

■ Tips of the Paint Shop Masters

The title of this section has been chosen with care. Many of the basic ideas presented have been learnt at the feet of experts. Being experts you can be sure that they don't waste time with trivialities like personal hygiene, making the research of this section a particularly onerous, and possibly odorous task. These tips concern the things most people, myself included, wouldn't think about doing. The instructions given are deliberately vague as experimentation is the mother of invention. Frequent checkpointing is useful when exploring

A 24-bit scanned color photograph (actually it's my head). This has then been embossed. The result is certainly impressive, giving me that fossilized stone age look but would frighten off less than hardened Web surfers.

Embossed text is effective especially on navigation buttons.

The text can be given a nice rounded look by using the Softening filter first.

The chiseled look is achieved by the Color/Negative Image effect.

Figure 7.10   Embossed effects

PSP. From the Preferences option under the File menu select the New Windows dialog box and turn on *All Create*. Now each time a filter is applied a new image is created. This keeps an audit trail of images. Save interesting images and keep a note of how the effects were achieved.

Embossing

The favorite trick of the novice user is to emboss pictures but this filter is better applied to simple features such as text. Embossed text can be used on buttons and really entices viewers to press.

Textures

Embossing can be used to create textured effects. A texture, such as the weave of cloth or the grain of rock, is just a pattern with three-dimensional relief. Patterns are applied using the Add Noise special filter. Weave patterns tend to be a criss-cross and are created by applying uniform noise and then using one of the Edge filters before Embossing. The pattern can then be colorized.

Figure 7.11   Cloth weave

Figure 7.12   Wood grain

Figure 7.13   Chiselled rock

Wood, some papers and rock have a grain running in one direction. A horizontal grain can be added by using the Motion Blur deformations. The amount of noise and the application of other filters govern the density and hence the overall effect. The Wood Grain uses Uniform Noise which has been Edge Enhanced and then Deformed with Motion Blur before being embossed to add depth.

The Granite effect uses Random Noise which has been Eroded to give a coarser grain. It was then deformed with Wind and lettering was added using white text. Black text is used when the background is dark. The image was then embossed.

The Negative image option is used to raise 'chiseled' text. The image can be colored to enhance the effect or the palette can be edited to introduce colored veins into the strata. The examples have used both Background and Uniform Noise. The density of Uniform Noise is set with the % field and is identical to Random Noise when at 100%.

All of these techniques may be used to create background images for HTML 3.0 and Netscape pages. Many snazzy patterns can be generated without ever touching the Emboss filter. Backgrounds should be used with caution, a visual cue being taken from magazine design. Generally information is presented as black text on white paper. Where a background is used there will be a high contrast between it and the text. Heavily textured backgrounds also detract from the information.

Masks

The text of Figures 7.11 and 7.12 is applied using a mask. Masks are useful for creating transparent text, especially when it should follow a background pattern. Masks are used for the selective application of Filters. A blank mask is created from any image by using one of the following: the Create Mask

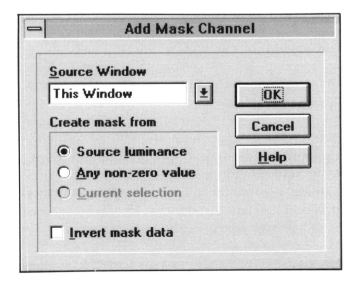

Figure 7.14 Mask dialog

The text is written in black. A duplicate image is created and smoothed. The duplicate is then applied to the original as a mask with the data inverted. Embossing produces the subtle raised effect.

This time the mask image has been deformed using Wind. This produces a light shadow and some interesting shading on the letters.

The original image was smoothed before being duplicated and the mask was deformed using motion blur. This gives a more pronounced shadow. All three examples are very effective when colored.

Figure 7.15   Masking text

menu option, the Copy and Paste commands, the Selection Tools or by simply creating a New image of the same dimensions.

Masks are grayscale images where black represents full off and white full on. When a new mask is created from the Image menu the background is set to black. If text is added in white and this mask applied to an image subsequent filter operations will only affect the text area. The effects illustrated were applied by varying the brightness or color of the masked area. The dialog box allows the mask data to be inverted before it is applied to the image. There are also checkboxes for Source Luminance and Any None-Zero Value. The latter sets any gray levels in a mask to white. The images in this chapter were produced with the Source Luminance option enabled.

Masking text

Text for headings, headline graphics and overlays can be produced easily with Paint Shop Pro. As calculating the width of text is problematic it is easier to work using a large image area and then cut the text out using the Select tools. Shadow text is provided by PSP as standard but should not be over used. Again other effects revolve around creating masks and embossing.

Double masking

The masking technique can be extended by taking a background pattern and double masking it, as shown in Figure 7.16.

Figure 7.16   Double masking

The following steps were used to create this image:

1. A new image was created and Random Noise added for the background pattern; this was Eroded to give a coarser texture.
2. A mask was created and the 'Rock' text added. The mask was then applied to the original and the brightness adjusted to remove the background.
3. The original mask was then deformed using the Wind option and applied to the original and the whole image embossed.

The Wind effect works better than Motion Blur with smaller text sizes.

3D buttons

3D buttons are little icons which, by virtue of shading, appear to stand out from the screen. The world has gone 3D crazy of late, use any Windows package and the toolbar icons simply beg to be pressed. The raised effect is a very good way of showing that an icon has an action associated with it. The world has also decided that all computer screens are lit from a light source somewhere off to the top left. Look at a NeXTSTEP system or Motif and you will notice the same pattern. Icons should be drawn with light top and left edges and shaded to the bottom and right.

An obvious candidate for drawing 3D images would be the Paint Shop Emboss feature. If the Emboss feature is applied to a black square on a white

Figure 7.17   Button styles

background it does indeed make a raised button. However Paint Shop thinks the light is arriving from the top right. This can be corrected using the Mirror option from the Image menu. Text may be embossed to give it a texture. Black will be raised and white depressed. Text should be written without aliasing, instead the softening filter is used for a rounded look. The fourth button in Figure 7.17 could almost be read by a blind person! The paint tools are used to produce really fancy variations as the end button shows.

More buttons

Now these buttons may not be quite fancy enough for some. Figure 7.19 shows some variations on the theme. Rounded buttons can be created using the following steps:

1. Draw a gray rectangle.
2. An off-white line is added to the top and left of this rectangle using the Add Border dialog box and a corresponding dark gray line is added to the bottom and right. The joins can be edited with a pen to give a butted corner.
3. The image is then Softened and Softened More giving the basic rounded button shape.

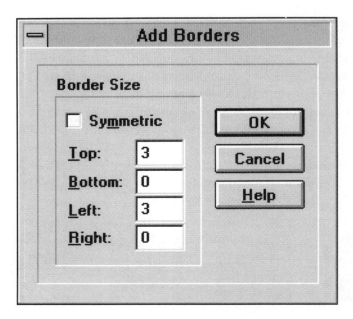

Figure 7.18   Adding borders

The 'tablet' shape uses a rectangle with line width of 4. Text can be added before embossing for a raised effect.

A Basic Rounded button. The button can be colored and text added directly from the text dialog.

Raised text is applied using masks.

A pattern can be added before the text by using the Apply Noise filter.

The noise can be filtered to produce a variety of patterns. Negative option was used to chisel the text.

Figure 7.19   Fancy buttons

Once a rounded button has been created the Resample menu option can be used to scale it for a variety of captions. The brightness of the button is adjusted with the Gamma Correct dialog box and the button may be colored. Text can be applied either before or after coloring.

Raised text on a button is created by carrying out the following:

1.   Create an empty mask with a white background, the text is written onto this mask in black and Softened.
2.   The mask is added to the button with the Invert Data box checked.
3.   The Brightness of the button image is then adjusted to -100% to leave black text.
4.   The original mask is then Softened some more and reapplied to the button.
5.   The button can now be embossed.

Leaving the mask applied allows the text to be colored separately from the button. Inverting the mask then allows the button to be colored without affecting the text.

■ Transparent GIFs

Transparent background support was added to Paint Shop Pro with the introduction of version 3.01, however, PSP doesn't allow a comment string to be
set. The transparent background color and comment trailer can be set from the
DOS command line using either Giftrans or my own GDIT.

The syntax for giftrans is:

```
C:\> GIFTRANS -c "comment string" -t <index> oldfile.gif
> newfile.gif
```

The index of the background color must first be identified by using the
Eyedropper tool in Paint Shop Pro.

GDIT is a 32-bit program so won't run on Windows for Workgroups. In
general, the background color is that found at the border of an image:

```
C:\> GDIT
> new oldfile.gif
> get pixel 0 0
index 66; RGB values are: 192,192,192
> set transparent 66
> ct "a comment"
> save newfile.gif
> bye
```

Obviously a number of GIF files can be converted in one GDIT session. A script
could be written to batch convert images, adding a comment string at the same
time. This may be an assertion of your copyright or a version number.

■ Scanning

Many sources of graphics will exist as hard copy only. These can be digitized
using a scanner. For the Web author three scanner types are worth considering:
hand held, **sheet feed** and **flatbed**.

Publishing houses also use drum scanners and specialized film scanners, but
these address the need of high-quality magazine production. This also high-
lights the problem of using a print bureau to scan images: the output is rarely
optimized for the Web and will require post processing.

- Handheld scanners are the cheapest to buy, the scan area is restricted,
  usually 4 inches (10 cm). They avoid the high cost associated with

other scanners by getting the user to drag the head across the image. A small wheel measures the scan speed and compensates for variations.

- Sheet feeders use modified fax machine technology to pass the image over the scan head.
- Flatbed scanners often offer a sheet-feed option for bulk scanning but normally the image is positioned on a flat plate of glass and the scan head moved, much like a photocopier. Flatbeds offer the best image registration and quality. The cheaper models use a three-pass process where the image is scanned repeatedly to capture the red, green and blue components. This process, as with sheet-feed and hand scanners, results in loss of registration that is visible as a slightly blurred image. It also slows the scan process. Single-pass scanners have three scan heads, one for each color.

The available resolution ranges from 400 dpi with hand-helds to 2,400 dpi for flatbeds, although these higher figures are achieved with clever software. This process is called **interpolation** and is basically guessing how a lower resolution image should really look based on known limitations with the scan process.

◼ Resolution

Dots per inch (dpi) is a reflection on how fine the imaging process is, however, an image scanned at 400 dpi wouldn't print at this resolution on a 400 dpi printer.

It's a common belief that the ideal scanner is the one which matches the resolution of the intended output device. Computer displays offer somewhat less than 100 dpi, color inkjets 300 dpi and high-quality lasers 600 dpi. However, there is a fundamental difference in the way images are rendered. With a printer any dot is either on or off, whereas pixels on a screen can vary in brightness. A printer fakes intensity and colors by dithering. Thus, a driver for a 300-dpi printer may sub-divide the resolution into blocks four dots square, this gives 16 gray levels and a real resolution of 75 dpi, about the same as a monitor. However, a computer graphics system can usually display at least 256 levels per pixel, giving it an effective resolution of 600 dpi, and it can also do this in color. Strike one to on-line versus printed graphics.

Scanning at higher resolutions uses more memory; four times as much to double the resolution. A good general rule for images targeted at printers is to scan at a quarter of the print resolution as the driver will simply discard extra information. This doesn't happen with displayed images, where there is a one-to-one correspondence of dots to pixels. A one-inch square image scanned at 75 dpi will have on-screen dimensions of 75 x 75 pixels, or one inch square on a monitor with a resolution of 75 dpi.

From this it would appear that low resolution hand scanners are ideal for Web and low-end print use, especially considering their cost. Higher resolution flatbed scanners have the significant advantage that they can be used to enlarge small images. The same one-inch square image could be scanned at 150 dpi, and assuming the original was of sufficient quality, it would be twice the size when displayed with no decrease in resolution. High scan resolutions are also important to avoid Moiré patterns where a dot screen has already been applied to the scanned photograph. Moiré patterns are those weird hallucinogenic effects which are visible on television when the weather forecaster wears a check jacket! High-quality flatbeds usually offer faster scan speeds and are also better for driving optical character recognition (OCR) software and for scanning line art. It would be very convenient if OCR software could produce HTML documents directly and no doubt this feature will be added.

The majority of scanners support the TWAIN standard which describes a common way for applications and scanners to interact. Driver writers have a fair degree of flexibility when deciding what features to support. The Hewlett Packard 3C scanner driver worked well from within Paint Shop Pro but it's a good idea to check the compliance of other combinations before purchase. This HP scanner can also be used with the NT operating system which is not widely supported by scanner manufacturers. However, only a 16-bit driver is currently available which is a problem for 32-bit applications wishing to access it directly.

A final class of input devices is digital cameras; these are quite expensive considering their low resolution but are ideal for the direct input of real-world scenes. Some Web sites have even linked cameras using server scripts for direct input to the site. A quick search of the Lycos index revealed the following interesting view of Pike's Peak from the roof of Softronic's headquarters at Colorado Springs.

The image is updated every minute and could be useful for walkers who want to know what the weather is doing 'up top'. There are a number of other mountaintop weather cameras and other sites feature interesting views of the company parking lot or carwash.

Figure 7.20 Pike's Peak `http://www.softronics.com/peak_cam.html`

■ Pre-scanning

Scanning isn't just a case of setting the resolution and letting rip, most drivers have a range of options which can be changed before the final pass is made. These give optimization for line art, colored artwork and monochrome and color photographs. It's usually much easier to apply these before the image is scanned rather than cleaning the image using a graphics package. For instance, a color photograph may feature a background that is predominantly one color. Scanned as a photograph even the most uniform area will actually comprise many tints. The Web designer may want to hide the background by making it transparent, leaving the subject 'floating' on the Web page but because the background isn't a single color this must be done by careful airbrushing. Some scanner drivers know about color artwork which features large areas of a single color. The driver sets similar shades to the same base color. This mode can be used to scan other kinds of images such as photographs. The result is a uniform background which can be changed to light gray using the color palette editor in Paint Shop Pro and the corresponding color index set to transparent under the File Save options.

Figure 7.21   Removal of unwanted detail

■ Post scanning

Scanned images may not be suitable for including directly within a HTML page. A graphics package such as Photoshop or Paint Shop Pro can be used to remove blemishes and other details, enhance colors and apply text effects.

Paint Shop's airbrush sprays too uniform a color for removing faults in the original but the Clone brush is ideal for this operation. It can pick up color from anywhere on the image and apply it with the brush. The density and size of the brush can be set for broad strokes or fine detail. Unwanted detail can be removed quickly and efficiently. In Figure 7.21 the two people in the background have been removed by overpainting with the surrounding color.

Figure 7.22   Cropping and resizing

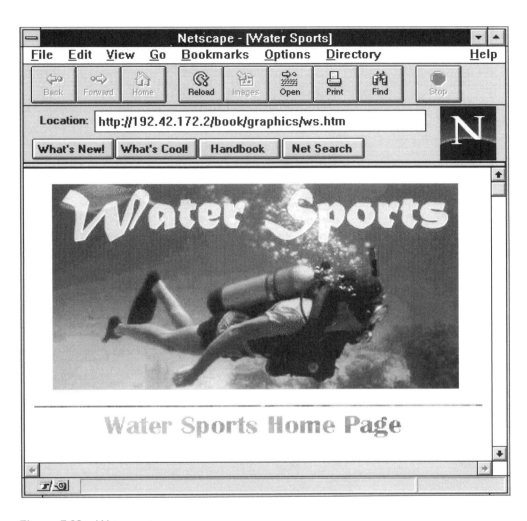

Figure 7.23 Watersports

Images may also be resized and cropped. The man in Figure 7.22 was taken from a much larger photograph. This was originally scanned at 400 dpi so the small selection could be enlarged without loss of detail. A scratch on the negative was removed using the Clone brush. The background around his feet has been cropped (and set to transparent); this gives an impression of movement, he's almost leaping from the page.

The translucent letters on the watersports page were applied using a mask in the following steps:

1. The original was scanned at 75 dpi and an empty mask created.
2. White text with a gray shadow was placed in the required position on the mask. This is not quite so easy as it sounds, the image and mask were aligned horizontally on the screen. Anti-aliasing was used to make the text outline smoother.
3. Finally, the mask was applied to the original image and the brightness adjusted from the Color menu.

The image was saved as a JPEG with a quality factor of 75, any less and the text would display the characteristic fringing distortion. Even at this level the image was over three times smaller than the equivalent GIF file. All that and true color too!

The custom rule was cut from a scanned image of the sea, as were the letters. In this case the reverse masking operation to the one above was used and the resulting white background set to a light-gray transparent color.

Many other interesting effects can be realized; for example, the text could extend off the image. To do this the original mask would have to be cropped at halfway across the text and reapplied to remove the background. With a graphics package the only limit is the user's imagination.

■ Summary

- The graphical content should reflect the audience of the Web site.
- The copyright status of graphics should be considered.
- Icons should be universally recognized and supported by text descriptions.
- Graphics act as signposts and help navigation. They also reinforce text.
- Charts clearly show trends in tabular data.
- When used, backgrounds should not interfere with legibility.
- Web graphics can be taken from existing sources or created directly with computer packages.
- Text on transparent backgrounds should not be anti-aliased, this produces a weird 'halo' effect.
- The JPEG format should not be used for working copy as it will suffer from accumulative losses.
- Photo retouching software is useful for enhancing and editing scanned images.

8 Running a server

To make Web documents available beyond the local network file system it is necessary to run a server. The server is responsible for fielding requests from Web browsers which arrive over the Internet and returning documents with the correct HTTP headers attached. It also enables the site builder to take advantage of one of the most exciting aspects of the Web, the ability to create dynamic documents. These are Web pages which are generated on the fly as a result of some external input. This input may be provided by the user through the submission of HTML forms data or by examining the operating environment or it may be some server-generated event such as a clock tick.

Back in the bad old days, installing and configuring a server was a job best left to a guru. Sources had to be downloaded, tweaked and built. The server was configured by editing lines in various files. These specified the TCP port, root server directory, MIME mappings and a program for processing image maps. The arrival of servers for the Windows operating systems has changed all that. Installing and running a server can be as simple as executing a set-up program. Configuration is normally through a graphical front end which provides structure to user selections and guards against garbage in, and out.

This chapter discusses the principal features offered by Web servers and takes a closer look at one of the most popular, the EMWAC's HTTPS server. Chapter 9 goes into more detail about how a Web server can be connected to user-written scripts and third-party applications.

Figure 8.1   Server comparison chart

Server Features	Alibaba	Commerce Builder	CL–HTTP	EMWACS	NaviServer	NetScape	Plexus	Purveyor	SAIC	WebQuest	WebSite
NT	✓	✓		✓	✓	✓	✓	✓	✓	✓	✓
95	✓	✓					✓	✓	✓	✓	✓
WWG			✓								
Multithreaded	✓	✓		✓	✓	✓	✓	✓	✓	✓	
Runs as NT Service	✓	✓		✓		✓		✓	✓	✓	
Enhanced CGI	WinCGI					NSAPI					WinCGI
Multi-homing	✓¹	✓			✓	✓				✓	
Multiple Servers					✓				✓	✓	✓
Log files	CLF	CLF	CLF	✓	CLF	CLF	✓	CLF	CLF	✓	✓
Extended Logging	✓	✓			✓	✓	✓	✓	✓	✓	
Server Side Includes					Q4/95	✓	✓	✓		✓	
Secure HTTP	Q4/96										v1.1
Secure Socket Layer	Q4/95										v1.1
User-Agent Support	✓	✓	✓		✓	✓		✓			
Proxy Server	✓	✓			✓	✓				✓	✓
Remote Administration									✓	✓	✓
Cost	$	$995	Free	Free	$	$$$	Free	$$	$$/Free	$$	$

¹NT version only

▓ Choosing a server

There are now a huge number of Windows servers to choose from. The widest selection is for Windows NT. NT combines a powerful and robust operating system with the familiar Windows front end. Unlike previous versions of Windows it runs on a variety of platforms including the Power PC and DEC's Alpha processor, although many of the Web servers are only available for Intel hardware. Some of the NT servers will also run directly under '95.

Figure 8.1 shows the main features supported by some of the most popular Web servers. This is by no means an exhaustive or complete list. New capabilities and servers are being forged daily in the white heat of global competition. (See Resource Guide for the server Web sites.) NetScape looks set to support the popular WinCGI script interface. This allows servers to talk to Windows-oriented programs such as Visual Basic applications. In fact NetScape have two different server products, the basic Communications Server and the Commerce Server which supports secure transactions. Purveyor is based on the free EMWACs server but has been extended for professional use. Bob Denny's Website also has a smaller sibling called HTTPD which runs on Windows for WorkGroups. It is free for non-commercial users and supports the WinCGI interface.

The following features are amongst the most important:

- **Multithreading** allows a server to answer many requests simultaneously. A thread is a lightweight control structure which shares data with other threads within a single task. It's much quicker to create a thread compared to a new task. On a multiprocessor machine, threads may be scheduled to run on separate processors. On a single-processor machine a thread may block waiting for a resource, such as a disk write, allowing another thread to run. This gives better throughput.
- **Enhanced CGI** (Common Gateway Interface) enables the server to talk with applications other than standard console applications. These are normally programs which can't use the standard input/output stream for transferring data. The server may communicate with these applications using Object Linking and Embedding (OLE) or Dynamic Data Exchange (DDE).

  The WinCGI interface is a well-supported enhanced CGI standard. It uses a normal file for transferring data between the server and application. Although this may appear slow, if there are sufficient disk buffers the data may not even be written to disk and the interface is considerably easier to use when compared with OLE and DDE.

- **Multihoming** is the ability to serve different Internet addresses with the one server. This is useful for providing customers with their own portable domain names.

- **Multiple servers** allow more than one instance of a Web server to run on the same host. For example, the main server may run using port 80, the well-known Web port. A second test server may run on port 8080. Actions affecting the test server will not impinge on the operation of the main server. Where many customers are supported by the one host each can run their own server with a unique server configuration.

- Most servers produce accounting and statistical output compliant with the **common log format**. Many utilities exist to analyze these logs. The log files contain an audit trail of page access and may highlight problems with site structure or indicate users trying to hack in to the system. Most servers also produce error log information. This is useful for debugging and with NT it may be examined using the Event Viewer found under the Administrative Tools window.

- Some servers offer **enhanced logging**. This can record user names, when available, and the site the user arrived from. This is handy for monitoring the effectiveness of external links, especially if they are being paid for.

- **Server side includes** are an alternative way to CGI for generating dynamic documents. They originated with the UNIX NCSA server http://www.ncsa.uiuc.edu but their simplicity has led to their wider adoption. Administrators should note that server side includes present security and performance problems and they are usually disabled on public sites. They are not discussed further in this book.

- Two alternative methods for directly securing data transfers over the Internet have attracted support. EIT's **Secure HTTP** (S-HTTP) is specific to the HyperText Transfer Protocol. Netscape's **Secure Socket Layer** (SSL) has added RSA encryption to sockets and can be used by other Internet applications besides the Web. The RSA encryption standard is classed as munitions and a less secure version is available for export outside of the United States. Microsoft has proposed **Secure Transaction Technology** (STT). Jointly developed with VISA it will be one to watch for the future.

- **User agent support** enables the server to provide different versions of the same document depending on the browser used. For instance, the default file for a table would be preformatted text but where the UDIwww browser is recognized a proper HTML 3.0 table could be returned.
- **Proxy servers** fetch documents on behalf of browsers or other servers. They can also provide a central cache for documents. A proxy is used as a part of a secure firewall system to give Internet access on a store and forward basis. A proxy is also necessary to give direct access to hosts where the internal network is not part of the Internet.
- **Remote administration** allows servers to be configured from another machine on the LAN or from a remote host, either over an Internet gateway or directly connected using the Remote Access Services (RAS).

Nearly all servers support the standard CGI script interface. Most offer a Windows-based configuration program, directory browsing and individual MIME configuration. Security is provided at the operating system level and on NT this is quite extensive, complying with the Department of Defense (DoD) Orange Book standards. Some servers have more extensive security features such as password protection on individual pages and can place restrictions on access by certain hosts. Computer security always follows a two-pronged approach of prevention and monitoring.

■ Server requirements

Windows NT offers a secure and robust platform for running Web servers. An NT Web server really needs a machine with at least 16 megabytes of RAM and a fast disk sub-system if the secure NT File System (NTFS) is used. Memory is much more important than processor speed, a 33 DX with 16 megabytes of memory will be faster then a 66 DX with only 8. Windows and '95 users can get away with only 8 megabytes of memory.

Processing requests and serving up a few HTML files is not a particularly intensive task so processor speed is not a big factor unless the Web server is hosted on a machine shared with other users. A more powerful machine may be required if the site involves running a lot of CGI scripts and third-party applications or is connected to a fast Internet link with many simultaneous users.

The NT operating system is supplied in the form of a workstation version or a more expensive server version. The workstation product has the same Internet support as the server version, the only restrictions are when running the system within the Windows networking environment. In fact, with less extraneous baggage the cheaper workstation option may even be a little quicker for Web work.

Another important factor to consider is administration and staffing. Personnel connected with the server will need to be trained and have time available to develop and maintain the site. The Web is not a nine-to-five system and where a certain level of access is guaranteed to the global Internet it may be necessary to have a member of staff on call at all times. These requirements may make it more convenient to use another organization's Web server where the cost of 24-hour support and a fast link is amortized over many customers.

■ External Web servers

Organizations which provide local Internet services normally run a Web server and will offer space on this to personal and commercial users. Users who take other services may even get a small amount of space for free. A number of specialist Web space providers exist as well, Turnpike Metropolis `http://turnpike.net/metro/metmktg.html` is one such and offers both personal and commercial space. In return for a fixed set-up fee and a monthly charge, external Web servers provide a certain amount of Web space. There are generally two access models employed:

1. **FTP**: customers transfer their files to the Web site using anonymous FTP. They must then email the system administrator who will move the files to the allocated home space.
2. **Full**: again FTP is used, but this time the customer has an account on the remote system and the files are transferred directly into the home space. The customer can then use a `telnet` client to connect to the remote system and perform administration tasks directly.

An external Web server has the advantage that it is normally well maintained and round-the-clock availability is often guaranteed. The server may also have a faster link than would be economically viable for a single user. This link may be shared with the other sites hosted on the server but this is not so bad considering that direct Internet access may also have been provided over this connection. However, potential clients should inquire about the link speed and the amount of data that is supplied by the server over this link.

The main problems with using an external site are updating the pages and access to CGI scripts. FTP access is especially irksome. Changes may take many days to be effected and some minor oversight may result in broken pages. These will have to be fixed and the whole update process repeated. With this kind of access it is especially important to test pages locally and be aware of differences on the remote Web server. Compare this to full telnet access where the user can connect to the server and fix any minor problems immediately. This type of access is almost as good as owning a server.

 Many sites restrict access to CGI scripts and almost never allow server side includes, viewing the idea of external users running programs locally as a security problem waiting to happen. Where CGI scripting is allowed it is often restricted to certain well-defined areas such as the Perl programming language. Some sites run an individual Web server for each customer and will offer to build and install specialist applications, for a price.

Multihoming is an important feature. It gives Web space customers their own domain name rather than using that of the Web server. A personalized name creates a more professional image and offers portability, enabling the site to be moved elsewhere with the minimum of fuss. This is very important where the domain name is well known with a large number of external links. Other features which may be important are the availability of log information and support for secure transactions. In the latter case the information must be secured not only from the user's browser to the server but also when it is sent from the server to your machine.

A local server should be used for testing, even when the site is hosted externally. Uploading single files and making fixes over a telnet connection can be tedious, it's better to test the site locally as far as is possible. This is especially true for any server scripts which can take some debugging.

The UNIX platform, the Sun operating system in particular, is popular with many Web service providers. This has implications for documents as well as the applications environment. Some providers expect files to take the four-letter extension .HTML, rather than .HTM. Both filenames and hyperlinks will have to be changed. This process can be automated with a script although it will need to differentiate between local and remote links (which should not be changed). Another complication is that UNIX is case sensitive so the filenames and hyperlink targets will have to agree.

The file extension problem can be easily resolved by persuading the Web provider to add a .HTM mapping in the configuration file. Some providers are reluctant to do this although they may offer a program to automate the conversion process. It may prove easier to find a provider that runs one of the Windows operating systems. If a site uses three-letter filename extensions there's is a good chance it runs a system like NT. This can be confirmed by mailing the Webmaster or sending an HTTP GET request as shown in Chapter 2. The application and scripting environment is less certain. The Perl language is available across most operating systems and there are versions for Windows, '95 and NT. The provider may offer some other utilities but full access to the system is rarely granted.

The remainder of this chapter discusses some server applications which don't require the site builder to develop scripts. The popular and free HTTPS server is used as an example.

■ The HTTPS server

Microsoft have charged the European Microsoft Windows NT Academic Center, thankfully known by the acronym EMWAC, with developing system applications for NT. The HTTPS Web server was one of the first fruits of this effort. It is supplied as standard on the NT resource disk and the latest version is available from the Microsoft or EMWAC FTP sites free of charge.

As Figure 8.1 shows, HTTPS is not the most feature rich of the Web servers. However, it supports CGI scripting and has an integrated search and image map facility. The simplicity of operation makes it a good choice for a first server on the NT platform. Its bigger brother, Purveyor has also been ported to Windows '95.

■ Basic configuration

The server is supplied as a single self-extracting ZIP archive. This contains full documentation for running HTTPS. The installation process is nothing more complicated than moving a few files to the SYSTEM32 directory. After installation HTTPS should br listed by the Services utility accessed from the Control Panel. The Control Panel window will have a new icon for the HTTPS Server. This starts a utility to configure the Server with five pieces of information:

1. the root directory of the document tree
2. the port number

3. transaction logging
4. directory browsing
5. the log file directory

The default options can be accepted, although normally the root of the HTTP hierarchy and the log file directory will be changed. It's often convenient to write log files into a sub-directory under root. The suggested port number of 80 is the well-known port for Web servers. Directory browsing allows clients to examine all of the files in a directory, not just those which form part of the Web site. Directory browsing can be turned off to stop users searching for and downloading files which may include scripts and other sensitive information.

Security is provided by the operating system; it's advisable to use the NT file system especially when FTP access is also offered. HTTPS does not allow access beyond its root directory; the previous directory '. .' or drive letters are ignored.

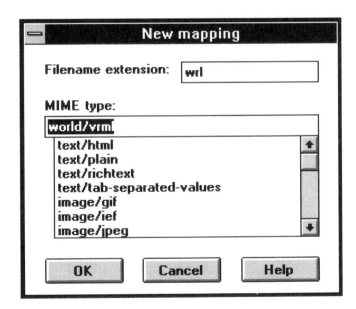

Figure 8.2 Configuring MIME types

■ Default documents

The default document in any directory is called, quite logically, DEFAULT.HTM. This file is returned when the client doesn't explicitly give the resource to be fetched.

```
http://hostname.com/
```

fetches the default file at the root of the document hierarchy. The presence of this file also inhibits directory browsing. An empty NOBROWSE file has the same effect.

■ MIME

One responsibility of a Web server is to attach the correct HTTP MIME header to a document. This gives information such as expiry date, status and document type. The server has no knowledge of the nature of the data contained within a document, instead it determines the MIME content type from the file extension. HTTPS has a number of these already configured but they can be augmented, changed and deleted.

Figure 8.2 shows how the MIME type for the Virtual Reality Modeling Language (VRML) is added. VRML files take the extension .WRL. When a request is made for this type of file the server generates the content header:

```
Content-type: world/vrml
```

Browsers use this information to determine which application should be launched to process the data.

■ Searchable documents

In Chapter 3 it was mentioned that a document can be made searchable by adding an ISINDEX element. This is of little use without some support in the server. EMWAC have ported the Wide Area Information Service (WAIS) search tool to the NT operating system and have integrated it into HTTPS as the standard way to carry out document searches.

WAIS allows users to search for keywords within many files in a directory tree, these can include documents generated automatically by other systems. A typical example would be Usenet newsgroups. Another application could be to look for bug reports on a technical support site. Rather than searching all the files each time a request is made WAIS builds an external index. HTTPS can reference this index to automatically generate hyperlinks to relevant documents. Using an external index makes searching very fast. WAIS works on all kinds of text file but as the actual contents are not altered the finest granularity of link is at the file level. HTML anchors are not inserted at keywords. This means that files should be organized on a per subject basis.

Setting up a WAIS index is very straightforward. HTTPS uses the WAIS-LOOK.EXE program to search the index file and it looks for this in the SYSTEM32 directory. A directory structure is created to hold the index files and data.

Figure 8.3 shows how a help system database might be organized. A top-level directory is created at the root of the HTTPS hierarchy, this will hold the HTML index document and the WAIS indexes. The DOCS directory contains reports organized by product. The hierarchical separation is necessary to avoid including the WAIS index files themselves when the index is rebuilt.

To create full URLs the documents must always be indexed from the root of the HTTP directory. The command WAISINDEX.EXE builds the various index files:

```
C:\HTTP> WAISINDEX -d HELPSYSTEM\INDEX -r HELPSYSTEM\DOCS
```

The -d flag gives the root name and location of the index files and the -r flag traverses the given sub-directory. All that remains is to create the HTML file to prompt for user input. This has the same name as the WAIS index files. In this example INDEX.HTM:

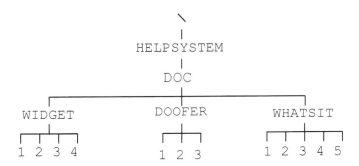

Figure 8.3 WAIS '*Help System*' directory hierarchy

```
<HEAD><TITLE>Widget Knowledge Base</TITLE></HEAD>
<BODY>
Search for problems in the knowledge base:
<ISINDEX>
</BODY>
```

One or more words can be entered in the input field and HTTPS will return an updated form with links to all the files where these keywords occur. The best matches are shown first. WAIS understands certain document formats and can show a more informative link text than just a plain filename. For instance with Usenet news messages the `Subject:` field can be used for the link text. The document type is specified by the `-t` flag:

```
C:\HTTP> WAISINDEX -d NEWS\INDEX -t netnews -r NEWS
\GROUPS
```

Figure 8.4 illustrates this type of indexing. The news articles containing information about the alibaba server are shown by subject. A new MIME mapping may need to be made for certain document types. The simple file-names used above (1, 2, 3...) will be served as the type `application/octet-string` which most browsers won't be configured to display directly. The default MIME mapping could be changed or as the files are plain text they may be renamed with a `.TXT` extension. The latter is the better solution.

When new documents are added the index files must be updated. WAISINDEX can either be run at the same time or overnight as a batch job. The program is quite resource intensive so batching the documents to be indexed and running during a quiet period may be preferable.

▪ Image maps

Image maps are not dynamic documents but need a server program to convert user input to a hyperlink. An image map is associated with a displayed image; when the user clicks the mouse on the image the cursor coordinates are returned to the Web server. The server looks for an area bounding these coordinates in a map file. This file consists of coordinate descriptions for various shapes and corresponding URLs.

An obvious candidate for an image map is a plan or photograph where clicking on points of interest (hotspots) brings up a description for that

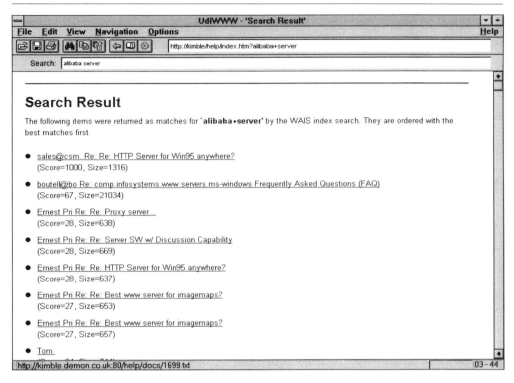

Figure 8.4 Searching News with WAIS

location. A camera sitting on the rooftop of the Olivetti building in Cambridge, UK `http://www.cam-orl.co.uk/cgi-bin/pangen` does exactly this. Using an image map, users can zoom in on buildings and then bring up an interesting description of the site. Button bars and lists of products can also be displayed with this feature but as they don't permit users with non-graphical browsers to view text alternatives these applications are best implemented with standard HTML constructs.

The HTTPS image map file format is the same as used by the original CERN Web server. The main difference is that the mapping program is built into the server which makes configuration easier. The HTML element will look like this:

```
<A HREF="http://yourhost.com/uk.map">
<IMG SRC="http://yourhost.com/ukmap.gif" ISMAP></A>
```

This example displays `UKMAP.GIF` in the browser window. The file `UK.MAP` contains entries of the form:

```
polygon (145,306) (145,360) (234,336) /UK/LONDON.HTM
```

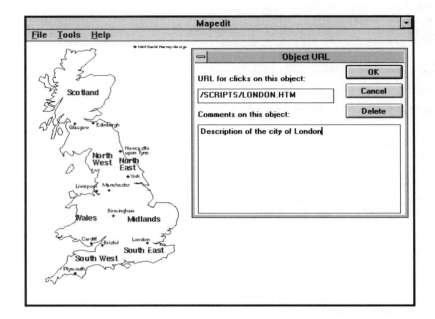

Figure 8.5 Creating image maps with Mapedit

Clicking on London would display a file about the City of London. The map file contains three kinds of shape:

1. circles   `circle (x,y) radius` *URL*
2. rectangles   `rectangle (x1,y1) (x2,y2)` *URL*
3. polygons   `polygon (x1,y1) (x2, y2) ... (xn,yn)` *URL*

Coordinates which don't lie within these areas can be associated with a default mapping. Coordinates are measured from the top left and a polygon can contain up to 100 coordinate pairs.

Describing hotspots by hand using these shapes is rather tedious and error prone. Thomas Boutell's Mapedit program enables developers to draw the hotspot areas directly on the image map. As each shape is entered a dialog box prompts for the associated URL and comment text. The map data is then saved directly to a file.

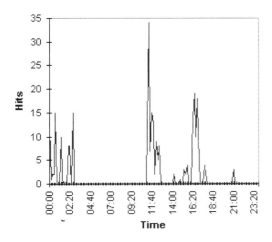

Figure 8.6   Daily usage from ANALYSE

■ Log analysis

Most Web servers can be configured to write log information about the hosts which have accessed the site. HTTPS generates a daily log file which contains the time and date of the access, the Internet address of the server and client, the HTTP command and the protocol version if it's not 0.9. The log files are used to determine patterns of site usage although seeing trends is as much an art as examining sheep entrails to predict the future.

ANALYSE processes HTTP log files to produce structured output which can be fed into a spreadsheet such as Excel. ANALYSE examines all the daily logs and generates four data files showing per page usage, hits by ten-minute intervals throughout the day, a weekly log of a hundred selected pages and visits by hosts. A fifth file gives a complete listing of all hosts that have visited the site.

This information is useful for confirming the overall success of a particular marketing strategy and to predict long-term resource needs. It's probably not sophisticated enough to form part of detailed analysis of site usage and referrals.

■ Summary

- A Web server is needed to give access to Internet users.
- Servers can link the site to other applications such as databases and search engines or custom scripts.
- A Web space provider can be used where there are insufficient resources to run a server internally.
- Web servers are available for all the Windows operating systems.
- Microsoft offer the popular `http://www.netcraft.co.uk/Survey` EMWAC Web server as standard with the NT Resource Kit: this server can be easily configured to search documents and process image maps.
- Log files provide information about site usage and trends.

9 Scripting

Users can interact with applications running on the Web server through the Common Gateway Interface (CGI). This defines a standard way for servers to communicate with backend scripts. These are known as CGI scripts. A typical use for a CGI script is to process information submitted from an HTML form. The script can handle the processing of the submitted information directly or it can access other resources such as a database. Generally it generates a new HTML document but can respond with any kind of data, for example GIF images, Excel worksheets or text files, but it must also generate the MIME header fields. The server can't do this itself because it has no way of telling what format the generated data is in.

CGI scripts can be written in any language including DOS batch files, the C language, Visual Basic and the ubiquitous Perl. Perl is ideal for many Web uses and its availability on a range of operating systems has turned it into something of a *de facto* standard for CGI scripts. Its chief advantages include:

- widespread support with many scripts freely available for a multitude of applications;
- it is free, and freely available, to quote Larry Wall;
- it is interpreted, good for rapid prototyping and provides a standard environment for running scripts;
- it is geared towards the processing of text and files and therefore ideal for many Web applications.

Perls are available as executables for all the Windows platforms, including the excellent Microsoft-sponsored NTPerl which also runs on '95.

The rest of this section looks at the Common Gateway Interface within the context of the HTTPS Web server. The main difference between this and other Web servers is that HTTPS can only launch .EXE programs directly. Information regarding the CGI interface remains common to all servers.

■ The HTTPS CGI interface

CGI scripts are invoked by specifying the program and its arguments in a URL. The HTTPS server will attempt to execute any program with a .EXE file extension. Unlike Windows itself HTTPS can't associate other extensions with applications, so specifying an Excel spreadsheet (.XLS) within a URL won't launch Excel, although it can return the file to be displayed by the browser.

URLs can be embedded within a hyperlink anchor or given directly to a browser. The format is:

```
http://hostname/PROGRAM.EXE/PATH_INFO?arg1+arg2...+argn
```

If a partial URL is used the program name can be either absolute (relative to the HTTPS root directory) or relative to the current directory. Given FILE.HTM in the sub-directory SUB the following URLs refer to the programs shown, all relative to the HTTPS root document directory:

```
"PROGRAM.EXE"                    \SUB\PROGRAM.EXE
"SCRIPTS\PROGRAM.EXE"            \SUB\SCRIPTS\PROGRAM.EXE
"..\SCRIPTS\PROGRAM.EXE"         \SCRIPTS\PROGRAM.EXE
"\SCRIPTS\PROGRAM.EXE"           \SCRIPTS\PROGRAM.EXE
```

The command must be located somewhere within the server's directory tree. The previous directory '..' string or the URL equivalent encoding %2E%2E cannot be used to access beyond the root of this tree. So in the above example ..\..\SCRIPTS is the same as ..\SCRIPTS.

Any characters after the program name and before the '?' character are assigned to the PATH_INFO environment variable. The text after the '?' character is passed to the program as command line arguments; these are separated by '+' characters.

■ The CGI bin

Anyone who's studied existing server documentation will have heard of the **CGI bin**. Now this isn't somewhere that you place bad CGI scripts, it's actually a reference to a feature of the UNIX operating system. UNIX doesn't identify programs by their file extension such as **.EXE**, **.COM** or **.BAT**. Instead a UNIX program has a flag which marks it as executable and an internal **magic number** which tells the utility that starts the program (called the loader) what type of data it is. File extensions are still used to aid user identification, thus **.pl** might be a Perl script, but they have no special meaning to the loader.

This magic number is most obvious in script files. Perl scripts ported from UNIX often feature the following first line:

```
#!/usr/bin/perl
```

The first couple of characters '#!' are the magic number **021441**, this tells the loader that the file is a script which can be executed by invoking the program **/usr/bin/perl**. There's that word **bin** again. On UNIX systems it is customary to place programs (binaries) in special directories much like the **WINNT** or **DOS** directories on Windows systems. Generally:

- **/bin** is for system programs
- **/usr/bin** for user programs and
- **./cgi-bin** for Web CGI scripts.

The normal way a UNIX Web server differentiates between a program and a file which must be returned to the user is to place it in a special location, the CGI bin. Windows identifies programs by their file extension and so Windows Web servers don't need a CGI bin, although some servers keep this convention and it may be a good organizational idea to keep all CGI scripts in one place.

```
<TITLE>Form Test</TITLE>
<FORM ACTION="EGI386.EXE" METHOD=POST>
<P>
Text Field: <INPUT TYPE="text" NAME="name" SIZE=40
VALUE="xxx">
<P>
<INPUT TYPE="submit" NAME="logon-b" VALUE="EGI386">
</FORM>
```

Figure 9.1 A simple form using **EGI386.EXE**

HTTPS comes with two example scripts, EG*cpu*.EXE and EG2*cpu*.EXE. The *cpu* part corresponds to the processor type, for example: I386, which we will use for the rest of this document. These are useful test harnesses especially when writing forms. The C language source code is also supplied and may be modified for a specific application.

EGI386.EXE is invoked by the server in response to a POST or GET request. POST requests that the input data be passed via the command's standard input stream. GET requests the data to be passed as command line arguments.

Supplying arguments in a URL query string as a result of a GET request can result in some of them being lost due to truncation as the string is passed back to the script. The POST method is preferred if a large amount of data is going to be sent. Normally a console application reads its standard input stream from the keyboard and writes its standard output stream to the monitor. When a CGI script is started directly by another program, such as a Web server, rather than from the console the standard input/output streams are redirected to the start-up program. GUI-oriented programs such as Visual Basic applications or Word have no concept of standard input/output streams and different techniques must be employed.

The form shown in Figure 9.1 will submit two values to EGI386.EXE using the POST method. This program is located in the same directory as the form. The program will output an HTML page showing the number of command line arguments, the current set of environment variables and the forms data. The forms data is sent as a set of name/value pairs:

```
name=xxx&logon-b=EGI386
```

EGI386.EXE parses this changing '=' signs for spaces and '&' for new lines.

```
name = xxx
logon-b = EGI386
```

The second program, EG2i386.EXE, performs the same trick only it writes the data to a file; this is identified by the PATH_INFO environment variable. The ACTION URL must be altered to add this field, the example below also uses the GET method. The programs automatically identify the selected method.

```
<FORM ACTION="EG2I386.EXE/SCRIPTS/FORM.HFO" METHOD
=GET>
```

The Web server and any CGI script is run as the SYSTEM user, therefore the file or directory used for output must have the appropriate write and create permissions set. Data is appended to the HFO file every time the form is submitted.

▨ Headers

Web document headers were discussed in detail in Chapter 6. The example programs output a minimalist header which merely identifies the type of the data returned:

```
Content-type: text/html

...Data
```

It's important to note that a new line separates the header from the data. If this is omitted the browser will interpret the data as header and then sit waiting for the data. This is the most common CGI bug.

▨ Environment

In addition to data submitted by the user a CGI script has access to environment variables. These are similar to variables set in scripts such as AUTOEXEC.BAT and may be used to determine the type of data returned to the browser. HTTPS supports the following set of environment variables:

- CONTENT_LENGTH
  The length of the data submitted by the user with the POST method.

- CONTENT_TYPE
  The content type of the data being Posted such as: `application/x-www-form-urlencoded`. The ENCTYPE attribute can be used to alter this field.

- GATEWAY_INTERFACE
  The CGI revision to which the server complies, for example: `CGI/1.1`.

- HTTP_ACCEPT
  The set of MIME content types which the browser can handle. A script may choose to return different data depending on the values in this field. For instance a GIF image could be substituted for the JPEG version.

- PATH_INFO
  The server sets this to the PATH_INFO part of the URL.

- QUERY_STRING
  The server sets this to the part of the URL following the '?' character. This data is also passed to the program on the command line. If the POST method is used data can be passed both on the standard input stream, say from forms data, and as a query string in the URL. This is useful for setting program options. Data submitted with the GET method overrides any URL query string and in addition '=' signs should be encoded as `%3D` when the data is passed on the command line.

- REMOTE_ADDR
  The dotted IP address of the host making the request; this may be a machine running a proxy server rather than the client's machine.

- REQUEST_METHOD
  The method used to make the request, for HTTPS this will be one of GET or POST.

- SCRIPT_NAME
  The path and name of the script being executed. Useful for where the script wishes to identify and run itself again without hard-coding its location. An example might be a form which generates a new form. The first command line argument also gives the script name.

- SERVER_NAME
  The name or IP address of the Web server's computer.

- SERVER_PROTOCOL
  The name and version of the requesting protocol. Typically HTTP/1.0.

- SERVER_PORT
  The port on which the request was sent, usually 80 or 8080.

- SERVER_SOFTWARE
  The name and version of the Web server, for the EMWAC's server this may be: HTTPS/0.96.

Browsers send other variables with the HTTP request and these are available in the environment prefixed with: HTTP_. Two useful variables are:

- HTTP_REFERER
  This identifies the document used to access the CGI script. For example a user may follow a link in the index.htm file on the machine www.zardoz.com. The referrer information would be http://www.zardoz.com/index.htm. This is a good way of tracking incoming links without resorting to such tricks as hidden data or multiple home pages. The script writer may also choose to display different documents based on the link value. A user arriving at an on-line sports shop from the *Haggis Hurlers* home page may be taken straight to features on haggis hurling equipment and sportswear. It is possible to be more generic, identifying the top-level domain; a user traveling from inria.fr may be given ordering details and sales outlets for France rather than the United States.

- HTTP_USER_AGENT
  This identifies the Web browser and version used to view the documents. A common example would be: Mozilla/1.1N (Windows; I; 16bit), the 16-bit Windows version of Netscape. Knowing the browser may influence the level of document returned, Netscape users may get a Mozilla version of the document, UDIwww users would see HTML 3.0 and Lynx good old version 2.0, with no images.

Some servers use these two variables directly, either to return different versions of a document or to extend the logging information available.

▓ Invoking CGI scripts

CGI scripts can be called to process forms data or given as a hyperlink either within a document or directly from a browser's URL field. HTTPS scripts invoked using the GET method, which includes any called directly from the browser, must specify a trailing '?' character in the URL. Otherwise HTTPS will send the script file to the browser with the MIME type of applica-tion/octet-string. Not an ideal situation for keeping scripts secret. When using the NT file system this can be prevented from the File Manager Security menu by making the script execute only for the SYSTEM user.

DOS batch files

DOS batch files can be used to generate dynamic documents. However, as they are not directly executable by HTTPS they must be run by calling the command processor, which has the required .EXE extension:

```
<A HREF=/SCRIPTS/CMD.EXE?/C+SCRIPTS\ENV.BAT>Script</A>
```

The command processor has been copied to a SCRIPTS sub-directory. It's better to link system utilities as this avoids data duplication. The link command LN.EXE can be found in the resource kit, available from: ftp.microsoft. com. By restricting programs to those found under the server's document tree HTTPS stops external users executing any program found on the system; an evident problem would be to give untrusted users access to the delete command! In the above URL the switch and the batch file name are passed in the query string part of the URL and separated by '+' signs. Note the use of Windows oriented '\' path separators in the batch filename passed as an argument to the command processor.

In this example the batch file has also been placed in the SCRIPTS sub-direc-tory. From the command line this would be run by invoking the command processor with the batch file as an argument:

```
C:\> CMD.EXE /C SCRIPTS\ENV.BAT
```

Of course the Windows command loader knows that a batch file has to be run by the command processor and would invoke it directly.

A simple batch script echoes the MIME content type followed by a new line and the data. The batch file below displays the whole operating environment as shown by the set command.

```
@echo off
echo Content-type: text/html
echo.
set
```

Perl

Perl scripts are equally awkward to invoke with HTTPS, the Perl command to process the script must be given explicitly. This is an advantage of the UNIX magic number scheme and the URLs of documents ported from UNIX to HTTPS will have to be modified:

```
cgi-bin/form.pl -> /scripts/perl.exe?form.pl
```

Again `PERL.EXE` will live under the HTTPS document tree or be a link to the actual program. Arguments can be passed to the Perl script using the '+' separators:

```
/scripts/perl.exe?form.pl+rewrite+1000
```

▨ Processing data

The example scripts discussed previously can be used to process forms data or the source code taken as a framework and modified for other purposes. Libraries are also available which can identify whether data is posted to standard input or submitted as part of the URL. They will usually package the data and runtime environment into an easy-to-use format.

One such library is Steven Brenner's `CGI-LIB.PL` `http://mole.bio.cam.ac.uk/web/form.html` for the Perl language. This can be installed in the Perl library or under the server's document tree. In the latter case the location will have to be specified using the '-I' flag and the permissions on the library set so that it is readable by `SYSTEM`, otherwise the server will complain that the requested URL cannot be found. To call a Perl script to process the form in Figure 9.1 the `ACTION` field would have to be changed to:

```
/SCRIPTS/PERL.EXE?-ISCRIPTS+SCRIPTS/DEMO.PL
```

`CGI-LIB.PL` has been placed in the `SCRIPTS` directory. A simple script could read the input data and print this out along with the correct MIME header:

```perl
require "cgi-lib.pl";

if (&ReadParse(*input)) {
  print &PrintHeader, &PrintVariablesShort(%input);
  } else {
    print &PrintHeader,"Gimme Some Data!";
  }
```

ReadParse determines if the data is sent using the GET or the POST method and reads it into an associative array. PrintHeader outputs the standard MIME header for an HTML document and PrintVariablesShort prints the associative array as an HTML list. CGI-LIB.PL has other useful subroutines:

- CgiError outputs an error message. If no parameter is given this is a generic message otherwise the first parameter is used as the HTML TITLE and subsequent parameters form paragraphs on the page.
- PrintVariables is the long form of PrintVariablesShort.
- MethGet returns true if the script was called using the GET method.
- MyURL returns the full URL of the script.

■ Debugging, security and common pitfalls

CGI scripts are initially debugged outside of the Web environment. A Perl script can be called directly from the command line using either the '-w' trace switch or '-d' for interactive debugging mode. Make sure all paths are exercised and in particular ensure that the MIME header is output correctly including the blank line separating it from the data. Check permissions on CGI scripts to ensure that the SYSTEM user can execute .EXE programs and read or write script and data files.

Permitting external users to run programs creates security problems. In particular, don't permit clients to pass unverified strings to popen, eval, system or exec commands as these can be used to launch unauthorized programs. Remember that characters can be encoded in the URL with the % notation, so don't just check user input for the obvious.

■ Dynamic documents and caching

Caching is the enemy of dynamic documents. A cache is a local copy of a document which is referenced for speed until the original is updated. Both proxy servers and browsers can cache. Dynamic documents, by their very nature, shouldn't be cached and there are a couple of techniques to ensure this doesn't happen.

The headers shown till now have been fairly minimalist; a more complete form of MIME header includes the current date and an expiry date:

```
Date: Sunday, 13-Aug-95 18:17:57 GMT
Expires: Sunday, 20-Aug-95 18:17:57 GMT
```

■ Head requests

It's possible to manually get just the header for any document by sending a **HEAD** request using `telnet`:

```
C:\> telnet kimble.demon.co.uk 80
HEAD /default.htm HTTP/1.0
HTTP/1.0 200 OK
Server: HTTPS/0.96
Allow: GET HEAD POST
MIME-version: 1.0
Content-type: text/html
Date: Monday, 21-Aug-95 2:24.31 GMT
Last-modified: Monday, 21-Aug-95 2:25:37 GMT
Content-length: 567
Connection closed by foreign host.
C:\>
```

Cache managers do the same when they want to discover information about the document.

This tells the cache manager when the data was originated and the date and time after which the cached copy is considered stale. The document should not be held in cache after this date without referring to the original. The cache manager may refer back to the server every time the document is accessed although it will only need to check the header and not download the whole document.

Dynamic documents can set the `Expires:` date to be the same as the `Date:` field and the document will not be cached. Alternatively the header line:

```
Pragma: no-cache
```

can be used to stop document caching.

This is fine for a single document but doesn't help where it is a mixture of text and in-line graphics. The graphics will still be cached by the proxy. Netscape browsers offer a solution by supporting multipart MIME messages; these allow data to be split into separate sections for text, graphics and other sources. The no-cache directive would apply to the whole file. Another

```
#
# Perl script to produce a sample color.
#
print "Content-Type: text/html\nPragma: no-cache\n\n";
print "<HEAD><TITLE>Color Sampler</TITLE></HEAD>\n";
print "<H1 ALIGN=CENTER>GDIT Color Sampler</H1><P>";

if ($ENV{CONTENT_LENGTH} ne "") {
        read(STDIN, $content, $ENV{CONTENT_LENGTH});
        ($red,$green,$blue) = split('\&', $content);
        ($redvalue) = (split('=', $red))[1];
        ($greenvalue) = (split('=', $green))[1];
        ($bluevalue) = (split('=', $blue))[1];
        print "<P><IMG SRC=\"/scripts/perl.exe?scripts/generate.pl+";
        print $redvalue, "+", $greenvalue, "+", $bluevalue, "\"><P>";
} else {
        $redvalue = FF;
        $greenvalue = FF;
        $bluevalue = FF;
}

print "Sample what color different combinations of Red, Green and Blue make.";
print "<P><FORM METHOD=POST ACTION=\"/scripts/sample.pl\">";
print "<INPUT TYPE=text NAME=Red SIZE=2 VALUE=$redvalue> Red ";
print "<INPUT TYPE=text NAME=Green SIZE=2 VALUE=$greenvalue> Green ";
print "<INPUT TYPE=text NAME=Blue SIZE=2 VALUE=$bluevalue> Blue<P>";
print "<INPUT TYPE=submit NAME=submit VALUE=SAMPLE></FORM>";
print "</BODY>\n";




#
# Perl script to generate a color using GDIT.EXE
#
open GD, "| gdit" || die "can't run gdit: $!";
print "Content-type: image/gif\nPragma: no-cache\n\n";
printf GD "st c %d %d %d c1\n", hex($ARGV[0]), hex($ARGV[1]), hex($ARGV[2]);
printf GD "n 100 50 c1\ns\n\nq\n\n";
close(GD);
```

Figure 9.2   Color sampler

possibility is to include images dynamically. These would be referenced in the usual way using the image element:

```
<IMG SRC=SCRIPTS/PERL.EXE?SCRIPTS/IMAGE1.PL>
```

but rather than referencing a static data file the SRC attribute tells the server to invoke a program that generates the image, with the appropriate no-cache header field.

Figure 9.2 shows two Perl CGI scripts. The first displays a form that prompts for three color values corresponding to the red, green and blue components of a color. The form invokes itself and on the second pass references the image generated by the other program.

The second script generates a colored square based on the values of the three arguments. It uses GDIT, a program for image creation. This doesn't have to be located in the HTTPS document directory and is in fact found in C:\USR\LOCAL\BIN on this system: this must be in the SYSTEM user's PATH. Some versions of Perl won't allow OPEN() to perform both input and output and the GIF image will need to be written to a temporary file and returned separately.

The first script is interesting in a couple of ways, it shows how a form can call itself and how input values can be carried to the new form. Data could also be kept in META elements, hidden form fields or added to the URL query string. **Shopping basket** scripts perform exactly the same task and this program could be modified to act as a shopping basket. Generating forms on the fly is useful if some user information is included from the environment or the response from earlier forms may govern the questions asked. For example, users checking off 'non-smoker' on a medical questionnaire wouldn't be troubled with questions about how many cigarettes they smoke per day. The above code would be more elegant if it used the Perl CGI-LIB.

▓ Server push and client pull

Netscape have implemented two techniques for periodically updating documents. These are called **server push** and **client pull**.

Server push uses a form of multipart MIME message to keep a connection between a server and Netscape browser open and to periodically send data over this link. This can be used to repeatedly update a video image, for example in a security system or to redisplay share prices every few seconds. The server push content type is:

```
Content-type:multipart/mixed;boundary=Abracadabra
```

or:

```
Content-type:multipart/x-mixed-replace;boundary=
Zanzibar
```

The second type uses the unofficial x-mixed-replace subtype indicating that the data should overwrite rather than append to the existing data. The **boundary** string is used to separate each message part:

```
-Abracadabra
Content-type: image/gif

Data 1
-Abracadabra
Content-type: image/gif

Data Last
-Abracadabra
```

The server sends each part separately and determines the length of the intervening pause. Data types can vary from part to part. A server push script can be referenced from an IMAGE element as was previously shown in Figure 9.2. This will update the image in-line without touching the surrounding text.

Client pull does the same trick from the other direction. A new META tag has been added which tells the browser to reload the document after the number of seconds specified by the CONTENT field have elapsed. This has the same affect as an HTTP Refresh header line:

```
<META HTTP-EQUIV="Refresh" CONTENT=1>
<TITLE>Client Pull</TITLE>
<H1>This is an example of Client Pull</H1>
```

This document would be reloaded every second. Obviously the file could be changed dynamically on reload. Alternatively a URL can be given to tell the client to load a different document:

```
<META HTTP-EQUIV=Refresh CONTENT=1 URL=http://kimble/
doc2.htm>
```

which is equivalent to the HTTP header:

```
Refresh: 1; URL=http://kimble/doc2.htm
```

A full URL must be used. The refresh period and URL can be different with each load.

Server push is generally more efficient than client pull as only a single connection is made, however, while this connection is open resources are consumed at the server end.

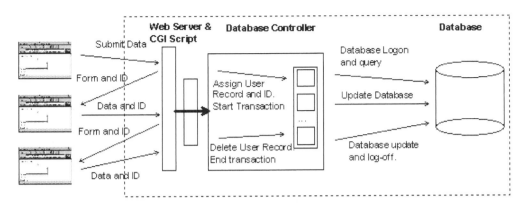

Figure 9.3 Database access with the Web

■ Tracking users and state

HTTP is a stateless protocol, information about the client is not retained between browser requests. This can be seen in the server log where each entry is an independent entity. It might be reasonable to infer that accesses to a group of pages from a single host occurring over a short period come from the same user, but they could equally be from many users simultaneously viewing the site from a single gateway or machine.

This lack of state is a problem when designing certain types of application. For example, when a client accesses a database the normal procedure is to log on, perform a sequence of actions which are often grouped into unique **transactions** and then log off. A transaction is any operation which results in input to or output from the database and may consist of many individual reads and writes. A Web front end might present these operations over a number of forms. For instance a booking system would make an inquiry about seat availability and then allow the user to reserve the seat. To do this state must be preserved from one screen to the next. A simple system may encode the entire user state in a hidden field within the form or add it as part of the URL.

A real database needs an intermediate controller program which takes responsibility for login, transaction management and logout. Users would be assigned an identifier token and this value would be passed from form to form. The token would be used as an index to a user record held by the database controller. The Web server could communicate with this program through a simple CGI backend using either Dynamic Data Exchange (DDE), Object Linking and Embedding (OLE), a shared file or even sockets, if it is located on a remote system.

Tracking a user around the Web site is an easier proposition. At first glance it would appear reasonable to use the CGI environment variables but user identification is only possible if both the server and client are running the **ident** protocol. The only reliable piece of information is the Internet address of the remote machine and this might be an intermediate proxy or gateway. These problems can be overcome by generating the initial home page with a CGI script. This would assign the new user an identifier (id), possibly the process number of the program. The id would be attached to all the URLs within a page. Figure 9.4 shows a listing in the C programming language for such a program.

```c
//      Tracker, add a unique user id to all URLs
//      (C) 1995 DB Harvey-George
//      Permission is granted to use and distribute this source.

#include <process.h>
#include <stdlib.h>
#include <stdio.h>
#define LEN 6
enum state {NORMAL, MAGIC} mode;

main(int argc, char *argv[])
{
        int user_id, count, ch;
        char id[LEN] = "cookie";      // magic string
        FILE *fp;

        printf("Content-Type: text/html\n\n");

        switch (argc) {
        case 2: // first invocation, get user id
                user_id = getpid(); // NT Posix Call
                break;
        case 3: // second invocation, user id is 2nd arg
                user_id = atoi(argv[2]);
                break;

        default:
                printf("Incorrect number of arguments: %d\n", argc);
                return 1;
        }/* switch */

        if ((fp = fopen(argv[1], "r")) == NULL) {
                printf("can't open input file: %s\n", argv[1]);
                return 1;
        }
```

```
        // Add user_ids, small finite state machine
        mode = NORMAL;
        while ((ch = fgetc(fp)) != EOF) {
                int     got_it;

                switch (mode) {
                case MAGIC: // eat cookies
                        if (id[count] != ch) {
                                got_it = 0; // bleugh, spit it out
                                fprintf(stdout, "%0.*s", count, id);
                                fputc(ch, stdout);
                                mode = NORMAL; // reset

                        } else {
                                count++;
                        }
                        if (count == LEN) {
                                if (got_it) {  // add cookie to URL
                                        fprintf(stdout, "%d", user_id);
                                }
                                mode = NORMAL; // reset
                        }
                        break;
                default:
                        if (ch == '+') {
                                count = 0;
                                got_it = 1;
                                mode = MAGIC;
                        }
                        fputc(ch, stdout);
                        break;
                }// switch
        }// while

        return 0;
}/* main */
```

Figure 9.4 Tracking users

The home page is output by invoking the program with the home page HTML document as the first argument:

```
http://<hostname>/TRACKER.EXE?DEFAULT.HTM
```

The program generates a user identifier and then parses the HTML document replacing every occurrence of `+cookie` with the `id`. The updated hyperlink anchors look like:

```
<A HREF=TRACKER.EXE?FILE.HTM+137>
```

The parsed document is sent to the standard output stream. The MIME header type must be added by the program as the server will not be able to identify the document as HTML from the file extension.

Following a hyperlink invokes TRACKER again, but this time the second argument, 137, is used as the identifier. The access log contains an audit trail of documents viewed by each user. This extra identifier information is useful for generating site usage patterns, normally log analysis tools would be created to provide more structure.

```
Sun Aug 13 17:04:10 1995 /tracker.exe?default.htm
Sun Aug 13 17:04:13 kimble.co.uk 1995 /tracker.exe?toc.htm?227
Sun Aug 13 17:04:10 1995 /tracker.exe?default.htm
Sun Aug 13 17:04:17 kimble.co.uk 1995 /tracker.exe?toc.htm+211
Sun Aug 13 17:04:52 kimble.co.uk 1995 /tracker.exe?index.htm+211
Sun Aug 13 17:05:18 kimble.co.uk /tracker.exe?news.htm+227
```

This is a minimalist program, but the basic technique can be applied to larger systems. In particular a simple shopping basket could either be implemented using the database scheme shown in Figure 9.3 or the list of items in the basket may be held in a hidden field. Forms would be generated programatically carrying the basket with them. The program handling forms submissions would add the selected items to a basket list and output this along with the new form:

```
<INPUT TYPE=hidden NAME=basket VALUE=item1,item2,
...,itemn>
```

 The URL encoding scheme used in the tracker program is best avoided as the item list may overflow the maximum URL length. The POST method, which submits forms data through the standard input stream rather than as a URL argument list, is normally used for this type of application.

Netscape **cookies** are a similar scheme to allow state to be stored and retrieved from a client. The server generating a cookie adds the HTTP header field:

```
Set-Cookie: NAME=Value; expires-Date; path=Path;
domain=Name; secure
```

Secure indicates that the cookie should be sent out only where SSL security is employed. The browser stores this information locally and when making an HTTP request includes a cookie header field for all cookies whose domains and paths match the URL components:

```
Cookie: Name1=Opaque_String1; Name2=Opaque_String2 ...
```

Thus if the original cookie was sent by CATALOG.HTM running on www.widget.com it can be configured so that it will only be returned to this host or document.

▨ Off-the-shelf scripts

Writing code may be too complicated or difficult for the site builder to contemplate and nearly always involves maintenance effort. Many ready-made CGI applications exist. These can range from complete on-line shopping malls to simple programs which package and mail forms data.

Email is often used in CGI scripts to send data to individuals or groups. This may be ordering information or structured customer feedback. It isn't possible to drive GUI mail programs directly with HTTPS. Instead a command line mailer is used. One such program is Blat which will send a file to anyone on the Internet using an SMTP mail server. It's a 32-bit console application that runs on NT. Data must be packaged into a temporary file before being sent. There is a utility called WWWMail which does exactly that for forms; however it may be easier to use a single program, for example Brian Dorricott's Mailto.

Mailto processes forms data submitted with the POST method. Hidden fields are used to specify the name of the mail server, the recipient's email address and the subject.

```
<TITLE>Subscribe Now!</TITLE>
<FORM ACTION="/SCRIPTS/MAILTO.EXE" METHOD=POST>
<input type="hidden" NAME="sendto" VALUE="david@threewiz">
<Input type="hidden" Name="server" value="threewiz">
<INPUT TYPE="hidden" NAME="subject" value="Subscribe">
<PRE>
<B>Your details:</B*gt
Name:            <INPUT NAME="uname" SIZE=30>
Position:        <INPUT NAME="title" SIZE=30>
Company Name:    <INPUT NAME="company" SIZE=40>
E-Mail:          <INPUT NAME="email" SIZE=30>

<INPUT TYPE="submit" VALUE="Subscribe">
</FORM>
```

Figure 9.5 A subscription form using Mailto

■ Inter-application communication

Windows provides a number of mechanisms for inter-application communication. At the simplest level a normal file may be used. This is the basis of the WinCGI interface supported by some Web servers and is useful for interfacing with Visual applications such as Delphi or Visual Basic which cannot use CGI directly.

Servers using WinCGI write the data to a file and then launch the application, the application reads this file, performs some processing and writes its output to a second file. As many such requests may be running simultaneously the file names must be unique and are generated by the server and supplied to the backend script as command-line arguments. Where disk buffering is used this process can be quite fast and is certainly a lot simpler to set up compared to either DDE or OLE.

The HTTPS server doesn't support the WinCGI interface although an intermediate CGI script could be written to launch visual applications. This would involve an extra task and would be quite slow. A wealth of applications have been written for WinCGI in both Visual Basic and Delphi. These can talk to Access, FoxPro and other databases supported by ODBC.

Dynamic Data Exchange (DDE) is a more sophisticated mechanism. It provides a communications channel which is basically an area of shared memory accessed through a higher level message interface. Using DDE the CGI script acts as the client and a Windows application is the DDE server. The server must be running before the conversation is started but it can be launched from the script. Microsoft applications which support DDE have a unique and well-known application name.

Object Linking and Embedding (OLE) supersedes DDE by replacing the message interface with a distributed object. Rather than sending data and commands down a message queue the OLE application has a **handle** to an object in the remote application. Once the link is established it is a lot easier to use than DDE.

OLE can be used from a high-level language like C. NTPerl has direct support for OLE with objects for Word, Excel and Netscape. A Perl CGI script could create an instance of the Word basic object which will (if necessary) start the application. It could then load a document and save it as an HTML file. It's possible to control this from a remote browser running on a non-Windows operating system.

▩ Summary

- CGI scripts process user input and enable interaction with local applications.
- Any language can be used, including 'C', Visual Basic and DOS Batch.
- A script must generate its own MIME header.
- Header and data are always separated by a blank line.
- HTTPS can directly invoke console applications with the .EXE extension.
- Permissions must be set correctly for the SYSTEM user. Execute for programs, read only for script files.
- CGI scripts should first be debugged from the command line.
- Dynamic updating is possible on Netscape browsers using server push and client pull.
- Client state can be held in the URL query string, hidden fields, comments or Meta elements. Netscape cookies can also be used to maintain state.

10 Design

'I'm as mad as hell, and I'm not going to take it any more.' Don't worry, I've only been cruising the latest whiz-bang Web site put together by some suits on Madison Avenue. The opening graphic took me the better part of a minute to download and the pages were about as easy to navigate as the Osaka metro system. I don't even have a firm idea of what the site was about or who it was for but one thing is certain, it won't get bookmarked on my browser.

Now most people wouldn't have waited for that first graphic; after all, a minute is a long time in media, longer than it takes Ford to sell a car on TV. These site builders appear to have forgotten two basic rules:

1. Work within the medium. A designer wouldn't produce a color advert for a black and white publication and by the same token shouldn't try to emulate magazine design on-line.
2. Good design is not concerned with looking 'flash' or 'cool' but aims to help the reader locate and assimilate information more rapidly.

The dynamic nature of Web documents and the limited control offered by HTML over page layout frequently makes design a secondary consideration. Many sites begin as a single page and then grow organically by adding new and assimilating existing documents. More often than not the result looks like organic fertilizer (manure) rather than a consistent and well-structured information system. The importance of the information content has been placed out of all proportion to the way it is structured and presented. Even where sites belong to large companies they may be established and run by technical people from within the computer department and are not integrated into a global marketing strategy. The site builders may be programmers or system administrators with little or no formal expertise in designing user interfaces. No matter what the origins of the site builders a failure to consider and implement good design will lose the message, no matter how interesting or important.

The Web builder has few existing terms of reference when constructing a hypermedia system. The structures of books, journals and papers are well defined and appear cast in tablets of stone. Hypermedia, on the other hand, presents the designer with a heady combination of text, graphics and audio-visual information all of which can be linked in a bewildering number of ways. CD-ROM would at first appear to have numerous parallels to HTML but the bandwidth and storage available to the designer is an order of magnitude greater than that of most Web sites. Current CD-ROM titles are geared towards real-time audio-visual and graphical information. Although the Web offers designers great power and utility they must be careful as to how the multimedia aspects are exploited. Indeed, useful pointers to layout and structure of on-line documents can still be learnt from the design of printed publications.

■ Print design

Modern printing has been around for some 500 years. Its introduction brought books from a monastic environment into a much wider domain. In the beginning there was no widespread agreement about the structure of books. Elements as familiar as alphabetical ordering, page numbering, heading and table of contents grew out of a need to organize hundreds of pages of information in a way that could be readily understood and referenced. The availability of movable type led to experimentation in page layout and the effect of different fonts. A need to catalogue and index the growing range and quantity of books held in libraries brought further change. Early books often had rather vague titles much like *A few observations pertaining to the formation of on-line documents,* rather than a more precise, and easier to catalogue, *The HTML Style Guide.*

Books and other printed media are very familiar, a great deal of our early life is spent learning how to use them effectively. This deep understanding leads many to prefer printed rather than on-line information. It's instructive to ask just what key elements make a book easy to use and how they are relevant to a hypermedia system.

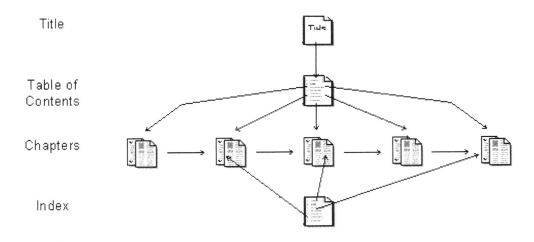

Figure 10.1 The hierarchical structure of a book

A technical book is organized in an information hierarchy of title, table of contents, chapters and pages. It may divide chapters into further levels of related information. Once a section is reached the pages are designed to be read sequentially although internal references, footnotes and an index permit individual paragraphs and sentences to be accessed directly. This structure enables us to find the desired information quickly – there is no constraint to read the book from cover to cover in order to find one small section. Books provide useful physical clues, so-called meta-information. The font style, the front cover and the page layout all intimate the intended audience. Knowing that a book is 500 pages long, the thickness is a good guide to where it should be opened to find any specific page. Of course, if it is the latest 2,500 page HTML epic it may be better employed as a door-stop!

Individual pages carry further information including a page number, book and chapter title. The text is normally broken into sections separated by various levels of headings. The depth of these headings depends on the nature of the material. A novel, which is designed to be read sequentially, will only organize the plot to as far as chapters, on the other hand a thesis may extend to four or more heading levels for easy reference.

■ The information hierarchy

Hierarchies are a common structure in society:

- king, lords, subjects
- boss, managers, workers
- library, categories, books, chapters, pages

Although many other meta-structures evolve (a book may directly reference a chapter in another publication) the hierarchy enables users to zoom in on the information required from a vague starting point. Hyperlinks allow the Web builder to contrive any type of structure. The Web itself is a complicated and seemingly random matrix of information but within the Web hierarchies are a common and useful feature. Site listings, like those carried by the Yahoo server, group pages under a hierarchy of subjects. Individual sites usually adopt the same arrangement with the root forming a home page.

 As in print the breadth and depth of a Web site obeys some loose rules. Documents are split into sections to aid the location of information. A Web site which is flat will be hard to navigate, its pages containing too many links for the user to mentally organize. Similarly sites which are too vertical won't give the reader an adequate overview of the contents and will force navigation up and down the hierarchy searching for data.

The flat site is often the result of organic growth. Links to new pages are continually added to some overall index and where a number of cross-links are also involved restructuring can prove a nightmare. It's worth drawing up a plan of the site before the first link is even made. This should not only cover the existing material but anticipate growth. A plan is especially useful where more than one person is responsible for adding and maintaining pages.

■ Pages and links

Users find it confusing when a large number of random links are shown on a single page and will tend to 'zap' to the first visible item of interest. The site ends up a bit like cable TV where nothing is watched for more than a few seconds. The short-term memory has a capacity for around half a dozen items. Once links are scrolled they are soon forgotten and the user will end up exploring only a limited part of the site. The site should ideally be structured to lead users through as much of the information as they find relevant and interesting.

The number of links that a user can handle on a single page is somewhat dependent on their organization. Where a page comprises links alone it should

Too High

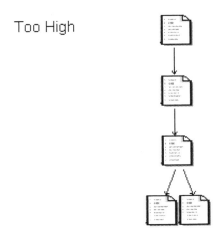

Too Flat

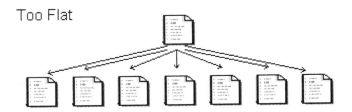

Figure 10.2 Flat and vertical hierarchies

be short, possibly only one screen full or about 20 lines. Longer sections of prose may run over many screens and there are numerous examples of whole chapters or documents structured as a single Web page. These have often been converted directly from existing sources. Full documents are convenient for reading off-line or printing but finding information is more difficult. Small movements of the scrollbar are magnified into large movements within the page. An index or table of contents helps internal navigation but for on-line use it's more convenient to break large sections into a number of pages of a few screens each. This eases maintenance especially where multifarious internal links are used.

The 'half dozen' link rule of thumb can be applied to most pages. This figure excludes standard structural links, such as to a home page. The disadvantage of using many small pages is that maintenance is more complicated and a logical naming scheme must be used. This may be based around title and page number, in which case a script can automatically generate the Next and Previous page links. A full version of the document may be offered through a link on the first page either to an FTP archive or, if scripting is used, it can be built programatically from the individual pages. Such documents should state the URL of the on-line version and where other resources are accessed this may be specified by a BASE element.

■ Advanced structures

A single tree is the most basic form of organization. With hyperlinks there is the power to impose various structures on the same set of pages. One link could lead users into an alphabetical list of subjects, much like the index in a book. Another could present a tutorial by linking the same basic data through some intermediate guide. With static pages, control should be exercised when imposing multiple organizations otherwise users may become lost in a maze of links. It is possible to keep the pages separate from the structure by generating the links dynamically using server scripts and this has many advantages.

Tim Berners-Lee, the inventor of the Web, has written that links should be used pervasively, in other words wherever a link can be made it should be made. While it is very convenient to be able to access related information a caveat should be applied to this general advice. A page full of links to people, software and other publications is like reading a book full of cross-references and footnotes or a program stuffed full of goto statements. They can impose an entirely different structure from the one intended by the designer. Where a document should be read sequentially it is better to group these links into a separate resource page or section. This division also makes revising the links easier.

■ Intrasite navigation

Users navigate about the Web by following hyperlinks and using the standard Back and Forward buttons. Where a site is entered through its home page these buttons can be used to move around even if subordinate pages feature no internal links. The buttons do not give any information about the context of a page within a site, they merely move users through a list of previously visited pages.

No matter what size a site is the user will only see the current page. This may be reached from within the site or directly from another location. URLs are also published in Usenet news articles and in journals. These links are like hyperspace, the only clue users have as to where they are is given by the page

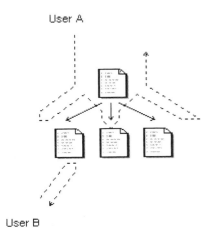

Figure 10.3   Intrasite navigation

in front of them. Consequently the site builder should not rely on the standard Back and Forward buttons for site navigation; instead each page should provide navigation links to anchor it within the site.

Figure 10.3 illustrates this problem. User A, entering the site from the home page, can navigate using the Back and Forward buttons but User B has no choice but to return through the entry point and will not see the remainder of the site.

 Every page should feature a link back to the home and possibly a `mailto` link to contact the author. Where a page forms part of a sequence, next and previous links should be added. This saves the user bobbing up and down via a contents page. These links should be included at both the top and bottom of the page and should be named consistently. HTML 3.0 formalizes various navigation links with the `LINK` element. This augments the standard browser Back and Forward buttons. It has the added advantage that the buttons are separate from the contents and do not get scrolled.

Images and icons are used to make navigation buttons more attractive. These can help to guide the eye and act as a mnemonic but an alternative text string should always be given for users running non-graphical browsers. For the same reason don't use image maps for button bars, instead build these from individual images which allow a text alternative to be specified. Icons present difficulties as there are few globally recognized symbols and their meaning may be unclear to other users. The server log file can be analyzed to see if visitors from particular geographic domains have difficulty exploring the site. Where an image and link are used together both should be made active.

■ The home page

The home page is the focus of any Web site. It provides general information about the contents, their purpose and the site identity. With the widespread use of computerized indexing it must also give enough information to persuade searchers to visit without it becoming a buzzword graveyard. The home page shouldn't carry information about subsidiary services, these can be given their own (possibly home) pages.

 First impressions last. Unless the target audience is well defined don't start with a 100,000-byte graphic. The page may have looked great over the company network but the vast majority of new Internet users are on dial-up modem lines running at speeds from 9,600 to 28,800 bps. This figure is a measure of the number of bits per second (bps) which can be transmitted, a bit represents a single 1 or 0. Even a super-fast Ethernet LAN will grind to a halt if too many people start accessing multimedia and large graphics, and if your boss wasn't interested in that 'Web thing' before, she soon will be!

■ Sizing the communication link

The speed of the connection to the Internet will have to be determined, based on projected traffic flow. A 28,800 bps link can carry about three kilobytes of data per second with compression. The communication protocols take up some capacity and it should be remembered that most audio-visual and graphics formats are already compressed so current modem ratios of 4:1 will only apply to text. Assuming a maximum acceptable download time of fifteen seconds per page this site can support two simultaneous users downloading a page featuring 20 kilobytes of text and graphics.

There is a less pronounced peak period on the Internet when compared, say, to the highway system. This is because the Internet is global, spanning many time zones. Users connecting to their local ISP may have trouble in the evenings but this is just a local jam, once down the on-ramp and out onto the super-highway traffic flows more smoothly. The ratio of off-peak to peak traffic is about 3 to 1 and average throughput is about a half to a third of peak. These figures were determined empirically by examining log files, your mileage may vary. The site described above could realistically serve about 5,000 of its pages per day or 150,000 in a month. This would make it moderately popular by Web standards.

Most sites quote their traffic in terms of **hits**. This is a measure of the number of resources accessed from a site. A home page with one graphic would register two hits, so the site we have described may be seeing 300,000 hits per month. In fact, the figure would lie between the two as some clients will run text-only browsers and so won't download the image. These will also put less load on the site.

Hits are a poor measure of how many people are viewing the pages as many ISPs and networks run proxy servers which cache pages. A cache is a fast local store of frequently accessed resources; it will only be updated when the original version changes. In the case of the Web, once fetched users will only see the local copy. No new hits will be registered at the site for the lifetime of the cached page unless the caching server sends a HEAD request to verify the modify time. The non-Internet providers usually offer Web access through a proxy server. Proxies are no bad thing – they let Web sites serve many more users than their hardware could otherwise support. However, as there is no record of who these users are it is largely irrelevant, except for marketing purposes. The most popular sites on the Web are currently seeing close to a million hits per day. Using the above model a site would require at least a 256 kbps connection to sustain that volume of traffic.

A 28,800 bps point-to-point connection is pretty slow. If the link is shared with other users, for instance site email and news, a faster leased line will be

■ How fast is the Internet?

Investing in a T1 link won't enable real-time video to be transmitted to similar computers across the Internet. The virtual connection is only as fast as its slowest link. As a rough guide, when the Internet backbone was upgraded to T3 connections (44.3 mbps) the average transfer speed I could get over my 256-kbps connection was about five thousand bytes per second. This was the average speed to a number of FTP sites throughout the world and was like an Internet speed of light. For a single connection the bottleneck was the wider Internet, not the local link. Working with this figure it can be seen that pages delivered over the Internet should not exceed a hundred thousand bytes including in-line graphics, no matter what type of connection is assumed at the client end.

required. ISDN provides 2 x 64,000 bps data channels and a single voice channel. It's still oriented towards dial-up operation and generally only one data channel is used for the Internet connection. Partial T1 offers speeds up to 1.54 million bps in multiples of 64 thousand and as has been shown it would be a very extensive and popular site which required a full T1 link. Getting the right link size for current and near-term growth is important because redundant capacity must still be paid for. The speed of the whole connection between the site and user has by far the greatest influence on the overall design and content.

■ Page design

HTML provides limited control over page layout. The Web author's primary concern is the effective organization of information using the HTML constructs. Incorrect use of these to achieve specific formatting for a particular browser is to be avoided. When used properly HTML is designed to correctly format documents on a wide variety of devices.

The argument over content as opposed to presentation is not black and white. Presentation is obviously very important to understanding a message. HTML markup provides a range of styles for the various elements of a document but there are still too many HTML 2.0 documents which are difficult to read because of poor application of this markup. With the greater control offered by Netscape and HTML 3.0, design is even more important.

A Web page can be mixed with a variety of structural elements in order to guide the eye, create interest, set the general tone and reinforce the text. The exact mix depends on the message and the audience. The key elements to Web pages are contrast, consistency and function.

■ Contrast

The more serious the text, the less contrast is used. A report or specification will have a gray, somber appearance with limited use of color and graphics. A home page may feature eye-catching graphics, color and plenty of white space. The aim is to grab the reader's attention by offering an interesting and visually exciting experience.

Contrast is provided by graphics, white space, rules and headings. Contrast on a Web page can seen by viewing it with a browser and doing a preview print. This can be resized to a point where the content no longer detracts from the presentation. Figure 10.4 shows the difference between two styles of page.

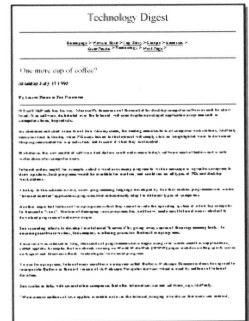
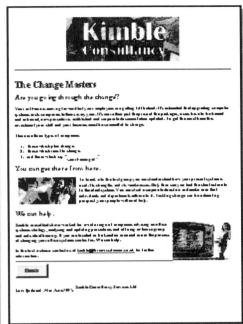

Figure 10.4 Contrasting page layout

It's a good idea to view related pages in this manner. The pages above wouldn't gel in a single document.

▪ Consistency

If contrast provides the excitement, consistency shows organization and planning. Related pages should be connected by a similar style otherwise they will give the impression that the site is a random collection of information with little thought or structure. Caution should be exercised when emulating the exact format of an organization's paper publications. The on-line *Financial Times* http://www.ft.com has got it about right, they use a pink background which is the same color as their newsprint. It's also one of the few good uses of a background color on the Web.

Designers working with more traditional media use a grid. This contains the features and structure which are common to all pages. The grid ensures page, project and personal consistency. Interest is maintained by minor variations on the basic structure. An HTML grid can be a template document or hard-copy layout. Version 3.0 of the language introduces banners and style sheets which help to maintain a consistent presentation across the entire document.

■ Function

When markup or graphical elements are introduced to a document they should serve a purpose. There is a tendency to get carried away with novel features, this is particularly prevalent with pages using the Netscapisms. Throwing everything at a page has origins in the design of community magazines and furniture warehouse mail shots. Just because a feature is there doesn't mean it should be used. Graphics must aid not obscure the understanding of the text.

■ Essential page elements

If a book is opened randomly the reader can place the page in context through information provided in special areas known as the header and footer. This often includes a chapter number and title, a page number and possibly a running head and book title. As two sides are visible this data is split between odd and even pages to avoid crowding.

While the home page is the focus of any Web site it is also likely that subordinate pages will be accessed directly. Users may bookmark pages they find interesting and plan to visit again. Other site builders can make links directly to relevant information bypassing the normal hierarchy. As in a book the context of a Web page must be clearly established. Generally each page will feature a reference to the originator and contact information. This may include the author's name or follow letterhead practice featuring a logo, telephone number and address. The logo can be a link back to the home page and it should never swamp the subsequent text. Email contacts can use the `mailto` URL or contain a link to a separate form where more structure is required for user response. This information is normally placed at the head of the page or in a banner page with HTML 3.0. A heading is also placed before any text and is a good idea even where a page is continued. This relation may be shown with the use of an ellipsis (...).

... The Project Life Cycle

Another important item is the revision date. This shows how stale the document is and whether the site is regularly maintained. If it is, readers may decide that it's worth a second look at a later date. If a revision control or other document management system is used this date can be inserted automatically.

A statement of copyright, although not normally a legal requirement, is a useful reminder that the law also covers the Internet. The HTML 3.0 link element provides a standard toolbar button to link a separate copyright statement.

▓ Titles

The page title will be used for browser bookmarks and may be displayed by on-line indexes and other search engines. The title will usually be seen within some context so can be short, serving more as a mnemonic. A reference to the 'Harley Home Page' in a document about motorbikes will refer to Harley-Davidsons, not London's famous Harley Street doctors. Then again, maybe not, considering the danger of riding bikes!

▓ Headings

Headings exist to help the reader decide what is of interest. They should be reasonably short and relevant. Upper case is not encountered in normal use and slows the reader, but the initial capitalization of words (other than the articles and prepositions) is normal practice. Centering should not extend over more than a couple of heading lines due to the difficulty of visual registration.

Main headings may be introduced with short phrases called kickers:

From the Man Who Wove the Web:
The Style Guide for On-line HyperText

These give further description of the text without detracting from the overall effect of the heading.

Subheadings break up the text and add contrast to a page and they can be read in isolation to provide a summary of the document. HTML has six levels of headings; they must be used in order with Heading 1 at the top of the document and others following below in strict sequence. Don't skip a heading level because of the way it is rendered on a particular browser and be aware that too many headings on a single page weakens the overall emphasis.

▓ Horizontal rules

Headings may be emphasized using horizontal rules. Netscape allows the width and thickness to be set but they shouldn't overwhelm the heading text. Custom graphics can be used for rules but their disadvantage is that they are not resized with the browser window. Assuming a default screen width of 640 pixels, a horizontal rule would extend no more than 600 pixels. Rules may also be used to separate topics or sections of a page, such as title or footer information.

■ Captions

Caption text can be added to in-line graphics and may be positioned using the Align attribute. The caption element has been formalized with HTML 3.0 figures and tables. The text should not be larger than the image and, when positioned above or below, of a similar width. To aid consistency the same alignment should be used for all captions in a document.

■ Text style

The font used to render text is browser dependent with the stalwart Times-Roman a common choice. The style can be changed for emphasis with underlining, italics and bold supported by the HTML 2.0 standard. Italics are useful where bold draws too much attention to a word, but it should not be overused in a document. Bold and italic can be combined for additional emphasis. Underlined text is harder to read and is generally avoided, as is the Netscape blinking text feature (pun intended). Fixed width fonts are useful for building tables, including indented code, and for emphasizing URLs or email addresses.

■ Images and multimedia

The decision to include images and other media depends on how much they will benefit the site and on the capacity of links both at the server and user end. Large in-line graphics can be particularly annoying, especially where no text alternative is offered. In general, images should fit within a browser window; exceptions can be made for maps and figures where detail would be obscured. This limits the width to about 400 pixels. Large images with lots of detail are also big and take longer to download. Many techniques have been developed to alleviate this problem.

GIF format files may be interlaced instead of displaying the image sequentially. An initial low-resolution image is displayed with the remainder built up over a number of passes. Not all browsers support this feature. HTML 3.0 and Netscape have introduced the height and width attributes. These aid rendering speed as there is no need to size an image before display and it also establishes the page layout so text doesn't jump about as images are downloaded.

Thumbnails show a small representation of the full image. Clicking a thumbnail hyperlink downloads a large, high-quality version of the same image. The height and width attributes may be used to stretch the thumbnail to the full image size. A combination of height, width and the Netscape LOWSRC attribute will automatically update a low-resolution image with its high-quality original:

```
<IMG LOWSRC=small.gif SRC=big.gif WIDTH=400 HEIGHT=250
ALT="The President">
```

The alternative text gives non-graphical browsers a description of the image. Where the image is used in conjunction with other text this may be unnecessary. The HTML 3.0 figure element offers more structure to the text description. When available use figures for image maps.

The size of an image reflects its importance in relation to the text. Different image dimensions on the same page build interest. Tabular data may be better presented and understood using graphs and charts. Images used in toolbars and logos should be consistent. A large home page logo can be resized using the height and width attributes for subordinate page banners. This has the advantage that when caching is used only the one file has to be downloaded.

▥ Bleeds

HTML 3.0 figures and tables can be positioned outside of the text margin, flush with the edge of the browser window. This is called a bleed. Bleeds enhance the impact of these elements. Movement can be added to a photograph by bleeding it to the edge of a page. This can be particularly effective if the background of the photograph has been cropped.

▥ Forms

Every form should have title and heading elements to identify its purpose. Instructions explaining how the form is to be completed can be given in a separate page. Surveys should make any rating scheme employed clear to participants, e.g. 1 – strongly disagree, 5 – strongly agree. Radio buttons may be clearer for this type of response.

Embedding a form in a table gives better positioning of fields, especially for order forms. Headers should identify the quantity, price and item number columns. If possible link the form to an on-line database allowing fields to be automatically updated. In this case the form may be generated from the same script which processes the data and a **form management** tool used. This can provide information such as stock counts and price before the final form is processed. Separate sections may be divided by horizontal rules and text fields should be large enough for input; if necessary they can be scrolled.

The old adage of 'be conservative in what you produce, liberal in what you accept' is especially applicable in the global Web marketplace. Don't enforce a particular address or telephone style where orders are accepted from many countries but remember to specify country names separately, a user may otherwise forget to include this information.

■ The details

 It's said that 'the devil is in the details' and nowhere is this more true than with electronically generated documents. All documents should be spell-checked and, depending on your competence with language, run through the grammar checker. This often produces interesting, if not always useful, insights. When writing this book one politically-correct grammar checker suggested the phrase 'I am a free non-gender specific individual' in place of 'I am a free man'. Remember that spellchecking won't find words which are correct but out of context, good examples being:

their, there, they're; to, two, too.

It's all *too* easy to mis-type these. As a final stage print the pages and get them proofread by another person. Small proofs are also good for examining the site as a whole. HTML compliance and hyperlinks can be checked with automated tools.

■ Designing the site

Pages should always be planned away from the computer although a thorough appreciation of the Web and the proposed site topology is necessary to avoid inappropriate design. The computer is a production tool and must not be allowed to dominate decisions. A fast way of working is to sketch initial ideas on paper. Designers can look at other sites and evaluate what looks good and works within the Web environment. It's usually quite easy to spot the sites which have been assembled by 'techies' or built by designers more familiar with print. The source for any page may be viewed to see exactly how it is coded.

It's worth experimenting with a number of small prototypes, user evaluation can then determine which ideas work best. Once the site is live a response form or email address is useful for garnering impressions but don't expect to be overwhelmed with user feedback. Certain ideas may not work on a particular type of browser which the designer never considered. If the documents comply with HTML 2.0 this should not happen. The server log files should also be monitored to see which areas are not explored.

■ Uniform Resource Locators

URL design is another neglected area. There's no point building a fantastic set of pages if the URL is hard to type or remember. The URL path consists of a hostname followed by a document path. If the document isn't specified a default may be served for that directory: `http://www.kimble.com` could return the file `default.htm`. Knowing the name of the company (Kimble Ltd) would allow users to guess the URL of the Web site.

Where a single machine supports a number of sites they are usually arranged as sub-directories under the root:

```
www.nemesis.com\
        kimble\
        widget\
         acme\
```

The URL for Kimble would then be: `http://www.nemesis.com/kimble/`, which is too long and obscure to be memorable.

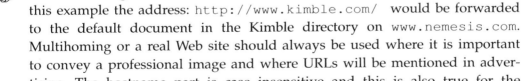 Multihoming enables a number of **virtual sites** to run on the same host. In this example the address: `http://www.kimble.com/` would be forwarded to the default document in the Kimble directory on `www.nemesis.com`. Multihoming or a real Web site should always be used where it is important to convey a professional image and where URLs will be mentioned in advertising. The hostname part is case insensitive and this is also true for the document path for servers running on Windows operating systems. As a general rule always specify the URL in lower case and use lower case where this matters.

■ Choosing a name

The www prefix has become a *de facto* standard for Web servers especially where a company also has email and runs other Internet services. All the different hostnames can be aliased to the same host with DNS giving an identical Internet address for each one. There is a great deal of controversy surrounding the distribution of hostnames with companies such as McDonalds claiming the existence of a trademark gives them the right to the same name on the Internet. The InterNIC, who manages the top level domains, has bowed to this pressure and won't register a name where a trademark is owned by another organization. As the registration process has in the past been free this is designed to prevent unscrupulous individuals who have been registering names in the hope of selling them to the trademark holders at a later date.

In general host names are 4 to 8 letters long. Shorter names are only registered in exceptional circumstance as they can be confused with the three-letter top-level domains and the two-letter country codes. Punctuation characters can be used but are confusing. All hosts live under a domain, for an international presence one of the top-level domains should be chosen:

.com	commercial companies
.org	other organizations
.edu	educational establishments, now restricted to large colleges
.net	network providers
.gov	US government facilities
.mil	US military installations

The .gov and .mil are restricted to the United States of America, and then to the government, asking for www.guns-ammo.mil will be met with a polite refusal. Hostnames using top-level domains can either be registered by an Internet Service Provider or directly with the InterNIC.

There are also national domains for each country. For the United Kingdom this is .uk and the registration process is governed by Eunet, based in England, who also manage the domain. A number of sub-domains have been established by Eunet for specific activities:

.co.uk	United Kingdom registered companies
.ac.uk	academic institutions
.gov.uk	UK government

Eunet do not apply exactly the same policies as the InterNIC or other countries. A country-specific domain will imply a geographic location and may be more appropriate for certain activities. Some supra-national domains exist; for instance, .eu represents the European Union.

■ Summary

- Good design guides the user to relevant information.
- Content and presentation are not separate issues, bad design will obscure content.
- Pages should be appropriate for the audience and material. Low-speed modem users will not appreciate the heavy use of graphics.
- Web design should take into account contrast, consistency and function.
- The context of each page should be clearly established to readers by the use of consistent headers and navigation links.
- Don't let the computer drive the design; work off-line.
- URLs should be short and relevant to the activity of the organization.

11 Marketing

An awareness of how to market the Web site should govern your every move. Now that may seem a bit extreme for the less commercially minded, but you must ask yourself the question: why bother to publish information which people are not going to read? And the more people who read and act upon it, the greater its value.

That's not to say that the approach to the market won't differ depending on the content that is offered. A non-commercial site giving details of French wines might need little planning and promotion. By providing comprehensive coverage of the subject matter it could establish itself by word of electronic mail as the place to go. The justification for the author would simply be a measure of the readership size. On the other hand a vintner `http://www.virtualvin.com` wishing to sell wine over the Internet would have to spend a lot more effort designing and promoting its Web site to achieve a return through increased sales. The exact approach taken is often referred to as the marketing mix and getting this mix right is one of the hardest tasks facing the Web builder.

Globalization

The Internet, and especially the Web, are leveling the global communications playing field, a trend which has its roots firmly in the personal computer revolution. To see how significant this is, it is necessary to look back to before industrialization. A couple of hundred years ago most people owned the tools of their chosen trade. There were few factories and even where labor was organized on this basis workers may still have used their own tools. The industrial revolution changed that – a great deal of capital was required to buy machinery and set up a factory. Workers became increasingly specialized, working at separate tasks on a production line. Henry Ford went as far as to state that the man who put the nut on the bolt was not the same as the one who put the bolt in the hole.

The personal computer has given the means of production back to the people with skill and ingenuity. Communications networks let groups of such people form virtual corporations to quickly exploit new situations and opportunities. Those same lines of communication provide individuals and small businesses with effective, low-cost access to the global market. A clever Internet campaign by a small outfit can have a more profound influence than the megabuck advertising budget of a large multinational corporation. This shift has occurred in tandem with a globalization of markets. Big companies are striving to establish brands with international recognition rather than targeting national markets with niche products.

There is a tendency to view the world as evolving slowly with progress continuing at a steady pace in a particular direction. Looking at the business environment many of the powerful industrial monoliths seem to have existed for ever. In reality, history is punctuated by a series of discontinuities. The Great Depression, the Second World War, oil shocks and the collapse of the Soviet Union. Each of these events changed markets – old companies withered and new ones sprang up to fill the void. Today's mainframe computer industry originated from the calculating engines used to crack German wartime ciphers. Similarly the microelectronics industry was fueled by the need to gain military advantage during the Cold War. The oil shocks led to the lingering deaths of Pan American and the gas guzzler.

The information age is another of history's grand events. It represents a shift in the way we work, make purchasing decisions, relax and talk. There will be both losers and winners. Some big companies are like the dinosaurs – entrenched in a comfortable corporate mentality they don't notice fleet-footed competitors moving into a new niche in the changing global marketplace. Geared for a bygone age their marketing strategy takes no account of the change in circumstance. It's like the old story of a board meeting in Detroit 20 years ago. The executives haggle over how much chromium the public want on the new model while down below the first few Japanese and European compacts negotiate the traffic.

A realization that 'everything we know is wrong', as the information hypemongers are fond of informing us, is only half the battle. We need some terms of reference in order to decide what is right. Where there are similarities with existing media we can draw inferences from the strategies employed. There is already a wealth of experience, much of it readily available on Web sites. However, caution is in order. The environment is evolving so rapidly that today's winning ideas may become tomorrow's lead balloons. The mentality of continuous change must be built into the core of any Web marketing strategy.

Web builders are faced by two marketing problems. Firstly they must convince the sponsoring organization that the Web is a viable mechanism to achieve the stated aims and secondly they must then market the site to the wider world. This is as true for a single person as it is for a large company. Convincing yourself that a Web site is a good idea is the easiest option, but the same criteria should apply.

■ What they won't tell you on Madison Avenue

Don't get me wrong, the best marketing people work in the world's advertising agencies but what they really excel at is marketing themselves. The marketplace is littered with expensive schemes which failed in one important aspect, increased business. Campaigns such as 'Where's the Beef?' are better remembered for their effect on a lightweight US Presidential challenger than hamburger sales. Even Chiat Day's seminal '1984' failed to stop the IBM PC steamroller, although that had as much to do with Apple's inability to capitalize on opportunities. Okay, so the account manager and a few execs from the sponsoring company got to fly to Cannes to pick up an award, but is that really a measure of success?

A great deal of science has been developed to support the marketing concept. Marketeers talk about social–psychological models and lifestyle choices, reference groups and behavior theories. Many of these concepts have been devised after extensive research but marketing remains an inexact science, as the many failures have shown. After all the data has been gathered the right combination is still based on guesswork and hunches. Without that seat-of-the-pants instinct marketing departments might as well consult the horoscope to decide which set of theories to follow. The science and statistics are useful as a back-up to convince hard-nosed business directors that they are making the correct decision.

The Web is a new game. It's very different from the other media. Existing theories on advertising and marketplace must be adapted and evolved. To some extent it is an advantage not being too deeply steeped in the accepted wisdom. With an understanding of the basics we can all play the Web marketing guru.

Many people confuse advertising with marketing. Advertising is just one important component of a successful marketing strategy. The basic tenets of marketing are the four Ps and remain as true for the Web as for any other area.

- **Product**: the product might be some existing good or service or it could be an entirely new concept taking advantage of economies offered by global networking. A site must be informative and of immediate interest to users. The aim is to get it 'bookmarked' to ensure continued visits and new business by referral. There is so much novel and interesting material out there that the competition for repeat business is fierce. Web users can be thought of as being more like cattle than surfers, continually migrating to newer and greener pastures.

- **Price**: users have been reared on a diet of free information and software. It's a dangerous attitude for commercial operators to automatically dismiss what is freely available as low quality. Users must find a compelling reason to pay for information which they may find elsewhere for free. If you are selling an existing product then the price may have already been established, but does it look competitive in the global marketplace? Should it differ from country to country to reflect different local costs? Should the on-line version of a magazine charge an access fee, bearing in mind that there are no print costs and the readers pick up the distribution charges. Organizations commissioning Web sites have also come to believe that the Web is, if not free, at least cheap. In reality it is often harder to successfully promote a product on the Web than on existing media.

  Web consultants have particular difficulties with price. Agencies working in traditional media get a commission on all the space they buy and this pays for the creative effort. Space in journals and on television is often reserved by agencies in advance of particular requirements. Customers don't get a reduction by going direct and so it is more expensive to do the work in-house. This strategy isn't an option for Web consultants where the cost of buying space is very small compared to the production costs. It usually appears cheaper for businesses to do the work themselves.

- **Place**: the Web site must be easy to locate. This means registering it with listing servers such as Yahoo and search engines like Lycos. The site should become part of a Web of related information rather than existing as a gossamer strand. This will mean trading links with other sites and the more relevant the link, the greater its value.
- **Promotion**: the site may be promoted by the placement of links from other areas and from Internet news announcements. There may be opportunities to follow up other news items with information about the site, but this shouldn't be blatant plugging. Existing promotional material and advertising can also carry the address of the site. A press release should be sent to relevant trade journals and many technology-related papers carry lists of interesting URLs.

Another marketing methodology is AIDAS: Attention, Interest, Desire, Action, Satisfaction. Like the proverbial horse, getting people to the site is only half the battle, it must be both interesting and designed so that the information is easy to locate. Remember that users are paying to view the material in the form of phone and on-line charges. The aim is to be given as much of that on-line time as possible and to get repeat visits. At any point another site is only a mouse click away.

With so many similar Web sites competing for attention users are looking for something different. For instance, a dictionary publisher won't get many visitors by offering a message from the CEO and a price list of the latest range. Put a thesaurus on-line and the number of accesses will soar. The site must stimulate interest beyond that of its competitors including the other media. As a general rule content is king, but content must remain relevant and current.

In general terms television and magazine advertising doesn't translate to the Web without introducing interminable delays, there just isn't the bandwidth. Think about it, TV viewers wouldn't tolerate a minute of blank screen in between advertisements, although they might wait if there is an interesting half-hour documentary. Web sites are better employed in increasing awareness of products and organizations as part of an integrated marketing strategy. With the rise of consumerism today's buyer is less likely to be convinced by simple advertising messages. Instead, technical information and reviews are gathered in an attempt to make an informed choice. A Web site can provide buyers with that information and feature links to on-line reviews and related data. It also provides a focus for customer feedback. Web sites offer a convenient way to support and help clients.

■ New directions

The Web's unique selling point (USP) is that it offers a low-cost, interactive, global communications mechanism. It is perfectly feasible for a small business or an individual to reach a worldwide audience without the huge advertising budget of a multinational corporation. Examples abound of small firms in the backwoods suddenly finding they have a ready market in Japan. The Net also provides a global delivery mechanism for software, be that information, computer programs or, in the case of the Internet Underground Music Archive (IUMA), music.

IUMA `http://www.iuma.com` have used both the promotional and delivery aspects of the Net to exploit a market segment which the large record labels are unable, or unwilling, to satisfy. These companies are interested in selling billions of discs, leaving small bands to press their own CDs and sell them to the limited audience who attend gigs. IUMA promote these bands over the Web and allow users to download music, for a fee. The economies of this mechanism mean that a band will receive a greater percentage of that fee than they would from a large label. The main limitations are bandwidth, a three-minute audio clip sampled at CD quality can take ten minutes to download over a modem. These problems have lead the IUMA into other fields and they are currently engaged in promoting their bands to the traditional record companies, a case of the tail wagging the dog.

■ Competition

 The Web provides further examples of businesses which have been able to utilize its unique characteristics to develop or create new markets. Other areas remain to be identified and exploited. Market segments can be analyzed using search engines such as Yahoo or Lycos. These reveal the extent and nature of competition. In some areas this competition is fierce, especially in the provision of information services where many free sources already exist. Pricing depends not only on costs but on the going rate. Information servers must add value by offering higher quality information or better organization. As Drucker points out 'it is the customer who determines what a business is . . . [by their] willingness to pay for goods and services'.

■ Demographics

With so much hype about the Web it's easy to forget that the audience is still relatively small and thinly spread. The Internet currently boasts about 40 million users but it is estimated that only a fifth use the Web on a regular basis. Eight million potential customers sounds like a lot, but a company offering a local service may find that only a few users are connected within its catchment area. The evening paper may prove to be a better advertising channel.

The demographics of this group are interesting, being predominantly young men with higher than average incomes. This may provide a critical mass for certain sectors. A case in point is job advertising, which currently works for hi-tech industries with a national or international marketplace. However, it is certainly too early to look for car mechanics amongst Web users.

The widespread availability of Internet access is slowly changing the demographics of Internet users. The GVU survey `http://www.cc.gatech.edu/gvu/user_surveys/User_Survey_Home.html` suggests that, although 82% of users are currently male, parity between the sexes may occur sometime in 1997. The GVU survey also found the average age of their sample to be 35 years, with no significance difference between men and women.

Large companies have gone in search of that elusive 25–35 age group on the Web. These consumers have been dubbed 'the Twirties' (twenties/thirties) and are thought to be cynical about traditional marketing approaches; being technically aware they are particularly hard to target. BMW have reputedly spent $750,000 on their Web site with a prestigious agency, although it remains to be seen if they will see a return. To a certain extent it doesn't matter to BMW, the very act of spending that sum is newsworthy. The message is in the medium, in this case a luxury car manufacturer spending (comparatively) enormous amounts on Net advertising.

■ Publicity

Web sites can be launched in traditional ways, for example by advertising in the old media and sending press releases to news organizations. News organizations largely rely on press releases for their output. The Web marketeer should prepare a press release and send it to all relevant groups followed up by a call to the news editor. To make news the site must have an interesting angle, perhaps showing how technology will make all our lives easier. Craft a press release with this in mind.

Internet news and mailing lists are also a good way to publicize the site. The Usenet group `comp.infosystems.announce` should be the first port of call. The charter of other groups and mailing lists should be read to see if a post is appropriate. A few days lurking to get the gist of **threads** and the feel of the group is also a good idea. Follow-ups to requests for related information are generally acceptable but blatant puffery and excessive cross-posting (known as spamming) will invoke the wrath of the Net community. The URL of the site may be included in the signature files of site personnel. This will be included at the end of any email or Usenet postings.

Depending on the available resources an individual should be assigned to monitor the mailing lists and net news. Companies can build up a good reputation by answering questions about their own or related products, not an easy task. In the mid-1980s a colleague of mine could read every post in the several hundred news groups that existed then. Nowadays it would take a whole team to monitor each and every message on the Internet. There is a similar problem with traditional media and clipping services have evolved to supply the need for market information. These companies keep a profile of the organization that employs them, culling and editing relevant stories in the day's press and magazines. A news filtering service fulfills a similar rôle on the net. Users enter a profile consisting of keywords and the service will forward any articles it sees by electronic mail. The service may cover Usenet news, email and possibly Web sites. The filter program may search only the subject line or the contents of the message. This allows a company to monitor articles about its own or related activities on the Internet without having to read large amounts of news. The Stanford SIFT `http://sift.stanford.edu/` service is a popular news filter.

 The Internet is a public forum. Companies must be prepared for users to discuss negative aspects of their products. A certain degree of anonymity means that Usenet users are unreserved with criticism, often to the point of being libelous. It's important to be indulgent to avoid alienating potential allies in these arguments. It is better to politely defend or rebuke by email than to enter into a public slanging match. Many net ranters are actually quite reasonable and will happily post a retraction where an error has been made. Care should be taken with the wording of email as this may be copied to Usenet news, a clear breach of netiquette by the perpetrator but potentially embarrassing nonetheless.

The effect of a single bad news article or message on the Internet is less than one in the traditional press. Where the criticism is harsh or unjustified users will jump to defend a product or service. However, the old adage of 'lose one customer, lose ten more' can turn into 'lose one, lose the world' where legitimate complaints are left unaddressed.

A public Web site should form part of a whole Internet strategy. Handle inquiries interactively rather than directing them to freephone or surface (snail) mail addresses. Freephone numbers are difficult to access outside the home country. Establish a mailing list server to offer users a forum for discussion, when traffic increases on this list create a new Usenet news group. When this is placed under the existing Usenet hierarchy a defined set-up procedure must be followed. Information about the news system can be found under the news.* groups.

Many sites have used competitions and similar promotions to attract users. These range from the simple 'first IP address out of the hat' approach to quizzes which require the user to visit each page on the site. Companies wishing to target a certain audience may also include questions to exclude competition groupies. Contests may be used to gather data for direct sales, however, it is advisable to inform users if this will happen. Holding information about individuals on computer can infringe privacy laws in some countries. Competition law is usually quite strong to prevent fraud and bogus events. Web sites are no exceptions to these rules.

 Web builders may find many related sites using search tools or through general exploration. These sites may be prepared to add or exchange links where they feel the information is beneficial and relevant. Provide such sites with a small anchor graphic to establish a Web personality.

■ Paying for links

Web sites which have built a substantial readership are now trying to capitalize on their success through sponsorship deals or by selling links. Sponsorship involves placing information or advertorial about the sponsoring company on various pages. It's a similar approach to the one adopted by the original soap operas. The advantage is exclusive coverage during the sponsoring period. An indirect benefit is that a sponsored site has money to invest to remain interesting thereby attracting further users.

Other sites may feel that their readership is of such quality or so large that they can charge for links. They often use traditional forms of promotion to attract and sustain readership and will quote their 'hit' rate and demographics as a justification for pricing. While it can be assumed (and surveys back up this impression) that a Web audience is young, reasonably well off and predominantly male, their interest in your site cannot be guaranteed. The readership of the PGA Golf Tour pages may have little motivation for following a link to the Rockie Mountain Ski Guide or worse the Widget and Sprocket sales line, but they may be very interested to find where they can buy Gary Player's new carbon–kevlar putter.

 Hit counts are very misleading. This figure is a measure of the resources accessed over a given period. Where a page features five images it will count six hits (five graphics plus one page). The hit count should relate to the page on which the link is being offered, not the overall rate for the site. It's a bit like the difference between being on the back cover of a magazine and a quarter page advert tucked away inside. Ask the site for last month's log file, especially if they can provide this in an easy-to-digest form showing new hosts and unique hosts. The domains of visitors gives some interesting demographic information, .edu are visits from colleges, .com companies, .ac.uk is a United Kingdom academic user.

Some companies have adopted the standard 'cost per thousand impressions' pricing structure and have developed quite complex formulas to translate their hit rate into a quantifiable price structure. These involve estimating the average number of hits per page and assigning a cost on repeat impressions, either from visits within the site or return trips at a later date. Although there is justification for this approach it is not the exact science the formulas and charts would imply. In particular, repeat visits over a very short period should count as a single hit as they may be due to the architecture of the site rather than a user's desire to revisit a particular page.

Whenever a link is taken it should be monitored very closely. The referer information (HTTP_REFERER) shows how users arrive at a site. If the server doesn't generate this data automatically it can be added to a custom log file by using a CGI script for the home page. Alternatively a unique identifier can be added to the query field of the link URL. Traditional (print/TV) advertising channels are harder to monitor without using distinct URLs and this goes against the concept of brand recognition.

The quality of the customers should be evaluated. The site may receive 18,000 users per month through one link but only 3,000 from another. However, the lower volume link may provide a quality audience that spends more time on the site.

The Web provides unique feedback about its users. Unlike print media it is possible to see if a user has visited a particular page. Special pages may be presented to users from certain Internet domains. As an example, those arriving from the America On-Line proxy server may see offers exclusive to AOL users or be referred to further local information on the AOL system.

Remember that electronic mail to people outside of the Internet should avoid using MIME.

▓ Commerce

The potential of the Web as a delivery mechanism for the sale of both products and services will only be realized with a secure mechanism for on-line funds transfer. The Internet is fundamentally insecure and is significantly worse than the public telephone system. Internet messages must pass through a number of hosts to reach their destination. The security of any of these may have been compromised. Once breached, hackers may be able to run software known as a **packet sniffer**, this examines the first few bytes of every packet for useful information such as credit card numbers.

The risk of a wily hacker intercepting any one credit card transaction is very small; the banks are concerned about the scale of the overall loss. Inviting users to send credit card details over the Internet unencrypted may lead to the Web site losing its merchant status with the bank.

There are a couple of solutions to this problem. The first is to encrypt credit card and other personal information. The Secure Sockets Layer (SSL) uses the RSA encryption algorithm to provide secure communications for any Internet service that uses the sockets library. SSL provides a solution for transactions within the United States where the secure 48-bit keys required by banks are used. Unfortunately the security algorithm is classed as munitions by the US government and the export version features a weaker 40-bit key. Data encrypted with this export version has already been cracked by a French cypherpunk using standard hardware. There is the additional problem that certain countries, including France, explicitly ban the transmission of encrypted messages. Secure HTTP is similar to SSL but is only applied to the HyperText Transfer Protocol.

As has been mentioned, the risk of interception en route is minimal. A greater problem lies with the server machine itself. Often credit card details are stored on-line in an unencrypted form. Cracking a single card number may take a few days, breaking into Internet hosts running Web servers may yield thousands of card numbers and personal details, a more lucrative proposition. Personal information should either be stored off-line or encrypted with a strong cypher.

Once compromised, the cyberthief can use the credit card information for a number of purchases limited only by certain restrictions placed on the card by the bank. Owners and merchants may be liable for a proportion of the lost funds. Credit cards are also inefficient for the transfer of small amounts. A future Web scenario may see certain sites paying users to visit, this requires the transfer of very small sums, maybe fractions of a cent (or ecu for Europeans). Digital cash solves both these problems by offering a virtual currency. Instead of providing an account code, as is the case with credit cards, virtual cash uses a key to represent a fixed sum of money. The key can only be used once, using it twice will raise an error with the bank. Further techniques are employed to prevent the key being intercepted en route and used for a different transaction. These involve identifier stamping and encryption with the exchange of public keys to verify authenticity. Most of the current proposals use U.S. dollars and few are recognized by the licensing authorities as banks.

When doing business over the Internet there is the problem of trust. Do you know if `gucci.co.it` will really supply tailor-made shoes or will they just steal your credit card details? The same problem exists for mail order operations but the Internet makes detection and prosecution more difficult, especially where the site is beyond the jurisdiction of the user's home country.

Many groups have been established to investigate and promote commerce on the Internet but a single set of standards has yet to be established. The whole area may simply be awaiting the involvement of some major players. This could take the form of Microsoft and VISA who have proposed Secure Transaction Technology (STT). A combination of the world's biggest software and credit card companies may make this the on-line payment system of choice.

■ Summary

- The Web offers small organizations a way of promoting themselves globally.
- Marketing is more than just advertising and promotion, it covers pricing, product and placement.
- Before starting the site ask some important questions. What Net benefit does the site bring? What resources are available to develop the site? What is the intended audience and will they pay for the product?
- Use the available Web search engines to evaluate competition.
- Keep abreast of the latest developments and technology by reading newsgroups and subscribing to mailing lists.
- Use a filtering service to track product information.

- Exchange links with related sites.
- Use the server log files to monitor the effectiveness of paid links and sponsorship.
- Integrate the Web site into the overall marketing campaign.
- Build a Net strategy by handling user requests through HTML forms and electronic mail.
- Secure electronic transactions and ensure that the Web site is also safe from attack.

12 | Epilog – new directions

The popularity of the Web has brought it to the attention of the world's computer manufacturers. Recent developments in offering **virtual reality** and **executable content** have been led by Silicon Graphics and Sun Microsystems. The fruits of these respective efforts have resulted in the Virtual Reality Modeling Language (VRML) and **Java**. Both technologies are being adopted by other leading players including Netscape.

This chapter introduces VRML and Java and presents some sample applications. It is not intended as a development guide but rather to give users the flavor of these exciting topics.

Virtual reality

People can navigate better around a three-dimensional (3D) rather than a two-dimensional (2D) world. A typical office is cluttered with three-dimensional objects, a filing cabinet can be opened to reveal other objects such as project reports or last week's sandwiches. The brain uses stereo vision to take a pair of 2D images and produce its own internal 3D representation of the world. Humans are very sensitive to depth – if two matchsticks are held at arms length and one is moved closer, the difference in distance is evident after just one match thickness of movement. The Windows, Icons, Mouse desktop metaphor is an attempt to model the 3D world (a desktop) onto a flat VDU screen and HTML presents a similar 2D view.

Large hypertext documents are difficult to navigate because the brain is poor at organizing complex hierarchies of information. Navigating around a 3D world is easier because it's more familiar and we remember signposts and features seen en route. One of the uses of graphics in Web documents is to provide these visual mnemonics.

The 1994 Geneva Web Conference addressed itself to this problem. Work commenced on a platform-independent virtual reality modeling language. The proposal, VRML, defines a world (**Home Space**) as a data set of 3D objects integrated within the Web paradigm. Strolling around a VRML house the user might spot a ghetto blaster and clicking the play button could download an MPEG file with some classical music. Touching a report marked 'Top Secret' lying on a desk may take the user to the CIA World Fact Book, an HTML document at the CIA's Web site.

VRML viewers are already available. The user interface still uses the VDU and mouse but objects are rendered as 3D shapes using perspective and lighting to show depth. As the format describes these objects as a set of points rather than using digitized images, it is reasonably compact. A small VRML world such as the house mentioned above may occupy as little as 200,000 bytes. Virtual reality is already being used in other sectors of computing such as computer aided design and tools are being developed to convert existing data to VRML formats.

VRML is still a way off the virtual reality database featured in the movie *Disclosure*. Web surfers won't be fighting over who got to the cyberdrinks machine first for a little while yet. The development of VRML does open a whole range of possibilities. The Internet itself could be modeled as a virtual world, a scenario foreseen by William Gibson in his 1980s Cyberpunk novels.

■ The VRML language

The Web community is impatient: rather than develop its own standards VRML is based on a subset of Silicon Graphic's (SGI) **Open Inventor** file format. It is not an extension to HTML – this would have slowed up the whole development process – instead it is a separate format with its own external viewing software. A VRML world is downloaded as a single file and, apart from hyperlinks to other resources, may be explored off-line. One aim has been to make the language compact and extraneous baggage from Open Inventor has been jettisoned. Only the commonly used subset has been employed for VRML, making it easier to implement viewing software, with less chance of incompatibility.

Real-world scenes can be thought of as a hierarchy. A garden may contain trees, shrubs, sheds and a house. The house contains further objects which exist, unless you are an ostrich, even though they are invisible. Entering the house reveals a whole new hierarchy of rooms, storage cupboards and furniture. In much the same way VRML uses a hierarchy to arrange its objects into structures called **scene graphs**.

A VRML file begins with the line:

```
#VRML V1.0 ASCII
```

This identifies both the language and version. The '#' character indicates the start of a comment. Servers may choose to strip comments and white space before the file is transmitted. After the header, the file contains exactly one VRML **node**, this is the root of the hierarchy and may contain other nodes. A node is an object which is useful for performing 3D graphics. Nodes fall into the categories of **shape**, **property** and **group**. Shapes are the components of the scene, VRML predefines `cone`, `cube`, `cylinder` and `sphere`. Properties have some effect on the components, a `material` can specify the surface texture of a shape. Some objects fall into both of these categories. A light source has both a position and properties which affect surrounding objects. A node that contains child nodes is called a **group**.

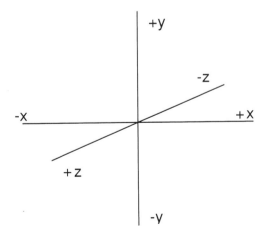

Figure 12.1 The VRML coordinate system

Scene graphs support the idea of state, nodes earlier in the scene affect those which appear later. A `material` node will change later shape nodes, a `separator` can be used to limit this scope. VRML uses the coordinate system shown in Figure 12.1.

The characteristics of any node can be changed by setting fields. For instance, the dimensions of a cuboid can be specified as follows:

```
#VRML V1.0 ascii
Cube { width 1 height 2 depth 0.5 }
```

This is a simple VRML world. If the code is saved to a file with extension `.WRL` it can be opened with a suitable VRML viewer such as Webspace. A large gray slab, a bit like a downtown office block, is displayed in the center of the window. The user can fly around this object by manipulating the control stick.

The position, rotation and appearance of an object can be altered by adding property nodes before it in the hierarchy. The user's view of the scene can be changed by specifying different **cameras** and **lighting**:

```
#VRML V1.0 ascii

DirectionalLight {
    direction 0 0 -1.5        # shine light towards the scene
}

PerspectiveCamera {          # position camera and rotate to cube
    position -9.2 2 6.5
    orientation -0.1352 -0.9831 -0.1233 1.1417
    focalDistance 6.8
}

Material {
    diffuseColor 0.8 0.2 0 # red/orange
}

  Transform {                # position and rotate cube
    translation -2.4 0 1
    rotation 0 1 0.5 .5
}

Cube { width 2 height 4 depth 1.2 }
```

The `DirectionalLight` fields gives the coordinates that the light source shines towards. This camera is located off to the left foreground slightly above

Figure 12.2 Cube and cylinder rendered by Webspace

the horizontal plane and has been rotated to look at the cube. The focalDistance sets the perspective of the scene. Objects within the scene are defined not only in terms of their dimensions but by their appearance and location with respect to the origin. The material and transform nodes alter these parameters for all subsequent nodes in the scene. Separators are used to limit the action of these properties.

```
#VRML V1.0 ascii

Separator {
   Separator { # Blue Cylinder
      Material {
         diffuseColor 0 0 1
      }
      Translation { translation 2 0 0 )
   Cylinder { radius 1.25 height 2.5 }
```

```
      }
Separator { # Red Cube
   Material {
         diffuseColor 1 0 0
   }

   Transform {
         translation -2 .4 .2
         rotation 0 1 1 .75
   }
   Cube { }
}
}
```

Cameras and lighting may be placed within separators. There can be many such nodes within a single VRML scene. For instance, walking from the garden into a house may change both the user's perspective and the lighting. VRML is low level in its description of shape objects, more complex polyhedrons are built from a combination of basic shapes or described by specifying the coordinates of their faces. It's likely that many libraries of shapes will be created.

Hyperlinks are not part of the original Open Inventor language but have been added to VRML:

```
Separator {
   Translation ( translation 0 1 0 }

   WWWAnchor { # about Saturn
      name "http://www.greenwich.org/planets/saturn.htm"
   }

   WWWInline {
      name "http://www.cosmos.com/vrml/saturn.wrl"
   }
}
```

This example will pull in the description of the Planet Saturn from a remote site after having first positioned it on the screen. The object is also linked back to a text description of the planet.

▪ Configuring a VRML viewer

Although VRML worlds can be explored off-line using the viewer as a stand-alone application, hyperlinks cannot be followed. The VRML viewer is designed to run in tandem with a Web browser, this handles the retrieval of VRML files and displays other resources. For example, the Webspace viewer can communicate with the Mosaic or Netscape browser using OLE. As hyperlink anchors are encountered they are passed back to the browser which fetches and displays the resource.

A VRML viewer must be configured as a helper application for the MIME: `x-world/x-vrml` type and subtype. The file extension is `.WRL` and this should launch the viewer. Many VRML files are first compressed with the GNU utility `GZIP`. This must also be configured using: `application/x-gzip` for the MIME type and `.GZ` as the file extension. The helper application is `GNUZIP.EXE`, which unpacks the file.

That's a brief look at writing VRML. VRML worlds are tedious to build by hand. The future lies in creating tools to rapidly generate new worlds or convert existing three-dimensional data sets. There are already some examples on the Web where topological information is used to render landscapes on demand, which the user can download and explore.

▪ Java

The Web can deliver any data format to a browser, including programs to be executed locally by the client. An administrator can configure a server to return a content type for scripts which will cause them to be executed locally. For instance Perl files could generate:

```
.pl  application/x-perl
```

and the browser may pass the returned data directly to the Perl interpreter. Of course, this relies on agreement between client and server and is dangerous because malicious users can deliver programs to delete or corrupt the local system. It's only practical when used within a closed and well regulated environment.

An advantage of running programs locally as opposed to using a CGI script is performance. Every time a user submits data a connection must be made across the Internet. This is undesirable when operations like simple input checking are required. A local script is also a good place to hold state variables.

Gopher —————┐   ┌———— SMTP
    FTP ————┐   ┌———— WAIS
  HTML ——┐   ┌———— NNTP

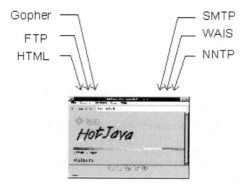

Figure 12.3   HotJava

Sun has introduced a new concept in browsers called HotJava. HotJava directly supports the Java programming language. Java is an object-oriented programming language similar to C++. Using the Java object library is not dissimilar to programming with the Microsoft Foundation Classes (MFC). The HotJava browser can interpret Java programs directly, this offers Web designers the possibility of including executable content within Web documents. This can be as trivial as a dancing blob in the middle of a page, like Sun's own Duke, or as extensive as a spreadsheet.

Java is an interpreted language; a Java program is compiled into an intermediate byte code which can be downloaded and interpreted by the HotJava browser. The browser provides a secure and defined environment for running Java code, guarding against malicious programs.

The HotJava browser is itself written in the Java language. It unbundles the browser from knowledge about specific Internet protocols, data types and navigation. New modules, called applets, can be added dynamically to the browser across the network and because they are interpreted there are no worries about language, CPU type and local application support. For speed, the Java interpreter turns the byte codes into native machine code.

The latest version of Java is available for free from Sun. It's a huge 4.5-megabyte ZIP archive and requires at least 11 megabytes of disk space when installed. It runs on both '95 and NT. Version 2.0 of the Netscape browser also supports Java and is available for '95.

To support Java applets HTML has been extended with the APPLET element; this may become a container class in the HTML 3.0 definition or be subsumed into FIG. This element references a Java application:

```
<APPLET CODE="ClassName"
  SRC="URL"
  ALIGN="Alignment"
  WIDTH="width in pixels"
  HEIGHT="height in pixels"
  AppSpecificAttributes="value">
```

Only the code attribute need be specified; Java will look for the applet in the `classes` sub-directory under the HTML document's current directory. A simple HTML file to call a HelloWorld applet is:

```
<HTML>
<HEAD>
<TITLE>A Simple Applet</TITLE>
</HEAD>
<BODY>
Here is a simple applet:
<APPLET CODE="HelloWorld">
</BODY>
</HTML>
```

Figure 12.4   Java HTML document

The applet source is called HelloWorld.java, and can be created in Notepad:

```
import browser.Applet;
import awt.Graphics;

class HelloWorld extends Applet {
  public void init() {
    resize(150, 25);
  }
  public void paint(Graphics g) {
    g.drawString("Bonjour le monde!", 50, 25);
  }
}
```

Figure 12.5   A Java applet

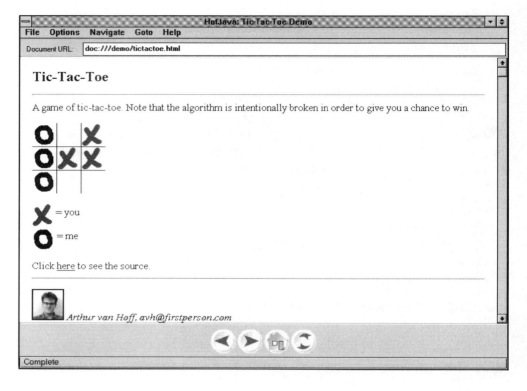

Figure 12.6 Tic-tac-toe with Java

This simple applet is taken straight from the Java programming manual but demonstrates the basic structure of a Java program. A subclass of the applet class is created, this extends the functionality of the `init` and `paint` methods. `Init` is called when the HelloWorld class is created, `paint` is called whenever a redraw event occurs, such as the window being uncovered. This is a bit like the MFC `CFrameWnd` class; declaring an instance of that class results in the initialization constructor being called and the window is redrawn when a *Paint* message is received.

A Java applet is compiled into the intermediate byte code:

```
javac HelloWorld.java
```

This creates a file with extension `.class`; this code can be downloaded by the browser and run. Java doesn't require any special Web server support.

When the HTML document in Figure 12.4 is loaded by HotJava it prints 'here is a simple applet' and then runs the applet shown in Figure 12.5. This displays 'Bonjour le monde!' Far more complex programs can be built using Java, including spreadsheets and word processors. Sun hopes that this will become the standard mechanism for accessing this class of application. Rather than buying software which sits idle on the hard disk for much of its life users will, for a small fee, download the latest version of an application on demand. This model will require faster networks, a billing mechanism and a willingness for management to let staff have control over software budgets. The last point is probably the greatest objection to be overcome.

Sun support their own Solaris operating system as well as '95 and NT. The source code is freely available and many third parties are working on Java ports.

▓ Summary

- VRML offers the possibility of modeling virtual worlds within the Web environment.
- VRML was developed from Silicon Graphic's Open Inventor file format.
- VRML worlds are compact, being represented by a set of data points rather than bitmap images.
- A VRML description forms a hierarchy of objects called a scene graph.
- Java is an object-oriented interpreted programming language developed by Sun Microsystems.
- HotJava is a Web browser, written in Java, which can execute graphical programs written in Java.
- Java programs, called applets, offer executable content to Web page designers.
- Java-aware browsers (including HotJava and Netscape 2.0) can dynamically extend their own functionality by downloading Java applets.
- Java browsers are available for '95, NT, Macintosh and UNIX systems.

Appendix A

ISO 8859-1 (Latin-1) character set

No computer book would be complete without an ASCII table in the back. This one shows the ISO Latin-1 character set used by HTML. It provides characters for most European languages, certain dialects of Gaelic excluded. Characters above 127 should use an HTML entity, either the symbol or &#nnn; where nnn is replaced by the corresponding decimal value. This is for compatibility with 7-bit ASCII systems. Entities are used for certain characters below 128 where they could be confused with special characters in a string.

There is no trademark ™ symbol in this set. This can be encoded by the entity ™ but this is non-standard and will only work on some browsers. Future versions of HTML will define a character set parameter to support other languages such as Arabic, Cyrillic and Japanese. Many operating systems provide this support through the 16-bit Unicode character set. The Netscape browsers already support Japanese Kanji characters.

Description	Decimal	Hex	HTML entity
	0–8		Unused
TAB	9	9	&#09;
Linefeed	10	a	&#10;
	11–31		Unused
Space	32	20	&#32;
!	33	21	
"	34	22	&quot;
#	35	23	
$	36	24	
%	37	25	
&	38	26	&amp;
'	39	27	
(	40	28	
)	41		
*	42	2a	
+	43	2b	
,	44	2c	
-	45	2d	
.	46	2e	
/	47	2f	
	48–57	30–39	Digits 0–9
:	58	3a	
;	59	3b	
<	60	3c	
=	61	3d	
>	62	3e	
?	63	3f	
@	64	40	
	65–90	41–5a	Letters A–Z
[	91	5b	
\	92	5c	
]	93	5d	
^	94	5e	
-	95	5f	
`	96	60	
	97–122	61–7a	Letters a–z
<	123	7b	
		124	7c	

Description	Decimal	Hex	HTML entity
}	125	7d	
~	126	7e	
	127–160	7f–a0	Unused
¡	161	a1	
¢	162	a2	
£	163	a3	
¤	164	a4	
¥	165	a5	
¦	166	a6	
§	167	a7	
¨	168	a8	
©	169	a9	
ª	170	aa	
«	171	ab	
¬	172	ac	
-	173	ad	
®	174	ae	
¯	175	af	
°	176	b0	
±	177	b1	
²	178	b2	
³	179	b3	
´	180	b4	
µ	181	b5	
¶	182	b6	
·	183	b7	
¸	184	b8	
¹	185	b9	
º	186	ba	
»	187	bb	
¼	188	bc	
½	189	bd	
¾	190	be	
¿	191	bf	
À	192	c0	&Agrave;
Á	193	c1	&Aacute;
Â	194	c2	&Acirc;
Ã	195	c3	&Atilde;

Description	Decimal	Hex	HTML entity
Ä	196	c4	&Auml;
Å	197	c5	&Aring;
Æ	198	c6	&AElig;
Ç	199	c7	&Ccedil;
È	200	c8	&Egrave;
É	201	c9	&Eacute;
Ê	202	ca	&Ecirc;
Ë	203	cb	&Euml;
Ì	204	cc	&Igrave;
Í	205	cd	&Iacute;
Î	206	ce	&Icirc;
Ï	207	cf	&Iuml;
Ð	208	d0	-
Ñ	209	d1	&Ntilde;
Ò	210	d2	&Ograve;
Ó	211	d3	&Oacute;
Ô	212	d4	&Ocirc;
Õ	213	d5	&Otilde;
Ö	214	d6	&Ouml;
×	215	d7	-
Ø	216	d8	&Oslash;
Ù	217	d9	&Ugrave;
Ú	218	da	&Uacute;
Û	219	db	&Ucirc;
Ü	220	dc	&Uuml;
Ý	221	dd	&Yacute;
þ	222	de	&Thorn;
ß	223	df	&szlig;
à	224	e0	&agrave;
á	225	e1	&aacute;
â	226	e2	&acirc;
ã	227	e3	&atilde;
ä	228	e4	&auml;
å	229	e5	&aring;
æ	230	e6	&aelig;
ç	231	e7	&ccedil;
è	232	e8	&egrave;
é	233	e9	&eacute;

Description	Decimal	Hex	HTML entity
ê	234	ea	&ecirc;
ë	235	eb	&euml;
ì	236	ec	&igrave;
í	237	ed	&iacute;
î	238	ee	&icirc;
ï	239	ef	&iuml;
ð	240	f0	&eth;
ñ	241	f1	&ntilde;
ò	242	f2	&ograve;
ó	243	f3	&oacute;
ô	244	f4	&ocirc;
õ	245	f5	&otilde;
ö	246	f6	&ouml;
÷	247	f7	
ø	248	f8	&oslash;
ù	249	f9	&ugrave;
ú	250	fa	&uacute;
û	251	fb	&ucirc;
ü	252	fc	&uuml;
ý	253	fd	&yacute;
þ	254	fe	&thorn;
ÿ	255	ff	&yuml;

Appendix B

Web MIME media types

MIME type/subtype	Windows file extension	Description
application/cybercash		electronic money
application/msword	DOC	Microsoft Word
application/octet-stream		binary data
application/pdf	PDF	Adobe Portable Document Format
application/postscript	PS, EPS, AI	Postscript
application/rtf	RTF	Microsoft Rich Text Format
application/wordperfect51	DOC, WP	Word Perfect
application/x-gzip	GZ	GNU GZIP compressed data
application/x-tar	TAR	UNIX tape archive
application/zip	ZIP	ZIP compressed archive
audio/basic	AU, SND	Sun/NeXT muLaw sound format
image/gif	GIF	CompuServe GIF
image/jpeg	JPG, JIF, JPEG, JFIF	JPEG image
image/tiff	TIF, TIFF	TIFF
text/html	HTM, HTML	HyperText Markup Language

MIME type/subtype	Windows file extension	Description
text/plain	TXT	Plain text file
text/richtext		
video/mpeg	MPG, MPEG	MPEG Movie
video/quicktime	QT, MOV	Apple Quicktime Movie
video/x-msvideo	AVI	Video for Windows
world/vrml	WRL	Virtual Reality Modeling Language (VRML)
x-world/x-vrml	WRL	VRML – unofficial

Example viewers

AI	Adobe Illustrator/GNU Ghostscript
DOC	Word
GIF	Browser
GZ	GNU gunzip
HTM	Browser
JPG	Browser/Paint Shop Pro
PDF	Adobe PDF Viewer for Windows
PS/EPS	GNU Ghostscript
RTF	Word
TAR	GNU gtar
TIF	Paint Shop Pro
TXT	Browser/Notepad
WP	Word Perfect
WRL	SGI Webspace
Z	GNU gunzip
ZIP	PKUNZIP

Glossary of terms

Anchor	Start of a hypertext link within an HTML document.
ASCII	ANSI Standard Code for Information Interchange.
Attribute	A parameter which alters the effect of an HTML element.
Bookmark	A user-compiled list of previously visited sites held by the browser.
Browser	A program for viewing Web documents.
CD-ROM	Compact Disc Read Only Memory, a high-capacity storage medium based on compact disc technology. Often used to deliver multimedia information.
CGI	Common Gateway Interface. A standard way for Web servers to communicate with external programs.
Clickable image	An image which features hotspots which when clicked with the mouse pointer initiate some event.
CompuServe	A proprietary computer network. Features gateways to the Internet.
Console application	A Windows program which runs in a DOS command window and communicates with the standard input and output streams (generally keyboard and screen).

Container	An HTML element which contains text and markup.
DNS	Domain Name System. A distributed database of Internet host-names. A bit like directory inquiries for computers.
DTD	SGML Document Type Definitions are used to provide a formal definition of HTML. The DTD specifies the type and order of markup permitted within each element.
Dynamic document	A document which is generated by the server in response to user or external input.
Edutainment	A contraction of education and entertainment.
Element	A structural component of an HTML document. It is usually identified by start and end tags.
Ethernet	A bus-based local area network architecture.
FTP	File Transfer Protocol. An Internet-based protocol for the reliable transmission of files.
GIF	Graphics Interchange Format. A graphics format developed by CompuServe.
GUI	Graphical User Interface (goo-ey). MS Windows is an example of a GUI.
Home page	First or welcome page in a Web site hierarchy.
Host	A computer hosting network services.
HotJava	Sun's browser which can run executable content written in the JAVA programming language.
HTML	HyperText Markup Language. The language used by the Web for describing documents.
HTTP	HyperText Transfer Protocol. Used for transferring files across the Web.
Hyperlink	Contraction of Hypertext link. The start of a hyperlink can also be an image.
HyperMedia	HyperText + Multimedia. CD-ROM and the Web are both examples of HyperMedia systems.
HyperText	Text which represents links to other documents. HyperText documents are designed to be read in a non-linear fashion.

Internet	A worldwide network of computers which communicate using the Internet Protocols.
IP	Internet Protocol. Sits above local network protocols permitting individual machines and networks to intercommunicate, hence Internet – Inter Networking.
ISDN	Integrated Services Digital Network. A digital communications network provided by telecom companies.
ISP	Internet Service Provider. An organization which provides Internet services to third parties. Often these are to home users with dial-up connections.
JAVA	An object-oriented programming language from Sun used for writing Web applets.
JFIF	JPEG File Interchange Format. Standard file format for JPEG images.
JPEG	Joint Photographic Experts Group. Usually associated with the image-compression format devised by the group.
LAN	Local Area Network. A physical network which is used over a limited geographical area.
Legacy documents	Existing documents in a format other than HTML which must be delivered using the Web.
LZW	Lempel–Zif data compression algorithm.
Markup	Text added to a document to describe its structure.
Markup language	A language which describes the structure of a page not the presentation. Heading and paragraph information is part of a markup language, font information isn't.
MIME	Multipurpose Internet Mail Extensions. A format for describing multimedia Internet message bodies.
MSNet	Microsoft Network. A proprietary network easily accessible from machines running the Windows '95 operating system.
Multihoming	The ability for different Internet hostnames to resolve to the same Web server but different home pages.
Netscape	A popular Web browser derived from the original Mosaic line.
NIC	Network Information Center. The central repository for Internet hostnames.

PKZIP	A popular DOS file compression and archiving utility based on the LZ77 compression algorithm.
Plain text	Text which is not encrypted and is plain for all to read.
Port	A number which names a particular service running on an Internet host.
PostScript	A page description language developed by Adobe Systems Inc.
Raster device	A device which uses a matrix of dots to produce an image. A television is a raster device. Conversely a plotter is a vector device.
Rendering	The formatting and presentation of a document.
RFC	Request For Comments. An initial document kicking off debate for a new standard. URIs are discussed in document RFC1630. This can be located on the Internet with a search engine such as Archie.
Server	A program which supplies services to clients via a communications channel (or port).
SGML	Standard Generalized Markup Language. An ISO standard for describing the structure of documents.
Standard I/O	Programs fall into two categories, GUI and console apps. GUI applications use Windows to display information, console applications use the standard input and output streams. These are normally connected to the keyboard and console output but can be linked up to the standard I/O streams of other applications.
Syquest drives	Removable hard drives popular with graphic designers for exchanging large volumes of data.
Tag	An item of descriptive markup.
TCP	Transmission Control Protocol. A reliable connection-oriented protocol.
Telnet	An Internet-based protocol and application. Used to get a command-line window on a remote host.
Thumbnail	Small (thumbnail size) representation of a large image.
Token ring	A local network architecture where machines are connected in a loop. A token is passed from machine to machine and data can be attached to this token. It has a predictable transmission time and unlike Ethernet is suitable for real-time use.

UDP   User Datagram Protocol. A connectionless and unreliable protocol using IP.

UNIX   Originally the name applied to a small, portable operating system developed by Bell Laboratories. Often used more loosely to describe operating systems with a UNIX-like interface.

URI   Uniform Resource Identifier. A standard way of naming resources on the Web.

URL   Uniform Resource Locator. The addressing scheme currently used by the Web.

URN   Uniform Resource Name. A proposed addressing scheme which will separate resource names from their physical locations.

Usenet news   Internet news service.

VRML   Virtual Reality Modeling Language. A compact language for describing three-dimensional scenes and used to deliver virtual reality over the Web.

WAIS   Wide Area Information Service. A system which allows keyword searches of documents over the Internet.

Web   The World Wide Web. A hypertext-based distributed information system.

WYSIWYG   'What You See Is What You Get' or 'whizzywig' is a desktop publishing term meaning that what is shown on the screen will be exactly what is printed.

XNS   Xerox Network System.

ZIP   See PKZIP.

Resource guide

'Every man is a piece of the continent'
– John Donne

A traditional bibliography is too exclusive for a book drawing on both on-line and printed references. Instead this section gives a potted listing of the resources used in the compilation of this book. This is just a snapshot of the vast amount of Web software and documentation available for the Microsoft platforms.

The CD-ROM contains much of the software described in Go Web! Where a program is distributed as *shareware* users should register the software after the evaluation period expires. This not only gives access to support but enables the developers to enhance their products. The ⊙ symbol marks the software that can be found on the CD-ROM.

16 bit Windows software, that is programs compiled for the older Windows 3.1 platform, will normally run on Windows 95 and Windows NT. Similarly 32 bit Windows software will normally run on both 95 and NT but not on Windows 3.1 (as an aside if the 32 bit DLL is available it may work on 3.1, but all bets are off). The structure of the CD-ROM reflects this situation. The programs found at the root of the directory tree will run on all platforms. Programs under the WIN16 directory will either only run on 16 bit Windows systems or there is a 32 bit version available under the WIN32 directory. Windows NT complicates the issue further as versions are available which run

on Intel, Power PC, Alpha and MIPS architectures. Usually 32 bit Intel versions will run on both NT and Windows 95, where this is not the case they are located under the `WINNT` subdirectory which also contains the software for the other NT architectures.

■ Installing software from the CD-ROM

The software on the CD-ROM is exactly as it is downloaded from the authors. Normally a ZIP archive, those ending in `.EXE` are self extracting. Self extracting archives must be copied from the CD-ROM and executed, either from the file manager or from the command line. `.ZIP` files must be unarchived with a special utility, for example `pkunzip` or Mark Adler's `unzip`. A copy of this second program can be found on the CD-ROM in the `WIN32\TOOLS` directory and it will also handle long file names. After the program is unarchived look at any `README` file for further installation notes; usually a Windows *SETUP* program is provided to install the software.

■ Bibliography

Meadows, J. (1989) *Information Technology, Changing the Way We Communicate*, Cassell, London.

Liu, C. and Albitz, P. (1994) *DNS and BIND*, O'Reilly & Associates Inc., Sebastopol, USA.

Kochan, S. and Wood P. (eds) (1990) *UNIX Networking*, Hayden Books, Carmel, USA.

Wall, L. and Schwartz, R. (1992) *Programing Perl*. O'Reilly & Associates Inc., Sebastopol, USA.

Ford, A. (1995) *Spinning the Web: How to Provide Information on the Internet*, International Thomson Computer Press, London.

Parker, R. (1990) *Looking Good in Print*, Ventana, USA.

Wilmshurst, J. (1978) *The Fundamentals and Practice of Marketing*, Heinemann, London.

Biesasa, A. (1993) Guerilla Marketers, how to make a splash without getting soaked, *UnixWorld*, May 1993, pp. 59-62.

■ On-line

■ Style

Paul Lynch has used his considerable experience with multimedia to produce a Web style manual. This is organized in the form of an on-line book, in this case the medium is part of the message. Many of the ideas in Chapter 10 are expounded in great detail by this manual.

> Lynch, P. *C/AIM WWW Style Manual*, Yale Center for Advanced Instructional Media, `http://info.med.yale.edu/caim/`.

The Style Guide for Online Hypertext, written by Tim Berners Lee, contains information relevant to the organization of Web documents.

> Berners Lee, T. *The Style Guide for Online Hypertext*, World Wide Web Consortium, `http://www.w3.org/pub/WWW/Provider/Style/Overview.html`.

■ Web specifications

The World Wide Web Consortium's server is a good source for many of the drafts and proposals concerning the Web. In particular descriptions of the HTML versions can be viewed and downloaded.

> *The HTML drafts*, World Wide Web Consortium, `http://www.w3.org/pub/WWW/MarkUp/`.

> *HTTP Protocol*, World Wide Web Consortium, `http://www.w3.org/hypertext/WWW/Protocols/`.

■ Web editors

Internet Assistant for Word

Organization	Microsoft Corporation
Reference	Chapter 5
URL	http://www.microsoft.com
⊙ 32 bit version	`WIN32\IA\WORDIA2B.EXE`
⊙ 16 bit version	`WIN16\IA\WORDIA.EXE`

Internet Assistant is an add-on for Microsoft Word. It is distributed free by Microsoft and the latest version can be found at their Web site. Internet

Assistant enables users to create and save Word documents in the Web's own HTML format. It also converts Word into a fully functional Web browser. There are currently two versions, the original 16-bit for Windows and a new, improved 32-bit NT/95 version. The 32-bit version supports some of the Netscapisms and is restricted to Word 32 running on NT and 95.

HotDog

Organization	Sausage Software
Reference	Chapter 5
URL	http://www.sausage.com
☉ 16 bit version	`HOTDOG\HDGSETUP.EXE`

HotDog is a shareware HTML editor that supports HTML versions 2.0 and 3.0 as well the Netscapisms. Users create pages by entering text and inserting markup from menu lists or using toolbar buttons and custom dialogs. The copy found on the CD-ROM may be evaluated for up to 30 days, after which users should purchase a license from Sausage Software.

Internet Publisher for WordPerfect

Organization	Novell Inc.
Reference	Chapter 5
URL	http://wp.novell.com

Novell produce a similar product to Internet Assistant called Internet Publisher. Full details can be found on their Web page. Users requiring a more rigorous approach may be interested in WordPerfect SGML edition.

Web Author for Word

Organization	Quarterdeck
Reference	Chapter 5
URL	http://www.qdeck.com

Web Author is a similar product to Internet Assistant and allows users to create and view Web documents from the familiar Microsoft Word environment.

HoTMetaL

Organization	SoftQuad
Reference	Chapter 5
URL	URL http://www.sq.com

HoTMetaL is a fully compliant HTML editor from SoftQuad. An unsupported version is available from SoftQuad's Web site. The Pro edition offers additional features. SoftQuad also produce Author/Editor, a fully fledged SGML editor that may be used to create Web documents. Author/Editor could prove extremely valuable where an organization must target multiple platforms, for example: Printed Reports, Books and the Web.

WebEdit

Organization	Kenn Nesbitt, Nesbitt Software
Reference	Chapter 5
URL	http://www.nesbitt.com/

WebEdit is a specialized HTML editor supporting both versions 2.0 and 3.0 of HTML. Language extensions such as Netscapisms, are also supported. WebEdit can also import comma separated data from spreadsheets and databases into HTML tables. It's available for 30 days evaluation from the Nesbitt Web site.

▨ Browsers

UDIwww

Organization	Bernd Richter. University of Ulm, Germany.
Reference	Chapter 4
URL	http://www.uni-ulm.de/~richter/udiwww/index.htm
⊙ 16 bit version	`WIN16\UDIWWW\UDIW1E05.EXE`
⊙ 32 bit version	`WIN32\UDIWWW\UDIW3E05.EXE`

The UDIwww browser supports many of the proposed HTML version 3.0 tags. It will also highlight what it believes to be bad markup tags. Versions are available for all the Microsoft operating systems and a German language version can also be found at the Web site. A nice browser for users wishing to explore version 3.0 on their system.

NetScape Navigator version 2.0

Organization	Netscape Communications Corporation
Reference	Chapter 4
URL	http://www.netscape.com

The most novel feature of the new NetScape Navigator is support for Java applets, although this is restricted to Windows 95 and NT platforms. NetScape also extends the Hypertext paradigm to News and Email with their integrated readers. News can also be threaded for easier reading. Progressive JPEG loading has been added for better performance.

The NetScape programmers are the source of those non-standard *Netscapisms* and are widely credited for bringing pictures to the Web.

Internet Explorer

Organization	Microsoft Corporation
Reference	Chapter 4
URL	http://www.microsoft.com

Could this be Microsoft's Netscape basher? It certainly proved a popular choice for many Web users in the first few weeks of its launch but in order to beat them you have to join them. Consequently Internet Explorer supports some of the more popular Netscapisms as well as VRML. There's no support for Java applets because Microsoft has it's own rival *Blackbird* system waiting in the wings. Blackbird is apparently restricted to Microsoft's own MSNet.

HotJava

Organization	Sun Microsystems Inc.
Reference	Chapter 12
URL	http://java.sun.com/

Sun's HotJava browser was built to prove the concept of executable content within Web documents. It certainly does that and is a fairly competent browser in its own right. Interestingly HotJava is written entirely in the Java programming language. HotJava will only run on Windows 95 and NT.

HotJava uses long filenames and the installation file system must support these (e.g. NTFS but not DOS FAT). The unzip utility will unzip archives containing long filenames.

▨ Checking HTML documents

HALSoft HTML Validation Service

Organization	HAL Computer Systems
Reference	Chapter 5
URL	http://www.halsoft.com/html-val-svc/

HAL Computer Systems provide an on-line HTML verifier. Documents to be checked must be accessible on the Internet. This entails running an HTTP (Web) Server locally. The verifier is based around an SGML parser and uses the Document Type Definitions, giving a rigorous analysis of the document to be checked.

Weblint

Organization	Neil Bowers, Khoral Research, Inc.
Reference	Chapter 5
URL	http://www.khoral.com/staff/neilb/weblint.html
⊙ Perl Code	WEBLINT\WEBLINT

Weblint is a syntax and style checker for HTML. It is written in Perl, an interpreted language, and this must be installed before lint can be run. Neil Bowers maintains two mailing lists giving information about Weblint:

```
weblint-announce@knoral.com
```

announcements of new versions;

```
weblint-victims@khoral.com
```

a support line.

Users should Email Neil: neilb@khoral.com, to join either list.

WebWatch

Organization	Specter Inc.
Reference	Chapter 5
URL	http://www.specter.com/users/janos/specter/

WebWatch is a tool for tracking changes to linked HTML pages. Given an HTML document WebWatch will produce a list of URLs which have changed since the page was last checked. This is useful for processing *hot lists* to decide which sites are worth another visit. Given a virgin page it will check the validity of all the URLs on that page.

Peruser

Organization	Real Time Internet Services
Reference	Chapter 5
URL	http://www.rtis.com/nat/software/peruser.htm

Peruser is a link validator for NT systems. It runs from the command line and checks all links in a Web of documents. Peruser produces a file listing the documents checked and showing the invalid links it found.

▪ Conversion tools

InterNotes

Organization	Lotus Development Corporation
Reference	Chapter 5
URL	http://www.internotes.lotus.com

InterNotes interfaces NT and OS/2 Web servers to Lotus Notes. It automatically converts Notes documents and views into HTML documents accessible from a Web server. An evaluation Beta is available from the Internotes Web site.

TILE

Organization	Walter Shelby Group Ltd
Reference	Chapter 5
URL	http://tile.net/info/index.html

TILE converts Lotus Notes databases into Web documents. Written in Perl the source code is provided with each license. The TILE-L mailing list discusses TILE; to subscribe send:

```
sub tile-l your name
```

to:

```
listproc@cren.net.
```

rtftohtml

Organization	Chris Hector
Reference	Chapter 5
URL	http://www.w3.org/pub/WWW/Tools/rtftohtml-DOS.html
⊙ 16 bit version	RTF2HTM\RTF2HTM.ZIP

rtftohtml is a command line utility that converts Rich Text Format documents to HTML.

PStoHTML

Organization	National Research Council of Italy
Reference	Chapter 5
URL	http://www.area.fi.cnr.it/area/ps2html.htm

PostScript files can be converted with PStoHTML. This program is happiest with the PostScript output from the Windows print drivers.

▓ Viewers

gsview

Organization	Free Software Foundation
Reference	Chapter 6
URL	http://www.cs.wisc.edu/~ghost
⊙ 16 bit version	GSVIEW\GS261WIN.ZIP

Ghostview is a PostScript viewer available from the Free Software Foundation. It uses Ghostscript, a version of PostScript written by Aladdin Enterprises, as the rasteriser. The additional files: GS261INI.ZIP and GSFONTS.ZIP contain test documents and fonts respectively. Directory information should be preserved when unzipping the fonts archive; with the PKZIP utility use the /d flag.

The Usenet news group: gnu.ghostscript.bug, announces bug reports and fixes to Ghostscript.

Acrobat

Organization	Adobe Systems Incorporated
Reference	Chapter 6
URL	http://www.adobe.com
⊙ 16 bit version	ACROBAT\ACROREAD.EXE

The Portable Document Format is a development of the PostScript language. Unlike PostScript, PDF supports hyperlinks and can be integrated with HTML documents using a suitable browser. The big advantage over HTML is close control over presentation. Adobe makes an Acrobat PDF reader available at its Web site.

Word Viewer

Organization	Microsoft Corporation
Reference	Chapter 6
URL	http://www.microsoft.com
⊙ 32 bit version	WIN32\WV\WD95VIEW.EXE
⊙ 16 bit version	WIN16\WV\WRD6VIEW.EXE

Word Viewer allows Web users to distribute and read Microsoft Word documents without having to invest in Word itself. The latest version of Word Viewer is freely available from Microsoft's Web site.

PowerPoint Viewer

Organization   Microsoft Corporation
Reference   Chapter 6
URL   http://www.microsoft.com

The PowerPoint viewer allows PowerPoint presentations to be viewed without running PowerPoint itself. It can be configured as an external viewer.

■ Other file formats

A good description of the various multimedia file formats and viewing software can be found in Allison Zhang's Web guide.

> Zhang, A. *Multimedia File Formats on the Internet*, `http://ac.dal.ca/ ~dong/contents.htm`.

■ Image manipulation

Paint Shop Pro

Organization   Jasc Corporation
Reference   Chapter 7
URL   http://www.winternet.com/~jasc/
⊙ 16 bit version   `PDP\PSP311.ZIP`

Paint Shop Pro is a general purpose image manipulation and creation utility. A fully featured version is available for a 30 day evaluation period.

LView Pro

Organization   Leonardo Haddad Loureiro
Reference   Chapter 7
URL   http://world.std.com/~mmedia/lviewp.html

LView Pro is another popular shareware program for image manipulation. The image editing and creation tools are more basic than those offered by Paint Shop Pro. Versions are available for Windows 3.1 and 95.

GDIT

Organization   David Harvey George, Kimble Consultancy
Reference   Chapter 7
URL   ftp://ftp.demon.co.uk/pub/nt/general/gdit.zip
⊙ 32 bit version   `WINNT\GDIT\GDIT.ZIP`

GDIT is a front end to Thom Boutell's gd library. GDIT reads drawing commands on the standard input stream creating a GIF format image. Useful for making GIF images on-the-fly as a result of some dynamic data. Can also be used to set the transparency index of GIF files.

▨ Languages

NTPerl

Organization	Hip Communications Inc.
Reference	Chapter 9
URL	http://info.hip.com/ntperl/
⊙ 32 bit version	`WIN32\PERL\NTPERL.ZIP`

NTPerl is a Microsoft sponsored port of Perl version 5 to Windows NT. It features tools and libraries for exploiting Object Linking and Embedding. The Intel version also runs on Windows 95 and versions are also provided for the Alpha, MIPS and Power PC architectures. These can be found under the `WIN32\WINNT` directory.

Two mailing lists exist to support NTPerl, these are:

● ntperl – discussion list
  send mail to: `majordomo@mail.hip.com`
    with: `subscribe ntperl`
    as the message body

● ntperl_announce – announcements
  send mail to: `majordomo@mail.hip.com`
    with: `subscribe ntperl_announce`
    as the message body

The newsgroup, `comp.lang.perl`, is where all the Perl programmers hang out.

Perl

Organization	Len Reed
Reference	Chapter 9
URL	ftp://ftp.cc.utexas.edu/microlib/dos/unix/ perl419x.zip
⊙ 16 bit version	`WIN16\PERL\PERL419X.ZIP`

Len Reed's port of Perl, version 4.19 for DOS systems.

JAVA

Organization	Sun Microsystems Inc.
Reference	Chapter 12
URL	http://java.sun.com/

JAVA is an interpreted object oriented project language. By using a compliant browser JAVA offers executable content in Web documents. The JAVA interpreter is currently distributed free of charge.

The Usenet newsgroup comp.lang.java discusses JAVA language related issues. Sun's JAVA Web site also carries details of various mailing lists related to the ongoing ports.

■ Search engines

WAIS

Organization	EMWAC
Reference	Chapter 8
URL	http://www.emwac.ed.ac.uk/
⊙ NT version	`WIN32\INTEL\WAIS\WTI386.ZIP`

WAIS or Wide Area Information Service is a set of tools for building document indexes; these enable information to be rapidly located via a keyword search. The EMWAC port includes an interface to the HTTPS Web server and can be interfaced to other servers with a CGI script. Versions for the Alpha, MIPS and Power PC can found on the CD-ROM under the appropriate sub-directories.

■ Web servers

HTTPS

Organization	EMWAC
Reference	Chapters 8, 9
URL	http://www.emwac.ed.ac.uk/
⊙ NT version	`WIN32\INTEL\HTTPS\HSI386.ZIP`

HTTPS is the official Microsoft sponsored Web Server, the same one that they supply with their resource kit and the one that runs the Microsoft World Wide Web site. Understandably it's amongst the more popular Windows Web servers. The CD-ROM has versions for Intel, Alpha, MIPS and Power PC architectures. A professional edition of HTTPS also exists called Purveyor and further information can be obtained from `http://www.process.com`.

▨ Other servers

Information on the servers shown in figure 8.1 can be found at their respective Web sites:

Alibaba	`http://www.csm.co.at/csm/`
Commerce Builder	`http://www.aristosoft.com/ifact/prod.htm`
CL-HTTP	`http://www.ai.mit.edu/projects/iiip/doc/cl-http/homepage.html`
EMWAC	`http://emwac.ed.ac.uk/html/internet_toolchest/https/`
HTTPS	`contents/htm`
Navi Server	`http://www.navisoft.com/products/server/server/htm`
NetScape	`http://www.rsa.com/netscape/`
Plexus	`http://www.bsdi.com/server/doc/plexus.html`
Purveyor	`http://www.process.com/`
SAIC	`http://wwwserver.itl.saic.com`
WebQuest	`http://www.questar.com/webquest.htm`
WebSite	`http://websute,ora.com/`
Folkweb	`http://www.ilar.com/folkweb.htm`
W4 Server	`http://wit381402.student.utwente.nl/index.html`
ZB Server	`http://bbgun.at.utm.edu/zbs/zbs.htm`
Win-HTTPD	`http://www.city.net/win-httpd/`

▨ CGI utilities

MailTo

Organization	Brian Dorricott, Internet Shopper
Reference	Chapter 9
URL	http://www.net-shopper.co.uk/software/index.htm
⊙ NT Version	`WIN32\WINNT\INTEL\MAILTO\MAILTO.ZIP`

MailTo will Email the results of an HTML form to a given user.

Blat

Organization	Mark Neal and Pedro Mendez
Reference	Chapter 9
URL	ftp://gepasi.dbs.aber.ac.uk/softw/blat.html

⊙ `WIN32\BLAT\BLAT14.ZIP`

Blat can be used in conjunction with a CGI script for more complex HTML form processing and forwarding. Blat is a Windows NT console utility that can Email a file to a user using SMTP.

Analyse

Organization	Brian Dorricott, Internet Shopper
Reference	Chapter 9
URL	http://www.net-shopper.co.uk/software/index.htm

⊙ NT Version `WIN32\WINNT\INTEL\ANALYSE\ANALYS11.ZIP`

Analyse is a tool for analyzing the log files produced by HTTPS. It generates data that can be manipulated by a spreadsheet, such as Excel. The latest version (available from the Web site) works with other log file formats.

MapEdit

Organization	Thomas Boutell
Reference	Chapter 8
URL	http://www.sunsite.unc.edu/boutell/mapedit/

Mapedit is a WYSIWYG image map editor for Windows. It saves having to determine and enter image map coordinates by hand.

■ Virtual Reality Modeling Language (VRML)

WebSpace

Organization	Silicon Graphics/Template Graphics Software
Reference	Chapter 12
URL	http://www.webspace.com

WebSpace is a VRML viewer for Windows. It runs in conjunction with a Web browser such as Netscape Navigator. Configured as an external viewer; users can explore 3D worlds and follow hyperlinks to other Web documents. WebSpace forms part of SGI's WebForce product range.

▨ Newsgroups

A number of Web groups exist under the `comp.infosystems` hierarchy. Your local Internet or Web provider may also have a group relating to issues on their Web server. Windows users will find the group: `comp.infosystems.www.servers.ms-windows` particularly interesting when configuring a Web server.

Internet Assistant for Word toolbar reference

Input Form

ab|	Text Field
⊠	Checkbox
▦	Select
Submit	Submit Button
Reset	Reset Button
▦	Input Attributes
▦	Shading
▤	Form Lock

Format

▨	Browse View
◀	Backwards
▶	Formwards
Normal,P ▼	Styles
B	Bold
I	Italic
U	Underline
▤	Ordered List
▤	Unordered List
▤	Decrease Indent
▤	Increase Indent
▬	Horizontal rule
▤	Anchor
▣	Image
◉	Hyperlink
ⓘ	Title

Standard

▯	New
▨	Open
▦	Save
▤	Print
▤	Preview
ᴬᴮᶜ	Spelling
✂	Cut
▤	Coppy
▤	Paste
▤	Format Painter
↻	Undo
↺	Redo
▤	Auto Text
¶	Show/Hide
{a}	HTML Hidden
100% ▼	Zoom
▶?	Help

Index

Go Web! CD-ROM

Products and Services that are referred to in this book and its accompanying CD-ROM may be either trademarks and/or registered trademarks of their respective owners. The Publisher/s and Author/s make no claim to these trademarks.

Please ensure that before using each program you read carefully and observe the conditions for its use. Individual program copyrights and notices are included with each package.

CD-ROM requirements

Data on the CD-ROM can be read by any Microsoft Windows system capable of reading CD-ROMs. A Web browser is recommended.

A Winsock compliant PCP/IP stack is necessary to run client/server software.

A minimum of a 386 IBM PC compatible with 4 MB RAM (486/66 with 8 MB RAM recommended) is required for client software.

A minimum of a 486/33 IBM PC compatible with 8 MB RAM (486/66 with 16 MB RAM recommended) is required for server software.

The software supplied on the CD-ROM runs on Microsoft Windows 3.1 or Windows for Workgroups. Please note that Windows 95 or Windows NT (workstation or server) are required for some software components. Please refer to the CD-ROM hypertext documentation for full system requirements of individual packages.